Dos Passos's Early Fiction, 1912–1938

Dos Passos's Early Fiction, 1912–1938

Michael Clark

Selingsgrove: Susquehanna University Press
London and Toronto: Associated University Presses

© 1987 by Associated University Presses, Inc.

Associated University Presses
440 Forsgate Drive
Cranbury, NJ 08512

Associated University Presses
25 Sicilian Avenue
London WC1A 2QH, England

Associated University Presses
2133 Royal Windsor Drive
Unit 1
Mississauga, Ontario
Canada L5J 1K5

The paper used in this publication meets the
requirements of the American National Standard for
Permanence of Paper for Printed Library Materials Z39.48-1984.

Library of Congress Cataloging-in-Publication Data

Clark, Michael, 1946 Jan. 16–
   Dos Passos's early fiction, 1912–1938.

   Bibliography: p.
   Includes index.
   1. Dos Passos, John, 1896–1970—Criticism and
interpretation. I. Title.
PS3507.O743Z555   1987   813'.52   85-63015
ISBN 0-941664-18-X (alk. paper)

Printed in the United States of America

*This book is for
Janis, Andrew, and Emily*

Contents

Acknowledgments		9
1	Introduction	13
2	Walt Whitman and John Dos Passos	18
3	William James and Dos Passos	24
4	The Early Short Stories and *Streets of Night*	29
5	*Seven Times Round the Walls of Jericho*	53
6	*One Man's Initiation: 1917*	62
7	*Three Soldiers*	76
8	*Manhattan Transfer*	97
9	The *U.S.A.* Trilogy	123
10	Conclusion	150
Notes		153
Bibliography		164
Index		170

Acknowledgments

In completing this manuscript, I have incurred many debts. I would like to give thanks in particular to a number of people who helped me along the way.

Ms. Susan Downing assisted in typing the manuscript; the staff members of Alderman Library, University of Virginia, gave me valuable assistance in my work with the Dos Passos Collection; the interlibrary loan departments of the University of Wisconsin Libraries in Madison and at Widener University provided much valuable assistance; Professor John Lyons and Professor William Gibson gave their time and many helpful suggestions.

Over the years, Professors Gerard Sweeney and Dale Doepke taught me much about literature and scholarship.

Professor Martin Bock, a very good friend, contributed many excellent suggestions for improving this study.

Professor Walter B. Rideout read the manuscript through several drafts and was most instructive. His good humor and astute criticisms helped me to avoid many pitfalls. Whatever pits I fall into in the present version of this manuscript, though, are of my own digging.

Widener University, and especially Professor Charles B. Smith, Professor Julian C. Skaggs, and Provost Lawrence Buck, provided much encouragement and support.

Mrs. Elizabeth Dos Passos was always very helpful in her kind responses to my inquiries and granted me permission to quote from her husband's work, published and unpublished.

Finally, this project would never have been completed without the enthusiasm and support of Janis Tenney Clark.

Dos Passos's
Early Fiction,
1912–1938

1
Introduction

This study attempts to show how American traditions can illuminate the aesthetics of John Dos Passos's early fiction. I believe that Dos Passos's novels can best be understood in light of their American intellectual background and that the compelling attributes of his aesthetic credo are distinctively and most emphatically American. John Dos Passos, in effect, fulfills Walt Whitman's prescription for "first-class song" by embodying a "sufficient Nationality" in his art. As Whitman knew, the artist and the country are organically related; in his preface "A Backward Glance," Whitman states that "one needs only a little penetration to see, at more or less removes, the material facts of their country and radius, . . . and its gloomy or hopeful prospects, behind all poets and each poet, and forming their birthmarks."[1] And indeed if one looks closely, the American birthmark is stamped indelibly on the work of John Dos Passos.

Whitman's remarks notwithstanding, the task is not a simple one. Dos Passos's literary career proved perplexing to his contemporaries, and an evaluation of his writing remains problematic because his work does not easily align itself with narrow categories, though it has affinities with numerous—and sometimes conflicting—tendencies and movements in art: imagism, impressionism, Marxism, naturalism, satire, and any number of other approaches. Dos Passos frequently expressed his dissatisfaction over the simple categorization of his writing and, indeed, even at one time questioned the seemingly obvious distinction between the fiction and nonfiction classifications into which his work is conveniently divided.[2] The fact that his prose is difficult to classify, however, is certainly one measure of its vitality.

This study will not attempt to trace the numerous authors and works that might be in any narrow sense literary influences on Dos Passos's work. In fact, such a study would be quite different and, I believe, less fruitful than the present approach. A listing of his early reading as mentioned in his letters, autobiography, and college diaries reveals the highly eclectic and generally European bent of his interests: Dante, Gibbon, Rabelais, Boccaccio, Robert Louis Stevenson, Baroja, the King James Bible, futurist poetry, Heine, and Joyce, to make only a short catalogue. By comparison, his references to American literature are scant. In a lecture entitled "The Great Tradition," Dos Passos traces the development of literature in English from Chaucer to the modern era, mentioning only one work in American literature, *The Adventures of Huckleberry Finn*.[3] In allusions to American literature throughout his long career, Dos Passos mentions only Walt Whitman's name often.

Perhaps it is because John Dos Passos read European literature with such a rare catholicity that so few critics have discussed his work in terms of its essential "Americanness." Of such studies only a few come quickly to mind: a number of articles discuss his debt to Walt Whitman, and a recent book, Linda Wagner's *Dos Passos: Artist as American*, treats the author in relation to his country. The latter study emphasizes the historical consciousness of Dos Passos and seems most illuminating when it discusses the later chronicles, which are more consciously historical interpretations of American culture. But Wagner is less instructive in analyzing the earlier works, although Dos Passos's most interesting—and, I believe, most successful—books are the novels that he published in the 1920s and 1930s. Clearly, what is lacking and what the present study attempts to provide is an examination of these early works that will discover the fundamental aesthetic principles and the central issues of these novels.

The reasons for the absence of an obvious American fabric in Dos Passos's work are clear. While at Harvard, Dos Passos took no course work in American literature, though there were a few such courses available to him.[4] In fact, there was little real interest in American colleges in examining the literature and history of America, as Malcolm Cowley succinctly notes in *Exile's Return:*

> It often seems to me that our years in school and after school, in college and later in the army, might be regarded as a long process of deracination. Looking backward, I feel that our whole training was involuntarily directed toward destroying whatever roots we had in the soil, toward eradicating our local and regional peculiarities, toward making us homeless citizens of the world.[5]

In spite of the general reluctance of Americans to look behind themselves, Dos Passos did come to do so. As shall be seen, while still in college, Dos Passos discovered important American traditions that were to have a significant impact on his art.

Dos Passos's roots in America can be traced throughout his life and art. Although he traveled widely overseas throughout his long life, he was

American-born and maintained a lifelong residence in Virginia. Furthermore, one can see that his American nationality is an important fact because time and again he muses over it. In *The Best Times,* his autobiography, he recalls an event from his childhood, when his father was to be presented to the king of England:

> To me the court dress seemed final. Here Dedi is on the edge of becoming an Englishman and I have been making a desperate plea to be allowed to go home to America to school. I didn't mind the hard study and I don't remember any particular fagging or bullying but I was an American and my entire small frame revolted at going to school in England. I can't remember what the upshot was right then but eventually I won my point.[6]

"I was an American"; he was indeed. The subsequent facts of Dos Passos's life assert his American identity. His college diaries, for example, record his persistent concern about defining the essential American experience; the following comment he records in 1916: "America has no ghosts! What is to take their place to give overtones to life, to keep it from being a mere scramble for the flesh pots?" Pages later he muses on a proposed essay entitled "Shelley and the Modern Age in America" and still later comments on the abstractness of American writing.[7] Although the stories he published in college generally had foreign locales, the same notebook records plans for a number of short stories with American settings. Furthermore, an unpublished essay that he wrote in college ("Art and Baseball") examines why "there is no art here in America." In response to this question, the young Dos Passos states that a truly American art is achieved not by living abroad, nor by copying foreign literature, but by "developing in America something new."[8]

After Dos Passos left Harvard, he was still grappling with the meaning of the American experience. His first publication in a national magazine, "Against American Literature" (in *The New Republic,* October 1916), is an enthusiastic plea for a genuine American literature.[9] The First World War especially seems to have served as a catalyst in his thinking, making him question the values implicit in American society. In a letter to his friend Arthur McComb in 1917, he reveals his unhappiness and at the same time his paradoxical attitude toward America: "But, god I'm glad to be out of the vast American wilderness and I don't feel now as if I could ever go back, though I know I shall."[10] Another letter two years later indicates the same contradictory feelings: "America is more dear to me than Europe—probably its colossal hideousness, its febrile insanity are evolving towards a better life for man."[11] In spite of his revulsion at the grossness of American values, then, he is still able to maintain an optimism about American life. He seems to have believed early in life, just as he did later on, that America's experiment with democracy, however flawed, was nevertheless the best political system in operation.

It is, perhaps, this basic optimism that drew him back to America after the war. One of his more militant statements written during this period illustrates this; he and his two close friends, Dos Passos notes, "are to return to America when we have served our terms & fight with pen & tooth & nail for free speech & general liberty—to try to make a splash, however small, in the stagnant puddle of the American mind."[12]

He did return to America, of course, and just as he had earlier noted in his college diaries, he again continued to ponder the complex problem of a vital art in America. In 1920 he writes to Stewart Mitchell (as so often, this letter is couched in highly dramatic terms) that "the *Dial* is the one hope of all the people who, like you and I, want to express themselves freely and still remain Americans." And in the same letter, he defines further the nature of this problem:

> I take it that you want to be literary, to embark on the grand vague sea of 100 per cent art. Well I don't think it is possible to do that without exhibiting some definite trend, and I think that the only trend which will interest the sort of person who will read the *Dial* . . . will be an attempt to exhibit or invent tendencies in American literature (of, for & by Americans). Of course you scorn politics; therefore you must have sex, and carefully chosen literary novelties that will stimulate without startling.[13]

This passage suggests two major subjects that would figure in Dos Passos's own fiction: sexuality and politics. It also reveals Dos Passos's attraction for "literary novelties"—presumably experimentation in technique (though it might be questionable whether Dos Passos stimulated "without startling" contemporary readers). But central to my purpose here is that the passage is a striking illustration of Dos Passos's concern at the beginning of his serious effort at a literary career. There is some wry humor in his phrase "100 per cent art," but there can be little doubt that Dos Passos is giving serious advice to his friend and that an essential component of art as Dos Passos conceives it is some definite American trend or "tendencies." The first task of this study is to define the nature of the "tendencies" that provide the skeleton of values in John Dos Passos's early fiction.

It has been suggested that Dos Passos was not consciously working in any literary tradition,[14] and indeed this may be the case; but as William Carlos Williams notes about American literature, "the blood means nothing; the spirit, the ghost of the land moves in the blood, moves the blood."[15] Ralph Barton Perry, in his study of American values, makes a similar, though less poetic distinction: "Americanism consists not of what Americans believe to be true, but rather of what they believe *in*—their attitudes, their sentiments, their hopes and resolves, their scruples and maxims, or what are sometimes called their 'valuations.' "[16] If one can discover the traditions that influenced the fiction of John Dos Passos—traditions that are also typically American—then one will be able to understand more readily the position that this author holds in American literary and cultural history, and one will be able to understand more clearly how his fiction speaks with a voice that is still important for America.

Each generation of Americans must face new problems—social, economic, philosophic, aesthetic—yet in some respects American culture in spite of its avowed dedication to heterogeneity has nurtured values that are homogeneous and that persist from one generation to another and oftentimes from one writer to another. In Dos Passos's letters, notebooks, essays, stories, and novels, there is ample evidence to suggest that two American "tendencies" in particular had a profound effect on the shape of his aesthetics. Dos Passos's readings in two American writers, Walt Whitman and William James, reflect his interest in the major ideas that led to the form and vision of his best work; Dos Passos's reactions to the poet and the philosopher were consistently positive to say the least, and as the following two chapters will illustrate, his perfervid response to these two authors is symptomatic of Dos Passos's own deepest convictions.

2
Walt Whitman and John Dos Passos

At first glance, there appears to be little similarity between the art of Walt Whitman and that of John Dos Passos. For example, the boasting, expansive, and cosmic persona of Whitman's "Song of Myself" seems to have little in common with the helpless, powerless figures in Dos Passos's *U.S.A.* trilogy. Dos Passos himself was a shy, retiring individual in his personal life and created fictional personages who are inhibited, restrained (when at their best), and generally of diminished stature. This apparent difference results from the fact that each author lived in what was, in fact, a different America. The sixty years or so between the inceptions of Whitman's and Dos Passos's careers saw tremendous changes in science, technology, and society in general, all of which changes affected the way man perceived himself. Man quite simply seems to matter less in the twentieth century than he did in the nineteenth. Charles Walcutt, for example, notes how the development of psychology has had a negative effect on man's self-image as it is reflected in literature:

> The special paradox of our time is that psychology in all its tremendous resources, which promised to open up depths and complexities of character for which there had been neither adequate concepts nor adequate modes of analysis in earlier times, has in fact witnessed (if not presided over) a steady diminution of the self.[1]

Nevertheless, there does seem to be a complex affinity between the two American authors, and Dos Passos recognized this by affirming throughout his career his indebtedness to Whitman.

Dos Passos found in Walt Whitman a stimulating American voice. His college diaries mention the American poet a number of times, and a college essay, "Art and Baseball," identifies Whitman's art as a prime expression of the natural vitality of American life.[2] In letters and novels throughout his life, Dos Passos always placed Whitman in a prominent position, and at one point he notes that "I read him a great deal as a kid and I rather imagine that a great deal of the original slant of my work comes from that vein in the American tradition."³ A close study of Dos Passos's fiction confirms that certain fundamental values are present that parallel those in Whitman's poetry and essays.

What Dos Passos responded to in Whitman is made clear in his essay "Against American Literature," published in 1916. In this piece, Dos Passos admires Whitman's art and—more specifically—the secure foundations that Whitman posits as anterior to his art. Such foundations, Dos Passos recognizes, are lacking in America; unlike most nations, America does not have a "landscape," no "primitive savageries, redolent with old cults of earth and harvest." Ordinarily, such realities, such myths, nurture the artist; "great writings," Dos Passos says, result from the writer's "unconscious intimacy with nature." But Whitman, Dos Passos observes, rose above that necessity by "founding his faith on himself, on the glowing life within him."⁴ The implicit assumption here is that the "natural" self still contains the residuum of nature that ties men to the natural landscape—or to the memory of it. What Dos Passos is advocating here is what Whitman affirmed repeatedly: to the degree that man can feel the ties to his natural condition, to his primal self, and to the world of nature, he can live a life that is organically whole and that escapes fragmentation. In Whitman's terms, the dichotomy of the one and the many, the self and the "En-Masse," man and nature, is resolvable: "Did you suppose that there could be only one Supreme? We affirm there can be unnumbered Supremes, and that one does not countervail another any more than one eyesight countervails another."⁵

Whitman's most persistently articulated article of faith is his belief in the individual, and the best example of the individual is the poet. In his 1855 "Preface" to *Leaves of Grass,* Whitman writes that the American poet is "the arbiter of the diverse and he is the key."⁶ There is no question here as to the source of moral and aesthetic values. "The best authority," he says, evolves from one's "own soul."⁷ The poet, he says further on, has nothing to do with "interpositions and coverings and turmoils and strategems" but with "first principles."⁸ This unqualified dedication to a fundamental subjective reality, self-generated, or at least self-discovered, remained throughout his career a central tenet in Whitman's aesthetic. For example, in the 1876 Preface, Whitman states that "to sing the Song of that divine law of Identity, and of Yourself, consistently with the Divine Law of the Universal, is a main intention of those *Leaves.*"⁹ Similarly, in 1888 he uses the term "Personality" but the purpose is the same. As *Leaves of Grass* evolved, he says, "I saw, from the time my enterprise and questionings positively shaped themselves . . . that the trunk and centre whence the answer was to radiate, and to which all should return from straying however far a distance, must be an identical body and soul, a personality."¹⁰ Whitman was a poet rather than a philosopher (as many critics have noted); thus the reader should not expect a detailed analysis from Whitman as to what he means by "Identity" or "Personality," but the image of the tree trunk and the inclusion of both body and soul suggest that the poet predicated a solid, interior foundation that assures an authentic relation to life. The image of the tree suggests that the individual is an organic entity who can enjoy a holistic relationship with the natural world.

For Whitman, the individual is not all. Standing in potential opposition to the individual but ideally congruent with it is the not-me—Nature:

> A fitly born and bred race, growing up in right conditions of out-door as much as in-door, harmony, activity and development, would probably, from and in those conditions, find it enough merely *to live*—and would, in their relations to the sky, air, water, trees, &c., and to the countless common shows, and in the fact of life itself, discover and achieve happiness—with Being suffused night and day by wholesome extasy, surpassing all the pleasures that wealth, amusement, and even gratified intellect, erudition, or the sense of art, can give.

To this end, to show mankind the true path, Whitman says, literature "needs tally and express Nature, and the spirit of Nature."[11] Through literature, man will know "the eternal beats, eternal systole and diastole of life in things."[12]

A good illustration of Whitman's conception of the individual's relation to nature occurs in his poem "There Was a Child Went Forth,"[13] which is an account of the process of maturation. By implication the poem suggests Whitman's view of the artist's development. This short poem can be conveniently divided into two parts, each of which is dominated by a distinctive catalog of visual images. Implicit throughout, however, is a world of isolated individuals. The child, who begins the poem as a solitary individual observing reality, ends in essentially the same condition; he is an isolated observer in spite of the fact that he has grown. Moreover, the characters who figure in the poem are also for the most part isolated. An "old drunkard" (l. 13) is staggering home. A schoolmistress is seen "on her way to the school" (l. 14), though the communal activity of teaching is not mentioned. Even when the poet mentions "the friendly boys that pass'd—and the quarrelsome boys" (l. 15), there is a sense of only minimal involvement or interaction: they pass. The one hint of a truly social situation is in the description of the child's parents. The mother is mentioned as having "mild words" (l. 23), and the father is "strong, self-sufficient, manly, mean, anger'd, unjust; / The blow, the quick loud word, the tight bargain, the crafty lure" (ll. 24–25). This first catalog, which deals largely with the human element, ends on a philosophical note, suggesting that all reality may be an illusion: "Whether that which appears so is so, or is it all flashes and specks?" (l. 29).

At this point the reader might assume that the remainder of the poem will be devoted to answering this troubling epistemological question, but it is not, or more correctly the second part of the poem (ll. 30–39) answers the question by ignoring it. The first catalog is notable for its treatment of the individual's relation to the human community; the second is significant for its transcending of the human, for its listing of the visual images of the physical world: a facade, a river, streets, vehicles, clouds, wharves, and so forth. The question as to whether these things are "flashes and specks" or reality is not asked again, presumably because the objects mentioned have an inherent interest apart from philosophical speculation. They are objects of overwhelming interest and importance to the child. His visual assimilation of these objects contributes to his identity, regardless of what their true nature might be.

In the largest sense, this poem is also about the nature of reality—about the nature of Nature in Whitman's definition of the term. "There Was a Child Went Forth" is a record of the poet's growing awareness of the manifold aspects of the world, whether the human (schoolteachers, drunks, parents) or the man-made (wharves, facades, streets), or the natural (the sunset, the river, mist, light, waves, clouds, mud). "These became part of that child," (l. 39) he says, and readers are to presume that he responds to and assimilates these various things because exterior nature and interior nature are intertwining and complementary. It is the poet's task, Whitman says in his 1855 Preface, "to indicate the path between reality" and men's "souls."[14]

In the course of the poem, metaphysical questions become irrelevant, because a pragmatic consciousness obviates such quibbling. It is experience in its widest definition with which the poem concerns itself, and the particular attitude toward experience that the poet assumes is essentially pragmatic. This can be seen in the beginning of the poem, which describes the melding of the objective and the subjective through perception:

> There was a child went forth every day;
> And the first object he look'd upon, that object he became;
> And that object became part of him for the day, or a
>   certain part of the day,
>   or for many years, or stretching cycles of years.
>   (Ll. 1–3)

The act of perception is itself a blurring of the objective/subjective distinction. The object further becomes "part of" the perceiver through memory "for many years." Whitman is not being philosophical here; he is just reporting the experience that a human mind participates in every day. One might presume that the mind of the poet—being more sensitive than the average—experiences this process more acutely. The process of perception is, nevertheless, an epistemological activity, and this complete identification of the perceiver and the perceived, however transient, is what William James calls "'pure' experience": "It is only virtually or potentially either object or subject as yet. For the time being, it is plain, unqualified actuality or existence, a simple *that*."[15] Such fundamental experience is the starting point in pragmatic philosophy, and it is an important element in the poetry of Walt Whitman.

William James, years after Whitman, would define pragmatism as "a method of settling metaphysical disputes that otherwise might be interminable."[16] And indeed the central metaphysical speculation in "There Was a Child Went Forth" involves just such a problem—appearance and reality. What is real? Whitman asks. And the answer implicit in the poem is consistent with the answer that James himself arrived at. For after Whitman asks the question, he drops it and subsequently examines only the practical effects of the experience of the boy confronting the world: "These became part of that child who went forth every day, and who now goes, and will always go forth every day" (l. 39). In James's words, the pragmatic approach attempts "to interpret each notion by tracing its respective practical consequences. What difference would it practically make to anyone if this notion rather than that notion were true? If no practical difference whatever can be traced, then the alternatives mean practically the same thing, and all dispute is idle."[17] That, essentially, is where Whitman ends his poem. The final emphasis is on the boy's learning experience, his confrontation with visible reality, nature. That fact is of paramount importance, next to which philosophical speculation fades to nothing. There is, finally, consolation in the mere fact of experience; whether it is flashing specks or reality itself makes no difference next to life lived.

There is some danger in reading intellectual history backward, in analyzing Whitman's poetry in terms of ideas that came to full flower some years later. But one must remember that American culture from the beginning had a strong bent toward the pragmatic. Furthermore, one must state that Whitman was no philosopher in any strictly analytical sense. As James E. Miller, Jr., notes, "Whitman was not stating philosophical truths so much as he was dramatizing himself and his life of the imagination."[18] Yet one is also forced to admit that there is a strong pragmatic emphasis in Whitman's aesthetic. It is undoubtedly for this reason that William James speaks so highly of the American poet. Unlike George Santayana, who sees Whitman as an uncouth barbarian, William James, referring specifically to Whitman, states that "the barbarians are in the line of mental growth, and those who insist that the ideal and the real are dynamically continuous are those by whom the world is to be saved."[19]

Whitman's rude pragmatism probably appealed to Dos Passos, but as this study proceeds, it will become increasingly apparent that Whitman's legacy to Dos Passos was indeed an appreciation of man's relationship to nature. It should not be surprising that such a theme should figure in Dos Passos's understanding of and enthusiasm for Whitman's poetry, for the received opinion by the time of Dos Passos's undergraduate years was that Whitman was first and foremost a spokesman for nature, however the critic might interpret that term. Thus in his biography of the poet, published in 1906, Bliss Perry notes that Whitman's poetry exhibits a reversion to "the 'natural man,' to the ego stripped of all artificial and social disguises."[20]

One of the more avid and unrelenting claims identifying Whitman with nature was made by John Burroughs in his study of the poet. By his own admission, Burroughs notes that his book has only "a single theme": "Whitman's reliance upon absolute nature."[21] To this critic, Whitman was like "Adamic man re-born here in the nineteenth century";[22] "he has the quality of things in the open air, the quality of the unhoused, the untamed, the elemental and aboriginal."[23] *Leaves of Grass,* Burroughs says, "aspires to a candor and directness like that of Nature herself."[24] Most important and in the same vein, exposure to Whitman's poetry gives the reader "direct contact with the elements in which are the sources of our life and health."[25]

For the purpose of this study, John Addington Symonds gives perhaps the clearest statement of Whitman's response to nature. In his early examination of the poet, this critic saw Whitmanesque man as having "sympathies with nature and sensibilities that link him to the world he lives in."[26] It is man's task to "live according to Nature,"[27] and to be "at harmony with the world."[28] Man at his best enjoys an "intimate relation" with the external world and is "trained and taught by nature more than by churches and traditions."[29]

Descriptions such as these bring to mind Jimmy Herf, perhaps, but they are indicative of the ideals of all of Dos Passos's protagonists: man's vibrant interior life naturally responds to his environment—but for Dos Passos the landscape most often is blighted and man's natural self is thwarted. There is no doubt though that a respect for nature—in the tradition of Walt Whitman—informs the very texture of all of Dos Passos's early fiction.[30]

3
William James and Dos Passos

Whitman serves as the ideal for Dos Passos because he founded his faith on himself, on the "glowing life within him." This seems to be a major discovery for the young Dos Passos: the self-formulated value can be discovered by the writer. And it is the individual, the sense of the free individual life, that is the basis for this self-generated core of value. This last metaphor—"the core"—is a term that appears repeatedly in Dos Passos's writings, and while it has to do with the "identity" of the individual in the tradition of Whitman, it can best be illuminated by a discussion of Dos Passos's affinities with William James's writings. For as has been suggested in the previous chapter, there are close parallels in Whitman's, James's and Dos Passos's conceptions of the individual's relationship with "nature." In particular, the individual with a pragmatized consciousness can find an authentic relationship with the external world: such is the force of Whitman's "There Was a Child Went Forth"; such is the point of James's philosophy; and such is the underlying theme in the early novels of John Dos Passos.

Dos Passos has often been mentioned in connection with the French *unamiste* movement, and perhaps in the fictive world of no other major twentieth-century American novelist has the individual character seemed to matter less. But the core of value that the individual represents is the central element in his fiction, though the idea is radically transformed as Dos Passos's career progresses. Dos Passos is from the first explicit about the importance of the individual. He notes in his college diary that "artistic beauty is first of all the manifestation of the individual—I mean, the first requisite for made beauty is the expression of the soul and the heart and the core of man."[1] The core here is the fundamental positive value inherent in each individual. In other instances, Dos Passos uses the term in the same way. Thus at one point he makes notes for a novel "which may be called Quest of the Core."[2] Another time he associates the phrase "core of . . . individualism" with "the conviction that only the individual soul is real."[3] This concept is the starting point for an understanding of

Dos Passos's fiction. For however much the traditional American emphasis on individualism is transmuted in Dos Passos's fiction—sometimes to the point that any real belief in the individual is obscured—it nevertheless is a recognizable standard of value that informs the novels through *U.S.A.*

Dos Passos states that in his sophomore year in college be began to discover that the real life of the individual was an affair quite different from the assumed faces of civilized man, "that the ingrained taboos were taboos & not fast in the core of things."[4] What is it that constitutes the core? A brief but suggestive entry in his diary provides one answer: "Hearking [sic] back to primitive emotion—for the communal life of the race—the tribal spirit, the comfort, the simplicity of life of flesh."[5] And a note for a projected short story provides more explicitness: "Man & wife—scientific travellers cold and unhuman—By strange chance forced to participate in African Dance. Carried away. The old inherited instincts come back. Passion. Find themselves in each others arms with real animal love—Result humanized and bettered."[6] To be fully human is to be able to experience the unalloyed pleasures of authentic emotions and instinct. These emotions represent man's original connection with nature and the natural processes, and they are the starting point in the individual's search for himself. The emotions provide man—in particular the artist—with a bedrock of subjective reality by which truth can be perceived.

This is not to say that Dos Passos is naive or simplistic. He certainly knew, at least when he came to write his best books, that man's emotions are not simple, and that they do not pave the road to freedom. But they are the starting point for a person's self-realization, just as they are the real subject of art. "Great art," he writes in 1917, "is possible only where individuals are full, consciously or not, of great longing, great discontent."[7] Emotions, feelings, the flesh even, may constitute a "core of value" that the individual can count on as a touchstone to judge reality, to connect him to the natural world. The modern industrialized world, however, has lost touch with nature. Because the average American is pursuing the "golden eggs" of commerce his life is "from one point of view, a constant succession of thwarted desires."[8] Many of his novels, especially early in his career, are devoted to examining this theme. Later in his career, he judged his early writing (not with total approval) as expressing "a boyish and possibly fanatical enthusiasm for freedom and growth as against slavery and death."[9] Just as Whitman discovers in "Out of the Cradle Endlessly Rocking" that youthful innocence cannot last and just as Bellow's heroes have their hearts tempered by "reality instructors," Dos Passos knows that the modern man has lost his ideal harmony with the natural world.

The pragmatic method is admirably suited to Dos Passos's wish to establish a bedrock core of value as a standard for judgment. The starting point for pragmatic thought is "the instant field of the present" which is a " 'pure' state, plain unqualified actuality, a simple *that,* as yet undifferentiated into thing and thought, and only virtually classifiable as objective fact or as someone's opinion about fact."[10] It is this identification with external reality that saves Dos Passos's "individuals"—or some few of them. The standard, the core of value, takes its measure from the mind's encounter with reality, when the mind is actually fused with that objective reality in the act of perception and when the perceiver is rooted to concrete reality. Since, as will be seen, Dos Passos found James's *Psychology* so inspiring, it is likely that he would have agreed with the following statement from the text, a statement that crystallizes in a short space the elements I have been discussing: "The very core and nucleus of our self, as we know it, the very sanctuary of our life, is the sense of activity which certain inner states possess. This sense of activity is often held to be a direct revelation of the living substance of our Soul."[11] Dos Passos's domain, like that of all artists, is this slippery, essentially indefinable and evanescent element, the soul: human passions, emotions, and feelings as revealed in action.

If the individual is the central concern of the artist, as Dos Passos asserts, the primary means by which the individual develops and maintains an authentic core of value is by adopting a pragmatic approach to life. Thus the problem that Dos Passos faces most directly is the issue of abstraction. Language, for example, quite simply can mislead. Plato, whose philosophy is antithetical to the pragmatic approach, Dos Passos says, is "an utter windbag."[12] And during the First World War, American propaganda causes Dos Passos to view the United States as "utter anathema—I cant [sic] think of it without belching disgust at the noisiness of it, the meaningless chatter of its lying tongues."[13] The problem of each individual is essentially the same as the problem of the literary man: how to make words honest. But a solution can be found: a person must be pragmatic, must test language and all experience constantly.

There is little doubt that Dos Passos found the pragmatic method hospitable to his own view of life. For example, in Brest in 1919, he records a conversation in which he "went quite wild on the subject of American psychology."[14] Dos Passos here is referring to the psychology of William James, a psychology that has a pragmatic basis. James had taught at Harvard for many years and had died shortly before Dos Passos began his undergraduate education there. It is known that Dos Passos read a number of James's books and that he reacted with utmost favor to what James had to say. In 1916, Dos Passos advises Rumsey Marvin to "get hold of William James' 'Shorter Psychology' or his 'Varieties of Religious Experience' and I think you will have an awfully interesting time, as they are wonderfully fascinating books and not a bit dry. And they are the most interesting books on psychology I know."[15] The next year he writes to

McComb, "I am very slowly reading William James' Essays in Radical Empiricism—I wish you'd read it as most of the ideas I find to be my very own."[16]

That he found James's psychology "fascinating" and James's philosophy to be his "very own" suggests that Dos Passos's own writings, in subject, theme, and method, would be consistent with Jamesian principles. There are numerous examples to reflect this. In *The Ground We Stand On* (1941), Dos Passos tells a delightful anecdote about the early American Roger Williams spending a winter in London:

> He managed to make himself practically useful. It was an unusually cold winter. The royalists in Newcastle had shut off the supply of coal that ordinarily came by sea from the Tyne to the Thames, so there was great suffering in London for lack of fuel. Roger Williams spent a large part of the winter out with a wagon-train collecting firewood from the country districts and bringing it in to London. He knew how to handle an ax; work in the open was a relief after the learned debates and the crowded London rooms.[17]

In contrast to the abstract discussions in crowded English rooms, the American likes to be in the open—and practical. Here is a man of action; and he does good. Dos Passos would value such things throughout his life.

Dos Passos credits his father, John R. Dos Passos, Sr., with valuing ideas gotten either "from experience or observation,"[18] and like his father Dos Passos throughout his career valued either method as opposed to mere intellectualizing. In his college journal, for example, he laments the "lack of tactile values in American writing—characters are abstract, collections of ideas—you can't touch them."[19] A few years later he compliments himself on achieving a pragmatic attitude: "I rejoice that I have at least got hold of *things* a little better in the six years that have gone by."[20] It is natural, therefore, that he admires the working man because doing unskilled labor, he says, "must make one lay hold on the elementary facts of existence in a wonderful way."[21] For the intellectuals, on the other hand, he has a cure (as he writes to Rumsey Marvin): "I approve highly of your idea of segregating the intellectuals—in large well padded asylums— The only way for them to escape would be for each man to commit an act—a grimy fleshly bedrock act. Devil a few of them would ever reappear."[22] To avoid the pitfalls of the intellectuals, a man must try "to dope things out directly from day to day—not accepting any ready made phrases without testing them."[23] The key words here are "directly" and "testing." For the pragmatist, an idea—or an ideal—can be true only if it "works" in experience. So in the mid-1930s Dos Passos expresses his skepticism about the Marxist experiment because it is mere "vocabulary": "I shall have to see people in action for it again to believe it."[24] And later in life he states the answer to the problem simply (and William James would have agreed wholeheartedly): "means and ends have got to be one."[25]

These pragmatic principles can be applied to Dos Passos's art. Dos Passos's self-professed ideal is to "live naked and clean—in the full blast of experience."[26] By exposing himself to experience, the individual artist can reproduce the illusion of reality directly observed. The image of the machine seems most appropriate here in discussing this process. Thus James says that "the whole neural organism, it will be remembered, is, physiologically considered, but a machine for converting stimuli into reactions; and the intellectual part of our life is knit up with the middle or 'central' part of the machine's operations."[27] Dos Passos would resort to similar metaphors: "The artist must record the fleeting world the way the motion picture film recorded it."[28] It is only a metaphor, of course; that is understood by both James and Dos Passos. Yet the important point is that the process, however it is accomplished, results in what William James calls "the power of imagining the world concretely."[29] It is this power that John Dos Passos grapples with in his initial literary endeavors *Streets of Night, One Man's Initiation* and *Three Soldiers;* and it is a power that he achieves brilliantly in his masterpieces, *Manhattan Transfer* and the *U.S.A.* trilogy. Dos Passos's vigorous reaction to William James's writings suggests a strong underpinning of pragmatic thought in his aesthetics. As shall be seen, this is reflected in his fiction.

4
The Early Short Stories and *Streets of Night*

In November of 1911, John Dos Passos was in England, and on the twenty-seventh of that month he recorded in his diary his reaction to Sir Herbert Tree's performance in *Macbeth:* "It was the most awe-inspiring play I have ever witnessed. There you see the resistless march of his ambition, helped by fate making him King. But he cannot enjoy the honors cast upon him."[1] Dos Passos at this time was only fifteen years old, but the central concerns of his later writing career are already apparent in germinal form: the questing individual is pitted against complex, unyielding, and essentially antagonistic forces. In short, the theme that arrests the attention of the young Dos Passos is that which both promises man a sense of grandeur but denies him fulfillment. This theme appears repeatedly in Dos Passos's early fiction.

Four years after seeing the London play, Dos Passos, a senior in college, wrote a short story, "Revolution," which treats essentially the same theme.[2] This piece is not especially successful in technique (the handling of the point of view, for example, is rather inept), and undoubtedly for that reason it was never published. For all its flaws, however, "Revolution" is an interesting shorter treatment of the theme that Dos Passos recognized in *Macbeth*. This story serves as a paradigm of the fictional worlds that Dos Passos was to create. Instead of portraying a king like Macbeth, the author presents a mock sovereign, Andrew King, a middle-aged bookkeeper in a New York architectural firm. Both as a child and as an adult, King is a timid and unassuming person. He is abused by his young classmates and later feels that he is unappreciated by his employer. His aspirations, however, are great; as a child and as a middle-aged man he dreams of being (among other heroes) another Napoleon (pp. 1, 5), and he fantasizes about leading crowds to a successful revolution. Labor unrest in the city provides the occasion for his long dormant desire to seize him, to make him walk out of his boring job so that he might go downtown to join in the agitation. Riding the streetcar on the way to the excitement, however, he is struck by an errant rock thrown by one of the strikers and is killed.

There is no internal logic to the conclusion of this story. King's death is pure accident and is not a necessary consequence of the preceding events, but anyone familiar with Dos Passos's later writings will quickly see a familiar tension. King suffers from repression of his natural instincts, a repression that apparently results in his daydreams of grandeur. Dos Passos clearly suggests that the repression is at least in part sexual, for accompanying the threat of a social revolution is King's accidental meeting with a prostitute, a woman with a "leering tone," "provocative eyes," and "red painted lips" (p. 8). Later, the thought of this woman fills him with "horror," and "he felt doors long barred flying open in his mind" (p. 8). He feels "strange naive indecencies hurtled together in his mind; he seemed to see the writhing of naked bodies, the flashing of the legs of dancers, to hear the thrum of wanton music" (p. 8). The social revolution that seems to be at hand, then, has a parallel in his personal life; his placid exterior hides the explosive undercurrent of his feelings, and this disturbance is echoed by the images of revolutionary violence: "as he read the accounts of small riots, of dynamite discovered under pavements, of agitators arrested, a tide of terrifying excitement rose within him" (p. 10). Riots, dynamite, agitators, and tide of terrifying excitement all suggest the libidinal instinct that must battle against the repression of "pavements" and threats of "arrest." Fittingly, the labor meeting is to be held at "Liberation Hall" (p. 12). The boss's son, Tommy Welford, summarizes King's condition accurately: "He's found his soul . . . and it must be upsetting after so many years" (p. 14). To find one's soul is to find something fundamental, but when Dos Passos's characters indulge in self-gratification, they invariably damn themselves. King's death, therefore, has a psychological appropriateness that is not apparent on the narrative level. Dos Passos's characters are damned if they do and damned if they don't. They either suffer in their isolation or decide to engage with the world and thus inevitably suffer defeat.

In "Revolution" the concern with pragmatic issues is apparent. Andrew King is obsessed with dreams. His infantile fantasies seem appropriate to his childhood, but when the same illusions persist into middle age and rule his actions, he is divorced from the essential principles of life, principles that for Dos Passos must be pragmatic. Thus the new revolution that seems imminent calls forth King's desire to be a new Robespierre (p. 5). He unrealistically pictures the revolution as including "men in uniforms,—like soldiers in engravings of the French revolution" (p. 14). To be in the grip of this fantasy, however, leads to his death in very mundane circumstances, with none of the glory that King associates with the past. Instead of attaining grandeur, he is felled by a stray rock. Such is life in an empirical world; since hard reality is the stuff of life, it is dangerous to live by dreams. King actually confronts the epistemological question that seeks to resolve the dichotomy of pragmatism and idealism: he wants "to make sure he himself was not the only reality in a world of shadows" (p. 7). In the best pragmatic method, the story is about King's testing of reality, about his attempt to distinguish shadow from reality, to see if he is in fact another Robespierre or some equally glorious personage. The story gives a resounding answer in his death. His demise affirms the fundmental empirical nature of reality against which dreams are but illusions. The stone that kills King is as solid as the one that Samuel Johnson is supposed to have kicked to refute the subjectivist Berkeley.

"Romantic Education," published in *Harvard Monthly* in Dos Passos's senior year, treats a similar theme.[3] John C. Ricker, a character reminiscent of many of Henry James's protagonists, is an American innocent traveling to Europe. On shipboard, he meets an opera singer, Madame d'Alvarina, whose worldly wisdom balances Ricker's naiveté. She tells Ricker that he does not know "what it is to love, to live, really to see the world" (p. 2), and then she proceeds to tell him of her own life, which is evidently an illustration of her prescription. Her story calls up for him "a huge vista filled with glitter and merriment, even with poetry" (p. 3). Consequently, with an "inrush of longing for beauty and life" (p. 4), he decides to "live." The ending is heavily ironic. He is last pictured in a disreputable bar with a woman whose "overpowered, coarse face was twisted into a nasty leering smile" (p. 4).

This story is deceptively simple. There is the slight suggestion in the ending that Ricker merely did not do as well as he might have; he thinks back to Madame d'Alvarina's "glowing narrative" and "for a moment he doubted whether this was the culmination of romance" (p. 4). Presumably, though, the doubt is only momentary. His situation at the story's end really is the condition of "romance," for the ending does not merely dispel Ricker's illusions, but strongly suggests that d'Alvarina's "glowing narrative" is an elaboration of similar sordid facts: "the cheap, heavy scent that the woman opposite him was wearing reminded him of the old singer's handkerchief" (p. 4). Obviously, the lives of the two women are similar. This is not to say that d'Alvarina herself is duplicitous, for when she speaks of "love, beauty, art," her words are "sincere" (p. 3). Rather, what Dos Passos is examining is the need to deal with life not through romantic notions but directly through experience. The author's bias is essentially pragmatic. Thus although Ricker is seduced by d'Alvarina's vision, his proper sphere of contentment is "the solid ground of facts" (p. 2). He is a mechanic by trade (p. 2). Only a pragmatic testing of experience will reveal the true nature of "romance." Both of these early stories show that Dos

Passos had an early affinity for pragmatic values. To live in a dreamworld is dangerous. The protagonist's real duty is to discover the true nature of reality—the flux of life beneath the veneer.

Although *Streets of Night* was not published until 1923, this novel was begun when Dos Passos was a senior in college.[4] It is not surprising then that the book suffers from many flaws, but a careful reader will be gratified by its many virtues. It is certainly a complex work that has received far too little attention from critics. Relying heavily on Dos Passos's reading at Harvard, it is highly allusive and shows the young author's preoccupation with aesthetic interests. Of particular interest here, moreover, is that the novel clearly reflects values in the tradition of both Walt Whitman and William James.

In *Streets of Night* the prevailing atmospheric conditions are cold and snow. The weather in this instance is an effective symbolic representation of the emotional lives of the characters and of the New England culture. The central problem of these characters is to break through the stultifying cultural restrictions and to find happiness. The repressive atmosphere of Boston, however, actually suggests a larger problem. Dos Passos is using this urban environment to illustrate the problems inherent in American culture. So, for example, Nan was born on Beacon Hill, but Wenny is from Washington, D.C., and Fanshaw from Omaha. As in several of his later books, Dos Passos is emphasizing geographical diversity, and in the case of each of the three characters it is not the atmosphere of Boston and Cambridge streets alone that is portrayed as stultifying. The streets have the potential for excitement,[5] and for the most part the three main characters do seem to enjoy themselves in their urban excursions. What is suggested, however, is that each suffers from a repressive upbringing and that the source of their problems lies in twentieth-century American culture at large as much as it does in Boston itself.

Blanche Gelfant defines the problem of Dos Passos's generic hero as "a quest for self-identity, for stability, and roots."[6] In *Streets of Night,* Nan and Fanshaw lack secure identities, and for much of the novel the same can be said of Wenny. They are in varying degrees alienated from their true selves. Nan, for example, states that she wishes that she were Marion, the Irish servant girl (p. 263). To escape the harsh realities of the present, Fanshaw consistently daydreams about the "safe" world of Renaissance life and art, and quite appropriate to his daydreams and to his obvious narcissism, he wishes that he were like the figure in Dürer's self-portrait (p. 94). Even Wenny, who of the three is most in contact with his true feelings, states at one point that his real wish is "not to be myself . . . to be anybody, any one of those people but myself" (p. 240).

While it may be true that these three characters cannot successfully integrate their selves with the world as they find it (and thus never can achieve a secure identity), Dos Passos himself had a clear conception of their identities, and to characterize them he made use in each case of allusions to figures in American literary history. These allusions serve as a foil to Fanshaw's escape to the Renaissance and to Nan's need for an ancient Greek ideal. Only Wenny, as shall be seen, exemplifies and endorses the American tradition, and consequently he serves as a standard of value by which the other characters can be judged.

Fanshaw clearly is a literary descendant of Fanshawe, the protagonist in Nathaniel Hawthorne's first novel. Like Hawthorne's character, Dos Passos's figure is associated with college life. Both characters are "bookish," and Fanshaw is similar to his predecessor, as Linda Wagner notes, in that he has a tendency to lose himself in "idylls."[7] The similarities go further, however, and suggest that Dos Passos had read Hawthorne's tale carefully. The original Fanshawe, for example, is incapable of finding "his happiness in the common occupation of the world."[8] He is "a ruler in a world of his own, and independent of the beings that surrounded him."[9] This surely is a good evaluation of Dos Passos's own alienated creature. In Fanshaw's frequent escapes to the Renaissance and in his neurotic rejection of the "ugly" world, Dos Passos's character is likewise consistent with Hawthorne's Fanshawe, who "called up in review the years, that, even at his early age, he had spent in solitary study—in conversation with the dead—while he had scorned to mingle with the living world, or to be actuated by any of its motives."[10] In addition, both Dos Passos's and Hawthorne's novels involve a love triangle, with two men—one effete and one masculine—vying for the same woman. Just as Hawthorne awards Ellen Langton to the stronger Edward Walcott, so too Nan prefers the memory of the dead Wenny to the ineffectual, half-living Fanshaw who, like his predecessor, fails in lovemaking.

The allusion to Hawthorne's novel serves two purposes for Dos Passos. First, by borrowing the name of Hawthorne's character, he reinforces the characterization of his protagonist. More important, however, the literary allusion serves a functional thematic role. In harking back to a figure in American literature, Dos Passos emphasizes the degree to which Fanshaw is alienated. He is an American who doesn't know he is an American, who insists on "living" in Renaissance Italy.

This is not to say that Dos Passos's Fanshaw is an atypical American. In his essay "The American Background: America and Alfred Stieglitz," William Carlos Williams tells the story of the early English settlers in America, who when confronting a strange bird knew not what to make of it. These settlers, Williams says, had "an alien mood toward the land."[11] Instead of naming the bird anew, they fell back on old ways and called it a robin, the bird in their past experience that approximated most closely the new species. Williams sees this event as indicative of the American experience: "To Americans the effort to appraise the real through the maze of a cut-off and imposed culture from Europe has been a vivid task, if very often too great for their realizations."[12] The solution as Williams sees it was (and is) for Americans to apply their minds to new confrontations with the situation as it actually exists.

Fanshaw is an excellent illustration of this problem. He is living in Cambridge and Boston, but he never *sees* the New England that is really there. There are many illustrations of this; a few will suffice. A number of times, for example, he remembers Nan—the woman he supposedly loves—as "a girl by a Lombard painter" (pp. 68, 98). Looking out the window at red berries lying on the snow, Fanshaw "sees" a "scene by Brueghel" (p. 95). In looking at the Atlantic Ocean, he does not see the New England shoreline at all, but rather an "English engraving" (p. 225) of a seascape (thus giving a description *twice* removed from reality). Fanshaw cannot stand the thought of making love to Elise, the good-hearted and fun-loving chorus girl (chapter 1 of the novel), but he fantasizes about approaching Nan "as one would have made love to a marquise with powdered hair in a garden by LeNotre" (p. 227). And how does Fanshaw describe the ecstatic feeling that Nan evokes in him? It is "unbearable . . . when I looked in her eyes and a light like the light bursting out from the center in that Greco Nativity shot all through me" (p. 228). Numerous similar examples can be adduced to show the extent to which Fanshaw is alienated from himself because he is alienated from his surroundings. His emotions do not respond to his environment in any authentic fashion. He himself recognizes his essential condition even if he cannot remedy it: "cultivated people in this generation . . . are like foreigners who suddenly find themselves in a country whose language they do not know, whose institutions they do not understand" (p. 155). And this indeed applies to Fanshaw. He comes from Omaha and physically finds himself in Boston, but his state of mind is strictly Renaissance Italy.

One of the few times that the reader sees Fanshaw actually engaged with the world is revealing. In the first chapter of the novel, Cham Mason talks the reluctant Fanshaw into going on a boating excursion and picnic with two chorus girls. Elise Montmorency, Fanshaw's date, is as inarticulate and unrefined as a chorus girl might be expected to be. "Silly, ain't they?" she says of Cham and Phoebe's flirting (p. 19). Fanshaw's response shows that he has nurtured an elaborate system of rationalizations to protect his overrefined sensibility: "The ain't stung in Fanshaw's ears. The girl was common. The thought made him blush" (p. 19). Confronting the "common" and even the everyday is the type of experience that Fanshaw tries desperately to avoid. He lives in a highly artificial world. Elise

Montmorency is more astute than she realizes when she says that "Fanshaw" is "a funny name like a stage name" (p. 18). She is right in spirit, for the artificial fabrication is an essential part of Fanshaw's world view.

The price that Fanshaw must pay for his sense of propriety is a fearful lifelessness. Unlike le Capitaine Eustache de la Potinière and Wenny, both of whom are men who value action, Fanshaw is "frozen and rigid in ferocious loneliness" (p. 78). The recurrent metaphor that most frequently illustrates his character is the enclosed space, of being within "protecting walls" (p. 204). When he buys the newspaper that reports Wenny's death, for example, he must bolt himself into his room before he will read about it (p. 208). He dreams of himself and Nan in a "garden walled against" the ugliness of modern society (p. 241). Earlier, in describing his condition to Wenny, he is exact in his use of metaphor: "You know all those desperate little Mid-Victorian knick-knacks put in the cabinet so that they won't have to be dusted. I think my mind is like that. It opens. You can put things in and they stay there, but nothing moves" (p. 76). Stasis here is the complement of enclosure. Thus a scene in chapter 3 ends with Fanshaw in his room pondering his books, "deciding what he should read" (p. 81). The scene that ends the novel is similar. Fanshaw, isolated in the ship's cabin in the harbor of Palermo, almost acts, almost resolves to stay in Italy; that he does not is a comment on his failure to grow in the course of the book. Stasis represents a failure of the mind to interact with reality. Action, on the other hand, involvement with the world, represents a pragmatic merging with the flux of reality.

As is the case with Fanshaw, the characterization of Nan is to a great extent dependent on allusions to a figure in American literary history. Dos Passos says of his childhood that "I read a lot of Poe,"[13] and in creating Nancibel Taylor he obviously relied heavily on the poem "Annabel Lee." It is somewhat surprising that critics have not recognized this, especially since the unusual name Nancibel is strongly suggestive of Poe's Annabel. Moreover, several lines from "Annabel Lee" are cited in *Streets of Night*. The most striking similarities between the poem and the novel, however, are thematic. It is Fanshaw who cites the lines from Poe's poem, and this is particularly illuminating, for just as Poe's narrator is in love with Annabel, Fanshaw is in love with Nan. Also, both Poe's and Dos Passos's characters fail to achieve a normal, adult sexuality. Certainly, Fanshaw's ineffective wooing of Nan is a testament to his complete failure to come to terms with his "festering web of desire" (p. 158). And he actually cites Poe's poem, it should be noted, not while professing his love of Nan, but rather while he is daydreaming and trying to avoid thinking of his failure at lovemaking with Elise, the chorus girl, in Norumbega Park.

The reference to "Annabel Lee," however, is most effective in defining Nan's character. Like Annabel Lee, who lives by the sea, Nan is repeatedly associated with the ocean. "If I had been a man," Nan says, "I should have gone to sea" (p. 99). Her eyes, "green and grey," are compared to the sea at least twice (pp. 123, 226). When buying a pair of gloves, she does not care about the material, but she vehemently insists that the color must be a "warm pearl-grey" (p. 268). By naming her apartment house in Boston, the Swansea (p. 251), after the seaport in Wales, Dos Passos again associates her with the sea, and all of these references suggest Annabel's seaside abode. The seaside resort of Marblehead, Nan declares, "would be a nice place to live" (p. 255); and when Nan and Fanshaw vacation for a day in Marblehead, their "love affair," which remains unconsummated, is no more satisfactory than that of Annabel Lee and her narrator-lover.

In the proper name Marblehead, Dos Passos found the happy conjunction of a number of motifs that have parallels in Poe's poem. First, as noted, it is by the sea. Second, the town's name—suggestive of "headstone" or "tombstone"—continues the mortuary theme of Poe's poem:

> In her sepulchre by the sea
> In her tomb by the sounding sea.

There is good reason to make this identification. Like Annabel, who has been "chilled" by the wind and is "dead," so too Nan (a character representative of the malaise infecting Dos Passos's characters) is sexually aloof, emotionally detached, and living a narcotized existence. When Wenny finally realizes that he has lost Nan, his beloved, forever, he also realizes that she had always been lost to him: "It was as if a rind had burst in him letting out warm, sweetish floods; as if he were crying beside a grave where she had lain dead for years and lifetimes, his memory full of an ivory body he had loved" (p. 181). Further associating her with marble, sepulchre, and death is the "marble" and "livid tomblike oblong" of the Dental Clinic (pp. 250, 177) near her apartment. Nancibel, then, takes her identity from Annabel. The meaning of this identification is further reinforced by a reference to John Greenleaf Whittier's "Skipper Ireson's Ride":

> Tarred and feathered and carried in a cart
> By the women of Marblehead
>
> (P. 309)

Wenny, the reader is told, used to sing these lines, and they suggest a similar antagonistic relationship between Wenny and Nan. Since Nan is the cold, Annabel Lee-type of character, she is responsible in some way for the unsuccessful relationship with Wenny.

Finally, it is worth pointing out that although the seashore location of

Poe's poem is relatively nondescript, the name Marblehead might very well have been naturally connected in Dos Passos's mind with Annabel's surname, Lee. The Jeremiah Lee Mansion, built in 1768, a relic of America's past, was long a historic and architectural shrine, having entertained the Marquis de Lafayette, George Washington, James Monroe, and Andrew Jackson, among others.[14] Thus it is a place identified with America's glorious past, a suitable foil to the bleak present.

Allusions to New England's past as well as to the poems of Whittier and Poe, helpful as they are, merely reinforce the characterization of Nan made in the rest of the novel. A glimpse of her childhood reveals her once to have had an ebullient nature; she once spontaneously broke out singing "Clementine"—until she is told by her puritanical aunt that it is a "low vulgar" song (p. 53). Her upbringing, it seems, tames her. Dos Passos repeatedly points out her puritanic and New England nature (pp. 44, 49, 68, for examples), and like Fanshaw's reiteration of "Control," Nan's self-admonishment reads, "Careful Nancibel, careful Nancibel" (p. 37). Her words, the reader is told at one point, are "elaborately emotionless" (p. 123).

The most obvious effect of Nan's repression, of course, is its stultifying consequences in her love life. Although on the surface she seems to lack feeling, she does have a very strong emotional response to Wenny. She is obviously attracted to him. A passage will illustrate both the strength of her sexual urge and her problem:

> Somewhere at the end of a corridor of her mind she ran through the dappled shadow of woods, naked, swift, chased by someone brown, flushed, goatfooted. She could feel in her nostrils the roughness of the smell of Wenny's damp homespun suit. Apresmidi d'un Faune, the words formed in her mind, Music by Claude Debussy, Choreography by M. Nijinski; the big program in her hands with its smell of glazed printer's ink and the rustling of dresses about her at the Opera. (P. 44)

Linda Wagner (leaving off the critical last part of the final sentence) sees this description as "an erotic culmination" of Nan's daydream about Wenny.[15] But one should keep in mind that it is a daydream, that Nan can allow herself such thoughts only after Wenny has left her apartment, and that there is a question as to whether there is in fact an "erotic culmination" at all. Unless one wants to read the "big program" as phallic (which may be doubtful), then the episode has a bizarre progression that suggests how thoroughly Nan has learned about being careful: what begins as a sexual encounter becomes a highly formalized, safe activity of ballet (Nan participating) and then finally the unemotional, distanced activity of attending the opera. The sexual content of the daydream becomes sublimated to a "safe" daydream. If Nan is "curiously constrained" at being alone with Wenny in the kitchenette (p. 35), she is "curiously constrained" even in the solitude of her thoughts. The eroticism of this passage—or rather the lack of eroticism—is damning rather than positive.

Such an interpretation is confirmed in an incident just before the one discussed. Thinking of Wenny, Nan remembers "the warm bulge of his arm against her arm, hard, male, and the bright jelly of his eyes between black lashes, last evening looking at the star" (p. 42). Such a daydream is relatively innocuous, but "she tried to brush the memory off" (p. 42). That is not all the commentary that the memory requires: "She didn't want to think of Wenny that way, she told herself. It would spoil everything, she must have more self-control" (p. 43). The "opera" passage, then, rather than portraying an erotic culmination, is more likely Dos Passos's portrayal of an abnormal—though perhaps all too common—psychological state. Clearly, Nan shares with Fanshaw the effect of the "genteel paralysis of culture" (p. 102).

Besides being sexually repressed, Nan also shares Fanshaw's neurasthenia. She too finds that life—selected aspects of it and the greater part, at that—is offensive. Her sensibility is too refined to tolerate unsavory yet commonplace facts. When she disposes of the garbage, for example, she must hold "her face away from it" (p. 45). Her abnormal sensitivity manifests itself in a number of other ways as well. Like Fanshaw, Nan keeps herself aloof from people of other social classes. The fellow tenants in her apartment building, for example, are unknown to her; "there must be some queer fish," she notes (p. 266), without caring to know firsthand. In her aversion to the real nature of life, Nan, as much as Fanshaw, is ruled by dreams, as is suggested by her reading of Longfellow's "The Slave's Dream" (p. 53).

Like Fanshaw and Nan, Wenny's character is also elaborated upon by allusions to a figure in American literature, but whereas the first two characters are judged negatively by the references, Wenny's character is meant to achieve a certain grandeur. His prototype is none other than Walt Whitman himself, Dos Passos's literary idol. Indeed, one of the necessary texts for understanding *Streets of Night* is Whitman's "When Lilacs Last in the Dooryard Bloom'd." Just as Whitman celebrated the dead Lincoln in his poem, so too Dos Passos hoped to give Wenny a sense of heroic stature and to eulogize his death. Yet other Whitman poems are used to explore various facets of Wenny's life. It might be said that although Dos Passos's art may have failed him in this regard, his craft was both consistent and appropriate.

Early in *Streets of Night,* Fanshaw gives the reader his first memory of Wenny from several years before:

He had sat beside him in a classroom in front of the yellow varnished desk of the instructor. There was the dry smell of chalk and outside lilacs swayed against a blue sky full of little rosy clouds; the hideous lassitude of words in an even voice that smelt of chalk and blackboards, and besides [sic] him a thin brownfaced boy with moist brown eyes intent on everything, the chalky words of the instructor, the lilacs outside, the swallows that flashed against the sky. (Pp. 77–78)

It is fitting that the earliest memory of Wenny is associated with lilacs, for the reference foretells his tragic fate. Like Whitman's memory of Lincoln's death, Fanshaw's memory associates the springtime lilac with Wenny. Furthermore, after Wenny dies and Fanshaw visits his grave, the identification becomes inescapable; telling the reader his impressions of the cemetery, Fanshaw notes that "there was a smell of lilacs . . . When lilacs last in the dooryard bloomed. Perhaps that was what had made Wenny say that the smell of lilacs made him think of death" (p. 237). Moreover, in the penultimate chapter, when Nan has realized how much she misses the dead Wenny, the smell of lilacs from the Boston Public Garden intrudes upon her consciousness (pp. 288, 290). Whitman's influence on Dos Passos finds its expression most forcefully in this image of springtime and nature: the spirit of Wenny living on in the memory of his friends—living on through their contact with nature. In addition to the lilac motif, there are additional references to Whitman's poem. The "star in the west" (p. 60) that is associated with Nan and Wenny's love, the star that twice falls out of sight in the novel, is appropriated from Whitman's poem, where the western star symbolizes the fallen Lincoln. When, late in Dos Passos's novel, the "star sank flickering out of sight" (p. 243), the event is surely meant to invoke Nan's memory of the fallen Wenny, for at that point she rejects Fanshaw as her future husband. Clearly, Dos Passos means to suggest that just as Lincoln's memory is hallowed and that his presence prevails through memory even after death, so too Wenny is revered and remembered.

Other references to Whitman are scattered throughout *Streets of Night,* and they fall into four general categories: energy, work, death, and nature. Energy, of course, is the "American" element that Dos Passos identifies in "Art and Baseball." As Dos Passos states in that essay, it is Whitman who has best identified and embodied that principle. It represents for Dos Passos libidinal energies, the essential life force of man. Both Wenny and Fanshaw, as previously noted, are driven by desire, but it is Fanshaw who invokes Whitman explicitly. In noting his frustration over never having "held a woman in [his] arms and kissed her," Fanshaw mentions the title of a Whitman poem: "Pent up aching rivers" (p. 228). Still, Fanshaw lacks the essential energy to do anything about satisfying his desires. Wenny, on the other hand, recognizes that he must act. His life is a struggle to maintain his Whitmanesque sense of energy. It can be said that he succeeds in only a limited way.

In his life, Wenny exemplifies the dynamic. He is for the living rather than for the dead, he says (p. 36); and according to Nan, he has "vitality" and is "alive" (p. 62). The symbol that Dos Passos employs to illustrate his character is the engine. When Wenny is standing on the banks of the Charles River, "behind him was the throb of the power plant" (p. 120). Similarly, the desire that haunts him is that of walking with Nan down "streets unaccountable and dark between blind brick walls that tremble with the roar of engines" (p. 201; the image also appears on p. 112). In this respect, Wenny's character is a foil to Nan and Fanshaw, who are generally portrayed as static. Unlike Mabel Worthington, for example, Nan refuses to act.

If energy is the source of life, one of the ways it is made meaningful is through work. For the young Dos Passos, work did not mean grading art history exams (as Fanshaw occupies himself) but engaging in the practical aspects of the workaday world, preferably using one's hands. Like Whitman's rejection of perfumed houses in "Song of Myself" (section 2), Wenny rejects "culture," which only "mummifies" the past "with scented preservatives" (p. 185), and he admires outdoor laborers. He exclaims in wonder that "the world is full of people doing every conceivable sort of thing. The streets are full of them" (p. 192). "How many existences," he mutters another time, "Walt Whitman had it in The Song of Occupations" (p. 120). Fittingly, early in the novel, Wenny expresses a desire to work for the railroad (p. 71); later Fanshaw is right when he sees men working on the railroad tracks and states, not quite with approbation, that "Wenny would have wanted to be one of them, red-faced spitting men with skillful ugly hands" (p. 220).

Dos Passos's treatment of death is also Whitmanesque. A number of critics have found Wenny's suicide an ill-digested piece of writing. Linda Wagner notes, for example, that the event is simply not prepared for, that the psychological motivation is missing.[16] This is undoubtedly true, but an understanding of Whitman's influence on Dos Passos's novel may help to explain the event. Dos Passos seems to have wanted to express the cosmic optimism of Whitman's "Out of the Cradle Endlessly Rocking," which reconciles the ache of love with the acceptance of death. The young Whitman wades into the sea and is buoyed by the hiss of death. Similarly, Wenny feels "Nan's eyes, sea-grey, drowning him" (p. 141), and he also associates eros and thanatos: "spread out your bed for me Nan Ellen death" (p. 201). He says these last words just before he slides into the Charles River, a bullet in his head. Indeed, Wenny's death is not a culmination of the novel's action, though some critics have chosen to call it that and to see the last third of the novel as repetitive.[17] The last third of the novel is important in Dos Passos's design because it emphasizes the aftereffects of Wenny's death. The problem in interpretation arises because Dos Passos attempts to approximate Walt Whitman's nineteenth-century optimism in a twentieth-century novel; he echoes Whitman in emphasizing the process of the life cycle. Thus Whitman would have appreciated and approved of the irony of young couples "mashin' " and "spoonin' " on Wenny's grave (p. 238). To further emphasize the life process, Dos Passos transplants Whitman's "beautiful uncut hair of graves" ("Song of Myself," l. 102) to Wenny's grave: "On the reddish mound new grass fine as hair was sprouting" (p. 237). "Everywhere," Fanshaw says in the cemetery, "love springing like hair-fine grass to obliterate the new graves" (p. 239). And when he comments on that fact, it is clear that he never would have understood Whitman: "O, the pitiful cycle of it" (p. 239). Nor does he quite appreciate the quixotic—actually Whitmanesque—streak in Wenny, who advocated turning cemeteries into amusement parks (p. 237).

Wenny, of course, is not Walt Whitman, but in the course of the novel he does approximate his spirit. After Wenny's death, when Nan is reading Locke's *Beloved Vagabond* (and titles are always significant in Dos Passos's novel), the suggestion is that she has come to love the vagabond streak in Wenny, even though she could not accept the streak during his lifetime. The vagabond, of course, is that element in Whitman which Dos Passos was so enthusiastic about as a recent graduate of Harvard waiting to go to war: he read "Song of the Open Road" and "was frantic to be gone."[18] In addition, it is a vagabond in *Streets of Night* that first motivates Wenny to act out his dreams. There is little doubt that "Whitey," the hobo, is an avatar of Whitman's vagabond spirit.

Whitey's name suggests that he has devolved from Whitman, but there are substantive parallels as well. Whitey's vagabondage counts here as well as his encounter with the raw experiences of life, experiences as opposed to the dreams that rule Fanshaw and Nan. But the clue to Whitey's parentage comes when Wenny asks him where he has traveled in his lifetime. The answer is an inspired piece of writing that matches form and content to the context. Whitey answers in a free-flowing Whitmanesque catalog that advocates the free spirit as much as Whitman's own "Song of the Open Road":

> Jeeze, I been some places in the last year. I've worked in Akron an' Cleveland, an' Chicago, an' Atlanta, Georgia. If I'd had the sense to stay down south I wouldn't be freezin' to death at this minute. . . . An' Tallahassee an' Key West. . . . An' Galveston an' South Bend an' Topeka an' Pittsburgh. . . . An' Duluth an' Cairo an' Albany an' New Orleans. . . . I didn't get to the coast but I was in New York and Philly . . . (Pp. 132–33; first ellipses is Dos Passos's)

In many of his poems, Whitman uses such catalogs of American place names to suggest that he was spokesman for the American experience. To travel across the states is to be a vagabond, but that is not the only analogy that can be made between Whitey and Whitman. In one of his more famous passages (in "Song of Myself"), Whitman celebrates "loafing" on the grass, and Wenny at one point thinks of "Whitey loafing on street corners in New Orleans" (p. 136).

From all of this evidence, it is clear that Walt Whitman played a very active role in the conception of Dos Passos's fictive world, but there remains yet another way in which *Streets of Night* reflects a very strong influence by Whitman. This is in Dos Passos's use of nature as a positive ideal. Such a theme has already been suggested by the numerous references to Whitman's poems, but Dos Passos was so committed to such a program that it takes on an autonomous role in this first novel as well as in his subsequent fictions. The discussion that follows will make clear how deeply committed Dos Passos was to advocating a theory of nature very similar to Whitman's.

In the opening chapter of the novel, Fanshaw disappoints Elise Montmorency, who had been expecting a "good time." His sexual reticence is embarassing to himself as well as to the carefree chorus girl. Shortly afterward, he is pictured in a Harvard classroom taking an examination in Comparative Literature 1. He cannot keep his mind on the test, however, and his thoughts wander to the smell of new-cut grass outside the window, to Elise's perfume, and ultimately to an example of lovemaking more successful than his own:

> And there on beds of violets blue
> And freshblown roses washed in dew,
> Filled her with thee a daughter fair
> So buxom blithe and debonair
>
> (P. 29)

Fanshaw's memory here of Milton's "L'Allegro" is particularly apt, for throughout the novel he cannot deal adequately with the present reality, and he intuitively realizes that safety lies in removing himself a number of centuries to the past; thus to avoid thinking of his failure with Elise, he recites lines from Milton's "L'Allegro." The passage, however, is significant for another reason: for its association of roses with sexual love. The lines from the poem seem to have been chosen by Dos Passos to reinforce the rose symbolism in his novel.

Dos Passos weaves references to roses throughout *Streets of Night,* and the flower is in every instance associated with love in general or sexual love. Thus on this outing with Elise, Fanshaw notes that she wears a hat with "blue and pink roses on it" (p. 21). When Wenny engages with a prostitute and accompanies her to her apartment, he notices that "the carpet on the stairs had big roses on green; it was frayed and torn" (p. 139). The condition of the carpet here reflects the nature of the love. On other occasions, roses are connected with prurient sexuality, when Fanshaw twice remembers a smoker that he attended where someone told an off-color story about a rose (pp. 79, 205). In contrast to the off-color story, though, Fanshaw dreams of polite ways of making love, "a handing of old-fashioned bouquets with a rose in the center, red rose of passion, romaunt of the rose" (pp. 78–79). He imagines Nan and himself in Europe, where there will be "roses handed over suppertables at Capri" (p. 203). Nan is an object of both Wenny's and Fanshaw's love and, appropriately enough, at one point her neck is described as catching "a glow of creamy rose" (p. 178). Another time roses are associated with marriage: a girl on her way to Cham Mason's wedding carries "a large bunch of pink roses" (p. 143). These are just a few of the more obvious references.

Dos Passos uses roses as a sexual symbol most distinctly in his characterization of Fanshaw. Fanshaw believes that "one must try to be beautiful about life" (p. 160), and for him being "beautiful" means suppressing "the lowest in our natures" (p. 149). His aversion to the off-color story of the rose is one example of this; the most-telling illustration of his sexual repression is presented in a more elaborate passage. In chapter 7, when Nan and Fanshaw are spending the day at Marblehead and they take tea at the inn, the suggestion is that they will become lovers: "Nan put her hand out to him suddenly across the table. He pressed it gently with long, white fingers" (p. 230). What follows is a flashback that probes in a symbolic fashion the roots of Fanshaw's repression:

> He felt his carefully balanced restraint tottering. When he was very small once he had tried to balance himself on the fence of the back yard above a rosebush in flower, and somehow the drone of the bees and the fragrance of the dull carmine flowers had made him dizzy, and he had lost his balance and tottered and swung his arms wildly. Then he had fallen and lain crying on the path among the fallen petals, his face all scratched and bloody from the thorns. He patted her hand gently. Neither of them spoke. (P. 230)

In the face of a possible sexual encounter with Nan, Fanshaw retains his "balance," his control over his emotions and libido.[19] His memory suggests that he has learned not to "fall," that he has acquired a well-developed superego. His temptation passes. He and Nan then unexpectedly meet some friends, and they all return to Boston, a potential sexual escapade averted.

Roses are also employed as symbols of love in the story of Nan's Aunt M. An anecdote that the aunt relates about her youth (pp. 256–58) seems to have been meant to give a historical perspective to the modern repressive atmosphere that bothers Nan, Wenny, and Fanshaw. Aunt M never married, and the story she tells probes the sources of her sexual repression. She was once engaged, she tells Nan, to a "youth of good family and connections." There is no suggestion of real love, however. Before she has the opportunity to marry him, she fell deeply in love with an Englishman by the name of Verrey (the name suggests "true" love), who had skin so dark that "everyone thought him an Italian." "Everyday of my life," she goes on, "he sent me a great bunch of Malmaison roses." Unfortunately, her family "hated young Verrey because he looked so foreign." They refused to let her marry him, and she agreed to follow their directions. As a result of her repressing her natural instincts, she became "awfully ill" with "brain fever." "From that day to this," she concludes, "I've never been able to abide the smell of roses." The "flower of Venus" has an obvious symbolic value here, and the story is meant by Dos Passos to serve as an instructive lesson to Nan, who should recognize more clearly her mistake in rejecting the "foreign-looking" (p. 36) Wenny.

Flowers, then, serve as apt symbols to expound upon a specific problem: the need to fuse the discrete but related worlds of nature and human nature. Flowers serve as symbols for the healthy sexuality that is necessary for a happy, fulfilled life. Just like the grass on Wenny's grave, flowers here serve to indicate a Whitmanesque ideal: the harmony of inner nature and outer nature is the goal of life.

From the foregoing, it is clear that Walt Whitman's ideas provided a conceptual framework for Dos Passos in the writing of his first novel. And it is clear that Wenny is the character who most closely matches the Whitmanesque prescription. Other substantive issues concerning Wenny still need to be examined later in this chapter, but two things remain to be said concerning Wenny's American background. First, while Wenny is clearly Dos Passos's protagonist-ideal, he is also problematic. Just as Fanshaw (for all his obvious shortcomings) actually seems attractive to Dos Passos in some ways (Dos Passos cannot seem to feel idealism to be all bad), Wenny's character also reflects Dos Passos's fundamentally ambivalent frame of mind. F. Scott Fitzgerald's well-known dictum, perhaps, is operative here: "The test of a first-rate intelligence is the ability to hold two opposed ideals in the mind at the same time, and still retain the ability to function." Such an ambivalence typically inheres in many of Dos Passos's characters. This perhaps reflects Dos Passos's own psychological ambivalence, which manifests itself in numerous aspects of the fictional process—the bifurcation of characters into protagonist/antagonist, for instance (Wenny and Fanshaw are good examples of this). So Wenny is essentially a positive figure, the only character who represents the strength of the American tradition, slight as Dos Passos knew that tradition to be, and it is appropriate that Wenny appears in one scene with a "chromo of George Washington" (p. 134). It is curious, however, that Washington's portrait is looking over a bar scene in which Wenny makes arrangements with a prostitute. It is almost as if Fanshaw's reiterated lamentations over the lost, ideal past and over the sordid present are to be taken as valid—even though Dos Passos, through Wenny, expends much heated argument against such a view. Second, although Wenny is a representation of American energy (in Freudian terms, the id), Dos Passos seems reluctant to give such values his unqualified approval. Note, for example, the symbolic value of the scene in which Wenny catches a ride on a streetcar:

> The blundering yellow oblong of a car came towards him along the black straight track through the rutted snow. He ran, slipped and with a laugh landed on the step.
> "Wait till the car stops," said the conductor mechanically. "Safety first." (P. 117)

Here one sees the classic confrontation of libidinal energy versus the repressiveness of the superego (suggested by the "straight track" and the mechanical reponse). This incident in a minor way foretells Wenny's tragic fate, for libidinal exuberance unless contained will inevitably suffer in the confrontation with reality. As seen in "Revolution," this is one of the paradigms of Dos Passos's fiction.

The use of American literary antecedents contributes to the complexity of *Streets of Night*. Their use was a conscious effort on Dos Passos's part to make his writing richer, for in college this is what was on his mind. An entry in his college diary notes "the thinness of American writing: [its] lack of richness & texture."[20] Literary allusions alone may or may not have been a sufficient response to the problem, but Dos Passos saw that problem as a serious one. In 1916 he reiterates his concern about "thinness" by noting that American literature is "a rootless product" (echoing Henry James, and others), and mentions that "in other countries literature is the result of long evolution, based on primitive folklore."[21] Dos Passos in *Streets of Night* compensated for the lack of a rich American background by resorting to other "lore" as well—to the primitive folk variety, which he apparently gleaned from his study of anthropology. As an undergraduate at Harvard (1912–16), Dos Passos took an introductory anthropology course; in addition, he was extremely familiar with ancient Greek literature and culture, having taken a large number of courses in the subjects.[22] This academic background also contributed to his first novel, for Dos Passos gives *Streets of Night* a mythic basis by characterizing Wenny as a conflation of three mythic figures. From *The Golden Bough* he used Adonis, and from Greek myth he used Dionysus and Apollo. The skeins of symbolic parallels make Dos Passos's intentions clear, intentions that are not otherwise always apparent in this first novel.

After Wenny dies, Fanshaw, still ignorant of the suicide, goes to his friend's room searching for him. He notices on the mantlepiece "a little snapshot of Nan propped against some volumes of the Golden Bough" (p. 206). Critics have not noted the significance of the allusion, though *The Golden Bough* seems to have been used to give "texture" and meaning to the novel. In particular, a close reading of *Streets of Night* makes it clear that Dos Passos attempted to give Wenny, the anthropology student (p. 101), a quality of timelessness. He does this by references to the vegetation myths cited by Frazer in his monumental study.

The use that Dos Passos makes of Frazer's book is apparent. For Nan, Wenny is an Adonis figure. His physical attractiveness almost causes her to overcome her sexual reticence. Furthermore, in the ancient Assyrian festival, Adonis is reputed to have been sacrificed in the Spring,[23] and Wenny, who according to Nan has an "Assyrian" appearance (p. 36), commits suicide on the first day of Spring (p. 177). Similar to Adonis, whose body was committed to the ocean,[24] Wenny slides into the Charles River (p. 201). Finally, Frazer notes that "the ceremony of the death and resurrection of Adonis must . . . have been a dramatic representation of the decay and revival of plant life."[25] Thus the morning after Wenny's death, Fanshaw, still unaware of the suicide, notes that "the snow had nearly vanished under the beat of the warm rain" (p. 206); then later in the morning "Fanshaw stopped a moment to sniff the moist air that for the first time that season smelt of earth and gardens. The rain had stopped, and there were breaks of blue in the brightening sky" (p. 207). The use of the ancient myth here is congruent with the use of Whitman: nature provides the axis on which man's spiritual life revolves. Wenny's suicide then seems less a sign of his failure than it is evidence of modern society's sacrifice of its best: society offered no viable alternative for Wenny. His death, like Adonis's, is a kind of apotheosis.

The figure of Dionysus, as Frazer points out, is the Greek equivalent of Adonis, both being major deities in the vegetation myths. Dos Passos drew on this god too in this characterization of Wenny. That Dionysus is "a personification of the vine"[26] seems to lie behind Wenny's love of wine. Thus he asserts that "the only genuine thing I ever did in my life was get drunk" (p. 192). Furthermore, a perplexing description in *Streets of Night* is elucidated by an understanding of Dos Passos's use of this Greek figure. The star that Wenny and Nan appropriate as their own shines with "green horns of light" (p. 38). This description occurs when Nan and Wenny stand next to each other looking at the star when Nan is sexually aroused. It is an unusual description. Perhaps Dos Passos is suggesting the intensity of the moment by employing a synaesthetic image: sound (horns) and light. That would effectively convey Nan's feelings. Perhaps the author is drawing on the traditional association of sexuality and "horns." It may be, however, that Dos Passos is specifically appropriating Frazer's commentary about Dionysus, who "was often conceived and represented in animal shape, especially in the form . . . of a bull." Thus the god is frequently identified as "horned" or "two-horned."[27] The latter case seems most likely, for Dos Passos stresses that Wenny represents the vital, physical nature of man; he is "alive" and has "vitality," says Nan (p. 62). Wenny's Dionysian animality is also suggested by his frequent passionate outbursts and in Nan's description of him as an "animal" (p. 40). Also, Wenny's animality is represented symbolically when shortly after the suicide Fanshaw visits Wenny's grave and notices "a rough smell of singed hides" from the nearby abattoir (p. 236).

Although the Dionysian and the Apollonian are normally considered contrasting principles, it seems that Dos Passos made use of the myth of Apollo too in delineating Wenny's character. Fanshaw says in passing that Wenny, like Pico della Mirandola, failed in his great work of reconciling Christ and Apollo. Fanshaw is not Dos Passos's spokesman in the novel, so he may be mistaken in his appraisal of Wenny. As a descendant of the Puritans, the son of a Congregational minister, Wenny does in one sense represent the Christian strain. To a greater degree, however, he also shares some of Apollo's attributes. Just as Wenny's and Adonis's deaths coincide with the advent of spring, for example, Apollo's appearance is associated with "the warm spring and summer."[28] Furthermore, the myth of Apollo seems to underlie Dos Passos's use of the shepherd motif, which pervades the novel.

In Greek myth, Apollo was often portrayed as a shepherd.[29] It is fitting, then, that the star that symbolizes Wenny and Nan's love is *L'étoile du berger* (p. 243), the star of the shepherd. Other allusions in the text are used to suggest Wenny's association with the pastoral and elemental facts of life. Indeed, it is difficult to tell whether Dos Passos meant the reader to see Wenny as a shepherd or as a sheep. Note, for example, that Nan describes Wenny as a "dirty little animal" (p. 40) and that she reflects on the "fuzziness" of his hair (p. 40). He wears a "woolly suit" (p. 38) and typically takes what might be described as a shepherd's meal—lamb chops (p. 188). These literal details contribute to one of the book's themes, for as Wenny notes, the modern problem lies in "sheepishness and cowardice" (p. 184). He elaborates on this further: "Wenny saw himself in bitter distortion, standing on a hydrant confessing idiocies to crowds who wore his face as a mask on their own and bleated like sheep, baa, baa, at every pause" (p. 184). Wenny's problem is everyman's problem: the herd instinct rules, and man can find no transcendence—unless one is an Apollo.

One final point needs to be made concerning Wenny as an avatar of

Apollo the shepherd. *Streets of Night,* as seen, contains numerous overt allusions to American authors and their works: Hawthorne, Poe, Whitman, Whittier, and Longfellow. It seems appropriate, then, that this novel about Boston would also draw upon the poetry of one of the most prominent Brahmins, James Russell Lowell. It seems apparent that Lowell's poem about Apollo, "The Shepherd of King Admetus," was the major source in Dos Passos's use of the Greek myth.[30]

In this poem, Apollo spending a year on earth in human form seems a "shiftless youth" but is in fact wise (ll. 21–24). Typically, he "sat and watched the dead leaves fall, / Or mused upon a common flower" (ll. 27–28). This description is very suggestive of Wenny. Furthermore, Wenny's appreciation of "the gorgeousness of matter" (p. 191), a love of the mundane, has a parallel in Lowell's Apollo:

> It seemed the loveliness of things
>   Did teach him all their use,
> For, in mere weeds, and stones, and springs,
> He found a healing power profuse.
>
> (Ll. 29–32)

Most important—and this seems the point of *Streets of Night*—it is the memory of Wenny, the hallowedness of his life in death, that serves as a redeeming factor in the novel. Lowell's comments on Apollo are an exact description of Wenny's legacy:

> Yet after he was dead and gone,
>   And e'en his memory dim,
> Earth seemed more sweet to live upon,
> More full of love, because of him.
>
> (Ll. 37–40)

The reader is to believe, I think, that Nan's rejection of the vapid Fanshaw is a positive step made possible by her belated awareness of her true love for Wenny. Her resorting to the ouija board to contact the spirit of Wenny is somewhat artificial, a good deal pitiful, and suggestive of the sterility of modern life, but Dos Passos seems to believe that in the bleakness of the twentieth century, such a spark of true feelings makes all the difference in the world.

In using Greek myths, Dos Passos is compensating for the lack of similar American resources. And the *kinds* of myths he uses tell the reader something important about his intentions in *Streets of Night,* intentions not always realized in this author's first novel. In particular, Dos Passos was not emphasizing modern despair so much as the inherent nobility of the average human being. Wenny is an "everyman," whose life is "sacrificed" needlessly. But a knowledge of what is lost, Dos Passos seems to be saying, can lead to an affirmative vision.

One of the salient features of *Streets of Night,* as the foregoing analysis has made clear, is Dos Passos's attempt to make use of ready-made values in constructing his novel. Whitman, Poe, Hawthorne, and Greek myths all contribute to the meaning of his story. The physical descriptions of his characters serve a similar purpose, and in these, too, Dos Passos relies on an *a priori* valuation to portray his characters. A notation in one of his college diaries reads, "describe people's hands."[31] The role of such descriptions is suggested in one of Dos Passos's plays, *The Garbage Man* (1926). Mrs. Halloran admonishes Tom for "talkin' " instead of "doin' " and notes that "you can tell by their hands what folks has done."[32] So in *Streets of Night* the over-refined Fanshaw has "limp" (p. 40) hands and Wenny's are "hard" (p. 40), but Dos Passos goes further. Describing hands is Dos Passos's ways of separating the doers from the talkers. A bellboy has "red" hands (p. 16). The man who works renting canoes has a "big red hand, like a bunch of sausages" (p. 20), and Fanshaw is repulsed by the sight of raw knuckles of a counterboy in a soda fountain: "Fanshaw found himself staring with a faint internal shudder at the red knuckles as his fingers moved round swiftly in glass under [*sic*] glass under the faucet" (p. 76). Fanshaw here reveals his hyperesthesia. He is alienated from the world of experience, actually repulsed by that world; Wenny, however, is noted for his desire to engage with the world. Appropriately, he has "ditchdigger's hands" (p. 40). The physical description here is a convenient way to show the degree of a character's involvement with the real world.

The basic distinction between approaches to life—the "talkers" and the "doers"—is essentially a pragmatic concern and parallels William James's contrasting definitions of the "saltatory" versus the "ambulatory."[33] The former consists of words and ideas, while the latter takes account of the immediate reality that a person confronts. An exchange of dialogue between Fanshaw and Wenny illustrates this fundamental conflict:

> "I've often thought," Fanshaw said, "that there was something that cut us three off together, like people in a carnival in Venice who might drift in their wonderfully carved state gondola down a dark canal . . ."
> "And find themselves in the Charles . . . Exactly!" cried Wenny laughing. (Pp. 103–4)

Fanshaw is controlled by his neuroses to such an extent that unlike Wenny he lacks the ability to see directly, to see that he must place himself in the context of twentieth-century Boston and not in the Venice of another time. Thus both Fanshaw and Nan are enslaved by their dreams, and though

Wenny is too in some respects, he at least resolves to act: "What's the good of dreams? It's hard actuality I want, will have" (p. 189). Fanshaw, the idealist, deludes himself into thinking that the world was once "much cleaner, fresher"; Wenny, pragmatically, realizes that the stuff of matter doesn't really change: "Can't things always have been muddled and sordid? I think they were" (p. 70). "Sordidness" in itself is not necessarily bad. Dos Passos firmly believed that a correct way of seeing meant having "that feeling of the infinite beauty and infinite poetry underlying things—love, war, sunsets, tin pans, lawnmowers, etc. etc."[34] Dos Passos believed that such a feeling would produce an American literature, and Wenny is his first major pragmatic protagonist.

To act is of primary importance in *Streets of Night*. Thus Wenny vows to change his relationship with Nan from a passive acquiesence to action (p. 116). Wenny's perceptions too have an empirical basis. The "gorgeousness of matter" predicates the way Wenny looks at the world. Unlike Fanshaw's perceptions, which are filtered through a knowledge of Renaissance art, Wenny sees life directly:

> Out in the streets the snowflakes danced dazzlingly, ruddy and green and shivered gold through flaws and cones and crystals of light from windows and arclights. Faces bloomed and faded through a jumbled luminous mist, white as plaster casts, red as raw steak, yellow and warted like summer squashes, smooth and expressionless like cantaloupes. Occasionally a door yawned black and real in the spinning flicker of the snow and the lights, or a wall seemed to bulge to splitting with its denseness. (Pp. 192–93)

The language here is chosen to suggest empirical sense impressions; the similes are drawn from the world of everyday experiences. A similar concern with concrete, empirical language is suggested when in eating Wenny notices the "taste of veal with tomato and peppers, savor of frizzled olive oil, little seeds mashed between the front teeth into a prickly faint aroma, and wine, the cool curve of the glass against my lips, the tang of it like rainy sunsets" (p. 191).

Wenny's pragmatic frame of mind is further certified by his refusal to be ruled by concepts. Fanshaw notes with great disapproval that Wenny rarely commits himself to an arguable statement (p. 80); in other words, Wenny prefers empirical reality to abstractions. He insists on the ever-present moment of being engaged with the world rather than proceeding through life with fixed ideas: "You have to put yourself out to live at all; every damn moment of your life you have to put yourself out not to fossilize. Most people are mere wax figures in a show window" (p. 88). A good pragmatist, Wenny values the flux of life and recognizes that reason, the conceptualizing faculty, is less important than living: "Who ever had any reason to use? It's an illusion, the result of thinking things over after they've happened" (p. 89). All of this is strongly suggestive of William James's devotion to the flux of life, of his refusal to believe in ultimate "statements": "So far as reality means experienceable reality, both it and the truths men gain about it are everlastingly in process of mutation—mutation towards a definite goal, it may be—but still mutation."[35] William James, the scientist, gives more credence to the use of reason than does Wenny, but for the sake of argument Wenny merely carries the pragmatic method to its extreme.

Wenny fails in life, of course, though it might be more proper to say that his failure illustrates a right action—his suicide is a triumph over a failure to live. But the values that Wenny advocates are actually illustrated and are inherent in the aesthetics of Dos Passos's writing. The true hero of *Streets of Night,* then, is none of the three main characters but rather the implied narrator, who in the act of writing succeeds in suggesting the values that Wenny lives and dies for. Thus when Wenny thinks back on his childhood, the reflection takes the form of a Whitmanesque catalog, mirroring a diverse world of empirical data:

> And the little funny store where they had candy canes striped like barberpoles and toy trumpets; tin shiny through green and red bright paint; and the feel of rough brown paper twisted funnel-shape, cornucopias, horns of plenty, Auntie said they were. And the smell of schoolrooms and ink on his fingers, and himself walking home fast to get away from Pug Williams, who said he'd smash his dirty mug in. Fire engines and bare, proud arms of firemen loafing in the enginehouse. (P. 113)

This passage illustrates the "gorgeousness of matter" not by reproducing matter, which is diverse and infinite, but by selecting impressions that give the illusion of reality, the illusion of memory.

The aesthetics of this novel is further suggested by the philosophizing of Nan and Wenny. Their statements of aesthetic principles reflect Dos Passos's own concerns. Wenny, for example, sees himself "riding days over parched hills to find the yellow, half-obliterated parchment that once spelled out would resolve the festering chaos of the world into radiant Elysian order" (pp. 135–36); he is "in search of words" (p. 137); he is looking to "explain all the joy and agony he felt in words so simple" that the people in the street would "tear off their masks and tell their lives too" (p. 183). At the point when Wenny realizes the futility of finding such words, though, the conversation he has been having with Fanshaw and Nan turns to the "langage des fleurs" (p. 183), which suggests that although Wenny fails, Dos Passos knows that he himself is not as limited as Wenny, that he himself can find the language appropriate to his subject.

Thus, although Wenny fails to find a way to "resolve the festering chaos of the world," the author has succeeded in giving form and substance to the potential chaos of the fictive world. By alluding to American literary traditions and to *The Golden Bough,* Dos Passos creates a complex fiction that has all the finality of truth with none of the limitations of life. Wenny has to deal with the irresolvable indeterminacy of life; the author captures in the novel that indeterminacy and its pragmatic basis.

The values of Wenny and the author converge in Nan's discussion of Greek epigrams. Like Wenny searching for the "word," Nan ponders the problem of capturing the transient moment:

> Beginnings of sentences flared and sputtered out in her mind like damp fireworks. Slowly the yellow fog, the cold enormous fog that had somehow a rhythm of slow vague swells out at sea sifted in upon her, blurred the focus of herself that had been for a moment intensely sharp. She so wanted to say something that would make that moment permanent, that would pin down forever the sudden harmony of the three of them so that she could always possess it, no matter what happened after. Epigram, that was the word. There had been Greeks who had cut the flame of an instant deep on stone in broad letters for centuries to read. (P. 64)

Here is the central aesthetic problem that is repeatedly tackled throughout Dos Passos's career: to find the verbal equivalent of the emotive state. Much later in his career, when he reached his highest achievement, he would again state his aesthetic intent; his method was "behavioristic," a matching in the word of the internal and the external.[36] This is not far different from Nan's comments on the Greek epigram, though between *Streets of Night* and the *U.S.A.* trilogy the difference in execution is great. Nevertheless, Dos Passos's lifelong preoccupation was in getting the right word to pin down permanently the sudden perception of harmony. Before he was to reach his first real success, his apprenticeship as a fiction writer would continue in his next three novels.

5
Seven Times Round the Walls of Jericho

Seven Times Round the Walls of Jericho, an unpublished manuscript, had its origin in 1917, when Dos Passos and Robert Hillyer decided to collaborate on a novel. The extant manuscript is largely in Dos Passos's handwriting, which suggests that the great majority of the novel was Dos Passos's own invention. However, even if the preponderance of Dos Passos's handwriting is not a final verification that the novel is unmistakably Dos Passos's, one could deduce that fact from the familiar thematic strands from which the novel is woven. In general, the novel deals with the "overwhelming darkness" of early twentieth century.[1] In addition, many of the issues that appear in Dos Passos's other novels also find expression here. In particular, there is a strong emphasis on pragmatic values that devolve from an appreciation of nature.

Seven Times Round the Walls of Jericho was originally executed as a four-part novel, but Dos Passos eventually revised Part Four, publishing it separately as *One Man's Initiation: 1917*. Parts One through Three, dealing with the early life of Martin Howe, lead up to the war experiences of *One Man's Initiation*. In *Seven Times Round the Walls of Jericho,* Howe, nicknamed "Fibbie," is developed in the tradition of the Bildungsroman. The novel opens with the childhood of Fibbie, barely old enough to understand the implications of his grandmother's death, and follows him through the various difficulties of maturation. In his case, the difficulties seem particularly trying since he proves to be acutely aware of the inevitable hypocrisies of life. Thus his early nickname of Fibbie, which comes from his supposed tendency to tell lies, actually is an indication of his prescient idealism, which presumably is connected with his ability to imagine:

> And when he grew up big and strong he'd go up in a balloon and get on the edge of the moon and beat it and beat it. How fine it would be! Mother and Nurse wouldn't be able to get up there to stop him, not even if they sent for a Policeman or the Bogey Man, as had been threatened before when he had been naughty. He'd beat so hard he'd scare them all

away; then he'd eat up the barley sugar trees and the almond paste mountains. . . . O dear, but if the moon's an Indian drum, it can't be made of candy, can it.[2]

Right from the beginning, one sees the difficulties that Dos Passos's protagonists suffer. The bold, heroic act is fraught with unexpected difficulties.

In Fibbie's late adolescence, the image returns to him with some refinement, but with little more sense of the difficulties of realization:

> Now again he wanted to wake people in the dark streets of the cities, to shake them out of the ruts of their lives, to what end he did not know. Formless exaltations leaped up suddenly through the soggy dullness of his mind . . . Like on a drum he'd beat a tune on the belly of the moon, and the walls of Jericho would fall down, and a strong white wind would blow through the cluttered streets of the cities. (I, p. 153)

As can be expected in Dos Passos's world, no white wind ever does blow. Fibbie's early idealism, reinforced by frequent references to Don Quixote, is never really satisfied, as he finds himself confronting a hypocritical social system. As Dos Passos describes the novel to Rumsey Marvin in a letter of 1918, "there's a general undercurrent of the feeling that instead of Fibbie being the liar—it is Society."[3]

The novel focuses on numerous aspects of Fibbie's youth. It begins with the repressive atmosphere of his aristocratic Bostonian upbringing, which differs little in its harsh discipline from his experience at an exclusive preparatory school. There, though, he at least finds comradeship, a cynical boy of the world—he's English—named Weston Nichols. Together they manage to make life palatable, both at the prep school and later at Harvard, through walking tours, drinking bouts, and heady discussions. At one point, they rent a boat for a summer, having the liberty of vagabonds. Particularly noteworthy is Fibbie's secretive association with his uncle, James Clough. Fibbie's family has rejected Clough and has forbidden Fibbie to associate with him.

Part Two of the novel, the Harvard years, provides what Dos Passos in his notes for the novel calls "The Last Boredom of College."[4] But just as in *Streets of Night,* the ancillary activities that go along with the college years provide some excitement. In college he experiences some sexual freedom and derives a great deal of satisfaction from witnessing and participating in the night life of the city. Among the full social life that he carries on is his acquaintance with John Andrews, the musician who will become the central character of *Three Soldiers.*

In Part Three, after Fibbie's graduation, Nichols leaves for England, joining the military there, and Fibbie decides that he too must do something to escape Boston. Familial pressures push him toward law school, but Fibbie rebels and leaves for New York, which presents an environment where he can finally escape his family's influence.

In New York, Fibbie is hired by a business firm but then shortly thereafter quits in disgust. He feels that he must assert his own individuality, living life by going "into the great alone" (III, p. 118). In the meantime, he carries on a relationship with Suzanne Lavonniere, the former lover of the deceased James Clough. Again, the city is a place of excitement. Fibbie spends his time eating, philosophizing, and pursuing his friendships with Suzanne and John Andrews, among others. His full realization of the meaning of the war is brought home to him by news concerning the death of Nichols. Part Three of the novel ends with Fibbie's joining the ambulance corps, thus insuring that he will experience the war firsthand. The suggestion is that Fibbie will experience a transformation, a new beginning.[5]

The characterization of Fibbie is consistent with Dos Passos's other central characters. The lone individual must confront a reality that is overwhelming. To a great extent, Fibbie is resigned to being a quiescent register of events. His early ambition, the reader is told, was to be a politician—until he discovered that politics consists mainly of lies (III, p. 37). He is consistently portrayed as having a great desire for some unspecified transcendent experience. For example, he tells Suzanne that he experiences the "misery of wanting to be Achilles and Helogabalus and Dr. Johnson and the prophet Habbakuk. I want more than my money's worth out of the world" (III, p. 96). But he discovers that reality proves too resistant to an easy romanticism.

The sources of repression are manifold, and Dos Passos does not tire of berating every possible element that affects the individual. The most obvious example is the family, which from first to last in this novel is a strong force, a palpable presence, that brings tremendous pressure to bear upon the individual. Scene after scene of the novel shows Fibbie's chafing under the restrictions that his mother, loving enough, places upon him. Having gained the freedom in New York, Fibbie returns home and can see clearly and judge harshly of his family:

> How divorced they were all of them from any reality, he thought to himself as he enumerated the people at the dinner table. It was as if they had been shut up all their lives in close rooms, where there reached no echo of the work and hunger and starvation, of the sowing and reaping of the rest of the world. Yet they, through accident or cunning, all possessed money, the symbol of plenty, the reins of power. (III, p. 141)

Another time he states the problem most succinctly: "the family, the home[,] was the one thing that enslaved and belittled people, more than any other" (III, p. 118).

Fibbie's adolescence is a particularly troubling time. At prep school, Fibbie experiences a similarly stifling environment. There he must endure Mr. Shavel's talks, which are about vapid "ideals" (I, p. 25) and which are "platitudinous" (I, p. 48). Similarly, religions promulgate "ridiculous phrases" (I, p. 90), and Puritanism in particular comes under attack for its repression of sexuality. Cabby Johnstone, a poet and Fibbie's Harvard acquaintance, notes that "Puritanism has distorted all our ideas of love and life." Fibbie responds affirmatively, noting that we need to "shovel off a little of the debris of dead convention that is choking us, a little of the mountain of damn falsehoods that clutter up everything under the sun" (II, p. 26).

After college, Fibbie continues to rail against the establishment—here the business world in particular. His stepfather, Mr. Marvel, gives the traditional Horatio Alger pep talk to Fibbie: "A boy without ambition who doesn't want to make a success in the world. . . . why to me it's inconceivable, abject" (III, p. 44). Though Fibbie goes to New York for freedom, he must work, and he does try his hand at corporate big business, only to resign because it nearly drove him "insane." "God," he reflects, "American business is asinine" (III, p. 99). Later he reflects on a scene that exemplifies a typical working day in New York: "And below, under the shadow of the flags, flocks of people, the day's work done, on foot, in omnibuses, in limousines, streamed uptown to their food and rest, proud to be cogs in the mighty advancing machine of the city's life" (III, p. 116).

What all of this adds up to is a vision of life that is bleak and unremitting in its severity. The general public is steeped in "stupid phrases" and has nothing to do with "life." Instead, it is duped by what Fibbie calls "ukioiu"—Japanese for "unreality" (III, pp. 37–38). The newspapers are essentially pandering to a vicious public demand for hatred (III, p. 143), and the larger structure of life in America is equally sinister: "The nation is the sledge hammer, industrial organization has taken into its hand to crush out life" (III, p. 121). Dos Passos allows the largest generalization to go to John Andrews: "Organization has given the governments all such tremendous power to repress" (III, p. 148). From small talk to the largest elements of the social organization, a "huge malignant force" (III, p. 49) seems to pervade all. American society is, Dos Passos says a number of times, a "whited sepulchre" (III, pp. 15, 25).

One might think that in the midst of such a bleak moral landscape that there was little room for hope. But *Seven Times Round the Walls of Jericho,* like all of Dos Passos's early work, contains the seeds for man's redemption—if he would only look. Fibbie does. The answer lies in nature. Dos Passos's most effective weapon in this novel is juxtaposition, for scene after scene takes its meaning from the contrast of various social obligations with nature. One example will reveal the methodology: Fibbie reflects on the restrictions of his mother's house and of school, but nature is never far away:

> He thought of his home on Beacon Hill, of the old genteel red brick house, of the smell of breakfast, and the chatter, like that of an aviary at the zoo, when his mother gave a luncheon to her women friends, and of the heavy solemnity of dinner at night. Even school, with masters always telling him what to do, and rules and admonitions hemming him in on every side, was better than that. It was at least among woods and hills where you could breathe free air. (I, p. 152)

The freedom of nature (as emphasized by way of natural description) is repeatedly juxtaposed with various types of imposed social activities: playing organized sports (I, p. 48), attending school (II, p. 52), studying (I, pp. 20–21), listening to abstractions—"Comradeship, Manliness, etc."—being bandied about (I, p. 49), and imagining the "pillars of ordered society" talking—a generalized view of humanity engaging in "glib banalities" while shut in a room, away from nature (III, pp. 15–16).

In this novel, as much as in *Streets of Night,* Dos Passos portrays nature as an active force for the good. The origins of America are rooted in the desire for individual freedom, Fibbie notes, and that freedom is exemplified by a vision of man in harmony with nature:

> "Certainly people who came to America wanted to be free. They came to live in the wild and think their own thoughts and act and talk as they wanted to. . . . Think of all the beauty and softness of life the immigrants gave up for one thing: freedom to breathe. And now the rank growth of industry has come up like strange steel mushrooms and stifled us again." (III, p. 131)

Fibbie feels that nature is "inspiriting" (III, p. 17); when he gets ideas, they "bubble" up as from a spring (III, p. 37). At one point, Fibbie imagines nature in terms of the sacrament: the "sunset stained the day like wine poured into water" (II, chap. 22, p. 6). Another time he notes that the breeze holds "a faint warmth as from contact with the young fervid body of a god" (I, p. 45). Nichols is probably correct, then, when he notes that Fibbie's family life—however unpleasant Fibbie may find it—"roots" him to the soil (I, p. 75). And when human beings *are* connected with the soil, with nature, they truly know life. John Andrews puts it best when he notes that authentic life truly lived does not have to do with organization but rather with feeling one's connections with the intangible sources of life, nature itself:

> John Andrews spread before Fibbie in his rich impulsive phrases, his vision of the world. He saw life as a river, flowing turbidly through all time. People's lives were more like eddies than anything else, forming

and fading in the swift stream. Temporal things didn't matter, governments, houses, small miseries and joys, were all just toys carried away on the undulating stream of generations. (II, pp. 5–6)

Fibbie does seem to have an innate connection with nature. His vision of people in love is connected to the natural landscape: he imagines that love with women of his own social class "was nothing hot and human and fecund, but phrases out of popular novels, grotesquely conventional posters, the wording [of] society notes in the newspapers" (I, p. 85). When he observes men and women in love, he sees them "talking, giggling, abandoning themselves to the intoxicant stream of life that rose from the bursting buds and the unfolding leaves and the black fecund earth of the gardens" (I, p. 64). Thus when he is in love with Suzanne, she is connected with a play called, appropriately, *Paradise Valley* (II, p. 39). Shortly afterward, he sends her flowers, roses (II, p. 45).

In this novel, not only love, but also death, is intimately connected with the natural world. According to Andrews, flower, animal, and man are all part of a larger natural cycle (II, p. 4). Fibbie's beloved Uncle James dies in the spring, and nature serves as an appropriate backdrop to the funeral, the lilacs of memory included: "sometime before his death James Clough had asked to have his body laid there in an old disused burying ground at the edge of a cliff, where the wind and rain of each season ate into the little plots of myrtle-covered tombs and scraggly lilacs and wild rose bushes" (I, p. 160).

In Dos Passos's early work, nature is a primary good, but there is an additional element that is necessary and that is connected to Dos Passos's conception of nature: a pragmatic appreciation of life. In his plans for *Seven Times Round the Walls of Jericho,* Dos Passos called this novel an "idolization of action."[6] There are numerous suggestions in the novel that action is idolized by way of a pragmatic predisposition. Thus, Fibbie is searching for the "essential things" in life (III, p. 50). In reacting to his life in Boston, he is capable of feeling a "cold hard core of hatred" of its inanities (III, p. 51). And his exodus to New York is an attempt "to begin at the bottom and start constructing an existence all over again. So, here's the Vita Nuova" (III, p. 66). Whereas the empty, meaningless phrases of so much language seem to hide the "gorgeousness of matter" (I, p. 91), a sexual experience with Suzanne—one form of concrete, real experience—made him "enthroned in the gorgeousness of matter" (I, p. 106). And though he makes a questionable evaluation of the American business world, it is clear that his objection is founded on pragmatic principles: "They don't produce anything. They don't help anybody to have food and clothes. They seem to be nothing but a vast juggling with symbols. Instead of for reality, we slave for pokerchips" (III, p. 101).

Seven Times Round the Walls of Jericho

For these reasons, his own ideal of work involves physical action. He admires "steam-riveters," for example (III, p. 59), a drug store clerk (I, p. 84), and a cart driver (I, p. 121), people who work with their hands. The ultimate reality is concrete reality: "everything is full of gods" (I, p. 86), though most people are stuck in an artificial "stage-box" and do not recognize the "grimy, striving reality" (II, chap. 22, p. 7). Dos Passos repeatedly emphasizes that Fibbie rejects the general run of society, which is subverted by false ideals, phrases, abstractions (see, for examples, II, pp. 30, 46, 50, 74). Even the relatively positive antiwar movement is pilloried for its use of empty phrases (III, p. 147). To Fibbie, none of this talk compares to the empirical world at one's fingertips: "The bed, his clothes, the bureau, the world, were there to his touch and sight and smell, hard and thick and still" (II, p. 12).

In addition to Fibbie, there are a number of characters in *Seven Times Round the Walls of Jericho* who are spokesmen for the author's values: Nichols, Johnstone, and Andrews to name just a few. But no one character is as consistently and lovingly portrayed as James Clough, the brother of Fibbie's mother. In a letter, Dos Passos describes this character as "the sensitive soul which the world ends by killing."[7]

James is everything that Fibbie admires: a staunch individualist who leads a fulfilling life. He holds values that are anathema to the puritanical Boston social class of Fibbie's parents. He writes material for an anarchist magazine (I, p. 77), and he lives out of wedlock with Suzanne in somewhat of an idealized love affair. They live on Martha's Vineyard, which here is portrayed as a quiet island utopia, apart from the narrow restrictions of the mainland. It is appropriate that Clough's play scandalizes New York and Boston, but its title—*The Dreamer Wakes*—also confirms the very theme of *Seven Times Round the Walls of Jericho*. Indeed, Clough points the way for Fibbie, who must awaken from the world of dreams into the world of action. Fibbie does so by taking Clough's place: having a relationship with Suzanne, visiting Clough's friend, old Mrs. Holmes, and being entitled a fellow "Anarch" like Clough (III, p. 39).[8] Thus, using some hyperbole, Fibbie comments on the individualism of both Clough and himself as being inimical to established values (the gods): "In James Clough the gods had tottered. With [Fibbie] they had fallen" (III, p. 139).

Though Dos Passos worked at revising *Seven Times Round the Walls of Jericho* a number of times, it does not have the finely wrought structure of a finished novel. This can be accounted for partially at least by the fact that Part Four—the most important section—was detached from the early chapters and published as a separate novel. But the three remaining parts do have a clear thematic coherence. Part of this comes from the fact that the criticisms of society add up to a dissection of American culture. "Laughter" is the solvent, Dos Passos says here. "Against laughter nothing could stand up." "Before the laughter of their trumpets and the rhythm of their drumbeat the walls of Jericho would fall down" (III, p. 39). And Fibbie knows that in order for that constructive act to happen, the individual must "formulate" his perceptions (III, p. 145), and he must "point . . . out" to people the true beauty in life (II, p. 3), which is founded in nature. Thus John Andrews speaks for the role of art in life: "That was the greatness of the music: it was the one thing in life that freed you from the illusion of personality, from the convention of organized life, and plunged you into the great stream, to the rhythm of which the blood beat in your veins and the moons and the suns spun through the sky" (II, p. 6).

Dos Passos's pragmatic concern—the melding of life and art—can be seen most clearly in his numerous descriptions of the city. Time after time, he translates the sights, sound, and feel of the cityscape into a language that approximates the reality of its "nature." Thus Fibbie and Andrews on one of their walks through the city find themselves imbibing the impressions of reality:

> After much walking through streets that had the dead dampness of caverns, where people's skins were corpselike from the lack of air and sun and from the reek of crowded half-fed lives, they came to a place under a bridge where in a glare of gas torches, old women with untidy hair, and grimy faces wrinkled and grey like fruit dried into uncouth shapes, haggled over piles of fish that gleamed in lurid colors above the black flagstones in the flickering red light. There was a deafening sound of cars crossing the iron bridge above pierced by the shrill voices of the women, like the cries of gulls above a thundering surf. The women picked up the fish with dark clawlike hands and carried them away hastily wrapped in newspapers, pressed like something very precious to their caved breasts. (III, pp. 81–82)

Fibbie's perceptions here—consciousness and reality in contact, without mediation—represent Dos Passos's pragmatic ideal. The pragmatic mind can *know* reality. It is the artist's obligation to translate that reality into art.

This then is Fibbie's charge. He has come to understand that the world is hypocritical, that in general the world is out of touch with empirical reality. And he has come to understand that something must be done about it. As in all the other early works, the problem is cast in terms of an aesthetic argument. He must come to terms with the world by way of pragmatic apperception of life. In particular, he must experience the war, and then he must formulate those experiences into a language that makes a difference, the language of art:

> He was too hot and seething with desire of life to die. Later he would die, when he had sucked dry the orange, when he had experienced all lands and peoples and sins and joys, when he had moulded them all into

a sentence, a verdict and was ready to throw off the worn out clothes, to shatter the lamp that had shone on all the varied world. (II, chap. 22, p. 8)

By 1921, Dos Passos had come to see *Seven Times Round the Walls of Jericho* as "raw juvenilia" and as "mere sub-structure" of what he wanted to do as a writer.[9] In fact, the novel is no worse than *Streets of Night*. And it has the added virtue of expressing most clearly and insistently the dominant ideas in Dos Passos's early fiction.

6
One Man's Initiation: 1917

Dos Passos's experience in World War I informed his next two novels, the first of which was *One Man's Initiation: 1917,* published in 1920.[1] This novel, like *Streets of Night,* is in many ways unsatisfactory. Dos Passos's use of language, for example, has not yet attained the mature style of his later accomplished fiction. Moreover, although the disjointed, episodic narrative is perhaps a purposeful approximation of the chaotic nature of the war experience, its final effect is disturbing. It leaves the reader disoriented without providing an obviously corrective viewpoint, without stressing a reintegrative redeeming vision. This missing element is most noticeable in the novel's ending. There Dos Passos fails to cast in satisfactory form his philosophic, moral, and aesthetic assumptions, although, as I will show, such beliefs are nonetheless implicit in the final vignettes.

One Man's Initiation for all its faults is an important book in the Dos Passos canon. In contrast to *Streets of Night,* there is a significant amount of realistic action. Instead of the seemingly interminable talk about social and aesthetic issues that informs the novel about Harvard and Boston, *One Man's Initiation* benefits from Dos Passos's accumulated experiences in the war: his protagonist has something to do. Also, the characters in general seem more substantial in the war novel. Most important, Dos Passos is here free from the extensive, even labored, use of literary allusions, a habit that slows down considerably the pace of *Streets of Night.* When Martin Howe, crossing the Atlantic, sits on deck with "an unopened book beside him" (p. 45), the scene is symptomatic of the change that Dos Passos's writing had undergone. Unlike the highly allusive college novel, *One Man's Initiation* represents a direct account of experience, an effort to come to terms with reality without belaboring his extensive accumulated knowledge of literature. America, the reader is told late in the book, means "freedom from the past" (p. 157). Indeed, in chapter 1 Howe is seen as an "American Adam": "the future is nothing to him, the past is nothing to him.... Now a leaf seems to have been turned and a new white page spread before him, clean and unwritten on" (p. 45, my ellipses). This suggests that Howe's condition—his mind a tabula rasa—predisposes him to a direct pragmatic appreciation of the succeeding events. As will be seen, it is because of this predisposition that Howe contrasts strongly with the other characters. Howe, in short, comes to affirm values in the tradition of Walt Whitman and William James.

In his study of the First World War, *No Man's Land,* Eric J. Leed notes that "with the conclusion of the war, there were many debates over whether the veteran had been brutalized or ennobled, infantilized or matured by his war experience; but there was no debate over whether a deep and profound alteration of identity had taken place."[2] Such radically disjunctive experiences, of course, are not peculiar to war, nor is the reporting of them the province of history only. Indeed, literature typically absorbs such experiences into its very structures: content and form are inseparable in the crisis autobiography, in the Bildungsroman, and in the war novel. In Dos Passos's case, the experience of the war can be said to have left two distinctive marks on the novel.

First, witnessing combat at close quarters left a marked impression on Dos Passos's sensibilities. When Martin Howe meets an old college chum and asks him if he remembers a conversation that they once had in Cambridge, he responds, "No. That was in another incarnation" (pp. 127–28). This attitude exemplifies what Leed identifies as "the discontinuity and distance . . . between the front and home."[3] Thus the image of the tabula rasa in chapter 1 has a psychological as well as a thematic basis, and it is not surprising that the scene is taken from Dos Passos's own experience. He writes in 1917 to his friend Rumsey Marvin about his trip overseas: "America seems infinitely far off now—I can hardly imagine it exists at all." He continues, "I've never experienced anything quite like the strange break with everything past that has seemed to come over me since that sleepy quiet trip."[4] As it was for Dos Passos, the journey into war is Martin's Howe's "initiation." The novel's title indicates as much.

The second effect of the wartime experience of destruction can be seen in the texture of Dos Passos's novel. Most fiction, of course, is in the mode of memory, a story told;[5] that is to say that the first page is written with one eye on the last page. Dos Passos's novel, like the Bildungsroman,[6] forms an impenetrable web in which later traumatic events actually illuminate earlier scenes and give meaning to these scenes. In *One Man's Initiation,* for example, one particular image is of central importance. Martin Howe, sitting at a café in Paris, notes that detritus of war, one of the wounded: "Between the pale-brown frightened eyes, where the nose should have been, was a triangular black patch that ended in some mechanical contrivance with shiny little black metal rods that took the place of the jaw" (p. 54). The image is spectacular in summing up the gruesome effects of war. As the novel proceeds, the memory of this man lingers with

Howe, and the protagonist's implicit condemnation of war becomes increasingly grim, culminating late in the book with a full-scale denunciation of the drift of civilization (chap. 9). It is appropriate then that the first chapter presents an image of New York embedded in a triangular form: as his ship leaves the harbor, Howe sees "the buildings of New York slide together into a pyramid" (p. 44). The implications are serious and appropriate to the "disjunctive experience" of war; Howe will never be able to "go home again." In fact, the novel's purpose is to show that there never was a home, at least not as Howe in his prewar innocence had thought. Even when he leaves New York, the city as emblem of civilization has implicit in it the destructiveness of war. Thus late in the novel, Howe remembers "the flags, the menacing exultant flags along all the streets before we went to war, the gradual unbaring of teeth" (p. 159).

It was noted earlier that *One Man's Initiation* gives the impression of formlessness, and critics generally charge that it does lack structure. Iain Colley notes, for example, that Dos Passos's first published novel is not "finished and harmonious"; it has a "loose arrangement" like "a series of autobiographical sketches."[7] Robert G. Davis gives a similar assessment: "The book is purely episodic, made up of unconnected scenes, but they take separate and satisfying shape as vignettes or short stories."[8] Linda Wagner notes the same problem but affirms the existence of a structural principle: "Instead of choosing a dramatic structure of rising action—climax—falling action, Dos Passos sets one scene against another." She notes that the book's structure is maintained by "the repetition of images and language."[9] This agreement among the critics is the result of the lack of narrative complexity in the novel. Although Wagner is partially correct in her assertion, it seems that Dos Passos was indeed concerned with giving his novel an overriding structure. When one keeps in mind the premises on which the novel is constructed, it becomes apparent that there is in fact a rising and falling action.

John W. Aldridge, who remains one of Dos Passos's most perceptive critics, notes that a change occurs in *One Man's Initiation* "somewhere in the middle of the book."[10] He might have said *exactly* in the middle of the book. There are eleven chapters; it is the middle chapter, the sixth, that represents the core of experience that Martin Howe is seeking. In this sense, the chapter is the "climax" of the novel. For a number of reasons, there can be little doubt that Dos Passos carefully planned such an organization. First, chapter 6 is one of the longest in the novel. Only chapter 7, which represents a final reiteration of the previous chapter's motifs, is longer, and then only slightly. Second, although Martin Howe participates in the war at various times throughout the novel, chapter 6 presents the war experience in its most intense form, particularly for Howe. It is near the beginning of chapter 6, for example, that Howe states most explicitly his and the novel's raison d'être: "I am going to do something some day, but first I must see. I want to be initiated in all the circles of hell" (p. 108). A few pages later, in the midst of battle, he exclaims, "Talk about the real thing!" (p. 110). Finally, chapter 6 is clearly antiedenic. In fact, it lacks any reference to gardens, yet the garden is elsewhere one of the most pervasive and important symbols in the novel. This chapter has only one purpose: to present graphically the horrors of war. In Dos Passos's aesthetics, this is climax enough.

In addition to employing a climactic middle chapter, Dos Passos also stressed the form of this novel by using a sustained image pattern: nature in general and gardens in particular. In the introductory chapters of this study, it has been shown that Dos Passos saw nature as a particularly important symbol. Indeed, he repeatedly patterned his early novels on the cycle of nature.

Martin Howe begins the novel by traveling to Europe in the summer (p. 55), and the novel ends in the fall, the "death of the year," a time "of leaves drying and falling, of ripened fruit and bursting seed-pods" (p. 153). On this general frame of the natural cycle, the novel is structured. The process of nature is meant to mirror Howe's own life in the novel: from the callowness of youth to his maturity, ripening, and in a sense, decay. It is fitting then that Dos Passos would also evoke a pastoral setting as an antiphony to the horrors of the war. References to gardens can be found in chapters 2, 3, 4, and 7. Even chapter 5, which reports Howe's adventures away from the war, his leave in Paris, stresses Howe's relationship with elemental nature. When Howe spends the night sleeping in front of the Notre Dame Cathedral, "he woke up and stretched himself stiffly, smelling grass and damp earth" (p. 99). It is the garden specifically, though, that gives added meaning to Howe's war experiences.

The essential contrast between war and the garden is most clearly evident in a scene in chapter 3 (pp. 62–66). Howe and another soldier visit a schoolmaster and his wife and take wine with them in their garden. On the road adjacent, camions full of troops are passing on their way to the front. Dos Passos's description emphasizes the disparity between the garden's tranquillity and the feverish activity of the troops: Howe and his friends sit "next to the vine-covered trellis that cut the garden off from the road." The garden here obviously represents a place where a separate—if temporary—peace can be enjoyed.

In the first five chapters, there are numerous other references to gardens.[11] At one point in chapter 2, for example, Howe sits at an outdoor Parisian restaurant, across from the Jardin du Luxembourg (pp. 53–55). In the next chapter, near the front, he is quartered in a "little arbour," a "weed-grown garden" (pp. 58–61). In chapter 4, in quarters at his beloved abbey, Howe works at "making flowers bloom in the garden" (p. 80), and in chapter 5, once more in Paris, Howe spends the night sleeping "on his back on the little grass plot of the Parvis Notre Dame" (p. 99).

Although, as I said, chapter 6 is devoted largely to the horrors of war, in chapter 7 the garden motif reappears, and its symbolic value becomes most apparent. Dos Passos's description neatly balances the fullness and beauty of nature against the ravages of war:

> Of the house, a little pale salmon-coloured villa, only a shell remained, but the garden was quite untouched; fall roses and bunches of white and pink and violet phlox bloomed there among the long grass and the intruding nettles. In the centre the round concrete fountain was no longer full of water, but a few brownish-green toads still inhabited it. The place smelt of box and sweetbriar and yew, and when you lay down on the grass where it grew short under the old yew tree by the fountain, you could see nothing but placid sky and waving green leaves. Martin Howe and Tom Randolph would spend there the quiet afternoons when they were off duty, sleeping in the languid sunlight, or chatting lazily, pointing out to each other tiny things, the pattern of snail-shells, the glitter of insects' wings, colours, fragrances that made vivid for them suddenly beauty and life, all that the shells that shrieked overhead, to explode on the road behind them, threatened to wipe out. (Pp. 141–42)

It is not just this garden that is threatened to be wiped out. This particular garden becomes a symbol for everything valued by the author. It is all nature, "beauty and life," that stands against the moral ugliness of destructive war. The lyric intensity of this passage reflects Howe's newly discovered profound appreciation for life, an appreciation that results from his confrontation in chapter 6 with the war.

As mentioned before, chapter 6 contains no references to the otherwise prevalent motif of gardens. In this chapter, Howe confronts battle directly. After he vows to "see" the war, his ambulance is directed toward the action "into the woods," past the *Camp des Pommiers* (which suggests the realm of experience, an expulsion from the garden of paradise), and then "deeper into the woods" (p. 112). He witnesses the burial of dead soldiers at the front (p. 113), experiences a shell bombardment (p. 115), and becomes lost briefly in the darkness (p. 115). His experiences in a gas attack are particularly vivid and harrowing (pp. 117–22). Finally, he delivers a patient to a hospital away from the lines—though the man is at the point of death (p. 125). In this one chapter, the sheer cumulative weight of the details of war is surely meant to represent the beginnings of Howe's "initiation." This impression is reinforced by Dos Passos's use of language in the chapter: it is spare and concrete and emphasizes the immediate, unmitigated presence of destruction and death.

If nature contributes to the larger structure of Dos Passos's novel, it also has specific thematic implications. First, the natural cycle mirrors Howe's development, the process of his life. Second, in chapter 10 the vignette of the cobbler making shoelaces by cutting up the boots of war victims affirms this same principle. The cobbler is a testament to the idea that life must go on. As such he is a figure that is reminiscent of Wenny in *Streets of Night* and also of Whitman, who could affirm a process that is greater than an individual life by saying, "If you want me again, look for me under your boot-soles" ("Song of Myself," l. 1337). As the cobbler is cutting up the boots, he says that someday someone else will be cutting up his own boots for the same purpose (p. 172). The ghastly picture of the man does not in any way suggest Whitman's cosmic optimism, but he is a twentieth-century example of the idea that life is a process of which all are a part. As John Brantley suggests, even Howe's buying shoelaces from the cobbler is a life-affirming act in the same spirit.[12] It is an act symbolic of the reknitting of the human fabric that war destroys.

In employing concrete language, Dos Passos in *One Man's Initiation* reflects Whitman's prescription for the great poet, who "has less a marked style and is more the channel of thoughts and things without increase or diminution."[13] Instead of being "meddlesome," Whitman says in his 1855 Preface, "I will not have in my writing any elegance or effect or originality to hang in the way between me and the rest like curtains. . . . What I tell I tell for precisely what it is."[14] This passage suggests empirical reporting. Although, of course, Whitman is speaking in general terms about his art, the sentiment is not far from William James's conception of "pure consciousness"—the undifferentiated merging of mind and matter, of subject and object. In World War I, Dos Passos's own interests were similar to Whitman's and James's: "I was in a passion to put down everything, immediately [as] it happened, exactly as I saw it."[15] This is not to say that either Whitman or Dos Passos was totally successful in living up to this rigorous aesthetic prescription. There are abstract passages in "Song of Myself" as well as in *One Man's Initiation*. But in both works, the unadorned immediacy of experience is also apparent and also a central concern.

In 1920, Dos Passos wrote to his British publisher that he had "tried to picture the state of mind of an American in his first contact with the war."[16] Martin Howe's state of mind may be naive—as Dos Passos's letter suggests it was—but it is also complex, a confused mixture of conflicting tendencies. A composite of two of the central characters of *Streets of Night,* Wenny and Fanshaw, Howe reflects both Fanshaw's regressiveness and Wenny's desire for engagement with the world. In fact, the novel might be said to be a record of the fitful development of Howe's moral and aesthetic sensibilities, from innocence to maturity. In Howe, Dos Passos attempts to portray a reintegrative vision—which in his previous novel no one character achieves.

Howe has many shortcomings, but one is led to believe that he will one day "do" something. Yet to do something he must first be initiated into a new life. The events of the novel serve to cut away the inessentials of his life so that he might become aware of the more profound reality of his existence. The latter phrase, which might be otherwise hopelessly meaningless, is made real by the narrator's aesthetic values, which can be further understood in light of Dos Passos's avowed appreciation of William James's philosophy, for Dos Passos's belief in pragmatic principles plays a crucial role in the shape of this novel.

Although Howe may be said to end up a pragmatist, he is not at every point in the novel devoted to pragmatic principles. When he thinks of the "cant of governments," he immediately falls to picturing himself as a medieval monk, "working in the fields, copying parchments in quaint letterings, drowsing his feverish desires to calm in the deep-throated passionate chanting of the endless offices of the Church" (p. 81). He imagines tales of the Middle Ages in which "the crude agony of life was seen through a dawn-like mist of gentle beauty" (p. 81). Another time he

> looked long at the little ranks of clouds that had begun to fill the sky, like ruffles on a woman's dress. Might not it really be, he kept asking himself, that the sky was a beneficent goddess who would stoop gently out of the infinite spaces and lift him to her breast, where he could lie amid the amber-fringed ruffles of cloud and look curiously down at the spinning ball of the earth? It might have beauty if he were far enough away to clear his nostrils of the stench of pain. (Pp. 70–71)

These yearnings for escape have a curiously sexual suggestiveness; it is a woman, a goddess, who will lift him up; his feverish desires will be quenched through "passionate chanting." In these moments, Howe seems to exhibit an infantilized sexuality, and his conceptions of "beauty," here associated with the exotic, are unlike Wenny's appreciation of the "gorgeousness of things." Instead, he carries the illusion of capturing the past. His true initiation, then, has to do with his conversion from idealist to pragmatist.

Just as the structure of *One Man's Initiation* is not readily apparent, the novel's resolution is somewhat confusing. The problem arises because at the novel's conclusion Martin Howe ceases to comment on and interpret experience and instead becomes a quiescent register of events. Such a condition, however, is congruent with the novel's theme; hence the ending is not necessarily flawed. Rather, Howe has reached the logical consequence of the author's own moral and aesthetic premises, and such a condition is mirrored in the final "objective" coda, the last two chapters. Furthermore, the last three chapters may treat Dos Passos's final position obliquely, but a close reading of the text will show that Dos Passos consciously attacked an idealistic approach to life in favor of a pragmatic acceptance of reality. *One Man's Initiation* is not a philosophical treatise, but Dos Passos must have recognized that the epistemological questions involved in Howe's experiences were more than theoretical issues; they were applicable to Howe's moral and aesthetic appreciation of events—to the very meaning of his life. It should not be surprising, therefore, that the conclusion of the novel examines thoroughly the philosophical issues involved and provides Howe with a final education in the relative values of pragmatic and idealistic thought.

Pragmatism, William James never tires of reiterating, means action. Ideas are valid only if they are capable of application. Truth, he says, is an action, a process, something that happens.[17] As mentioned in an earlier chapter, Dos Passos appreciated the philosopher's approach not only because it was a method for solving intellectual problems, but also because he recognized in James's thought an expression of his own deeply held beliefs, feelings, and attitudes. For both men, empirical reality stands at the center of human experience. It is not surprising therefore that Dos Passos contemplated the raw experiences of war both with moral outrage and with a certain amount of fascination. To *experience* the horrors of war, ironically, meant to live life in a most pragmatic sense. In the image of the "ethercone," Dos Passos found a suitable metaphor for the anesthetizing effect of college life; it is particularly appropriate that the war experience gave him the lasting memory of an antithetical image, the "gas-mask" tight about his forehead, "biting into the skin" (p. 117). The image is exact in describing the way that empirical reality impinges upon the self, which in turn must struggle for survival. Instead of having ether drug his senses, Howe is acutely conscious of the mortal danger he faces in the war. If college teaches one theoretical knowledge, the war teaches one the nature of empirical reality, and often teaches it in a deadly manner. "The chance of death," Dos Passos says in speaking of World War I, "sharpened the senses."[18]

Martin Howe journeys to war so that he might experience reality in its most intense form. In a wartime letter to McComb, Dos Passos distinguished between the pure experience of war as opposed to the climate of opinion, hearsay, and lies that deludes the rest of the world, which is innocent of the real nature of battle. "The joy of being at the front," he says, "is that one is away from the hubbub of tongues, from the miasma of lies that is suffocating the world."[19] Numerous examples of the "hubbub of tongues" are given in the novel's first chapter. Howe is at one point cornered by a woman who is eager to tell him a story about German atrocities:

> I know it'll make your blood boil. It's absolutely authentic, too. I heard it before I left New York from a girl who's really the best friend I have on

earth. She got it from a friend of hers who had got it directly from a little Belgian girl, poor little thing, who was in the convent at the time. (P. 48)

The air of unreal conjecture continues in the next scene, where two characters are reported in conversation:

"*They tell me* that Paris is some city."
"The most immoral place in the world . . ."
"*They tell me* that French people are regenerated . . ."
"*They say* the lack of food's something awful . . ."
"*Did you hear* what those fellows were saying about that new gas?"
(P. 49; my ellipses and italics)

The final comment on the dreadful "new gas" is particularly apt in suggesting an aura of dread about the war, but Dos Passos deflates the significance of hearsay by opening the next chapter with a description of Martin Howe arriving in Europe, filling "his lungs with the new, indefinably scented wind coming off the land" (p. 51). This juxtaposition suggests that in a paradoxical way the gas itself might be a "perfume" to Howe—to the extent that it represents the experience that he has been longing for. Even death—one might extrapolate—is preferable to lies.

Howe's pragmatic tendency—as opposed to culture's normative idealism—is revealed most clearly in his conversation with the young lady in chapter 1. She thinks that it is "splendid" of Howe to "come over this way to help France" and "to have understood the issues" (p. 47). In her allegiance to an *a priori* assessment of reality, she is akin to the rationalist philosophers. Truth to her is as it is to James's idealists—"supervenient, inert, static, a reflexion merely"; the pragmatist, on the other hand, keeps an open mind, "faces forward to the future."[20] Howe confesses to this lady that his real reason for going to France is more probably "curiosity," and he points out that the "issues," rather than being monolithic, were "hardly . . . defined then" (p. 47). The woman will not have occasion to go to the front to learn how wrong she is, and even if she did go, she (like so many others) would probably still be blinded by her preconceptions. Howe does go to the front, and his pragmatic attitudes (curiosity about the future) predispose him to accept at face value whatever he finds there: "I never did expect it to be what we were taught to believe. . . . Things aren't" (p. 60). Instead of confirming old beliefs, the war teaches him new things; before the war, for example, "he had not realized that torn flesh was such a black red, like sausage meat" (p. 99). The war is an effective, though brutal, instructor.

The degree to which Dos Passos identified with James's approach makes it natural that the pragmatic principles would permeate his fiction, as can

One Man's Initiation: 1917

be seen in this and the previous chapter. But if Dos Passos's pragmatism is unconscious, second-nature, it can be said that his attack on idealism in this novel is just as fervent and just as intentioned as William James's lifelong crusade. Of course, Dos Passos is not malicious. He sympathizes with the intentions of the idealists and respects them just as did James, who maintained a close friendship with his colleague Josiah Royce, a staunch proponent of idealism. But the pragmatic and idealist approaches lead to radically different consequences, and in chapter 9 Dos Passos presents a lengthy philosophic discussion, which precipitates the final stage of Howe's initiation.

The central argument is carried on by three characters with different points of view: the anarchistic Lully, the religious Chenier, and the socialist Dubois. In addition, the three American soldiers, Merrier, Randolph, and Howe, also contribute to the discussion, but on reading the chapter closely, one is struck by how little Dos Passos's protagonist adds to the argument. Certainly Howe, along with the rest, feels that civilization is in much need of reform; and when each of the three major spokesmen elucidates his respective position, Howe is an appreciative listener even if he does not endorse any single argument. Instead, he respects the good intentions of each and afterward, speaking to Randolph, praises them all by commenting that "with people like that we needn't despair of civilisation" (p. 169). Dos Passos also recognizes that civilization is in need of repair, and like William James he also believes that a good heart is oftentimes more important than the truth or falsehood of a particular theoretical position.[21] But Dos Passos also clearly does not share Howe's optimism in expecting the world to be reformed. Indeed, in chapter 11 he reveals how naive Howe's statement is by having Merrier, Lully, and Dubois all die as a result of a single bombardment. This conclusion is typical of the world view that informs all of Dos Passos's early fiction: objective reality is complex and will inevitably overwhelm the best of man's intentions. The three major spokesmen are simply blinded by their ideals.

Lest there should be any doubt as to his philosophic position in chapter 9, Dos Passos resorts to portraying the scene in a symbolic manner. No matter how much respect the author might have for the various arguments that are presented, his basic impulse is to reject any idealistic attempt to reform (actually, re-form) civilization. To show this, he appropriates a parable from the archidealist, Plato, and uses it much for his own purposes. Because Dos Passos was thoroughly familiar with ancient Greek culture, one might all the more expect that he would be familiar with one of the most famous of Plato's parables, the men chained in the cave, trying to divine the nature of reality though they can see only shadows cast by a fire behind them and by sunlight. To Plato, such a parable explained the predicament of mankind. Men are forced, he asserts, to gaze only at the "shadows," the world around them, sensible objects, while the true reality, the eternal form, intellectual truth, often eludes man's imperfect "vision." It is man's task to "rise" to a higher level, to perceive directly the higher reality of intellectual argument. In chapter 9 it seems likely that Dos Passos consciously used this parable but not as a validation of idealism. Rather, he is hoisting Plato with his own petard, showing the futility of the idealist's position.

Dos Passos's figures are similar to Plato's. They are congregated in a room discussing the nature of reality, here the social system, and offering alternative ways of structuring society. Dos Passos emphasizes their predicament by using imagery of fire and shadows that parallels Plato's: "A candle threw their huge and grotesque shadows on the floor and on the whitewashed walls" (p. 155). On the wall behind Martin Howe, "his arm and hand and the tumbler were shadowed huge" (p. 158). Dubois, who ironically appeals to the "Greek philosophers" to confirm the group's arguments, has his "shadow thrown by the candles on the white wall," and the shadow is "mocking him with huge blurred gestures" (p. 165). Man, Dubois concludes prophetically, has always been the "slave . . . of his own shadow" (p. 165). Toward the end of the discussion, "all the candles but one had guttered out. Their shadows swayed and darted in long arms and changing, grotesque limbs about the room" (p. 168).[22] Later, after Howe has left the group, the scene is raised to a more universal statement when Howe reflects that it seems "that all his friends were gathered in that room" (p. 170). If one keeps Plato's allegory in mind, "all his friends" were in that room, espousing representative solutions to political problems. The variety of their solutions, however, suggests a pragmatic pluralism rather than Plato's monism. Moreover, in the final chapter Dos Passos reveals his severe distrust of an idealistic solution to the complex problems of the modern world: Howe discovers from a critically wounded Chenier that Lully, Merrier, and Dubois have been killed. Their deaths serve as an ironic commentary on each of their intentions to improve society. In the face of their deaths, the ideas they advocated, Dos Passos seems to be saying, are as grotesque and as ephemeral as their shadows on the wall. Even the best-intentioned idealism has the possibility of misleading its followers by giving them a false sense of power and hope.

In the character of Martin Howe, Dos Passos offers an alternative to this seemingly unremitting bleak vision. Howe contributes nothing substantive to the issue of social reorganization. He stands apart from the idealists. Chenier calls for a Catholic theocracy, Dubois for an armed revolution and a socialist state. Lully is an anarchist in the extreme; for him "disorganisation . . . is the aim of life" (p. 165). Martin Howe, on the other hand, advocates no specific remedy to the problem. Rather than building visions of an idealistic society, he emphasizes the specific problems of being an individual in modern culture: empty "phrases" result in the "lulling to sleep of people's humanity and sense" (p. 159). In general, the other three might be said to take a macrocosmic view, stressing in their visions the wide sweep of the social system; Howe, on the other hand, sees the problems from the microcosmic and essentially aesthetic point of view, from the individual's expansive, expressive nature. In the vein of Whitman, he advocates "liberty" (p. 158). He values "faith" (p. 164), "courage" (p. 168), "energy" (p. 168), and "power" (p. 168). When, at the novel's conclusion, Chenier says that "everybody's dead" and asks if Howe too isn't, Howe replies, "No, I'm alive" (pp. 173-74). His "aliveness" is both literal and metaphorical.

To be alive at the novel's end entails specific considerations that are central to Dos Passos's fiction, and the novel's penultimate chapter gives an implicit assertion of the author's values. As noted before, Howe in chapter 10 buys shoelaces from the cobbler. Instead of the candlelight casting grotesque, exaggerated shadows on the wall, as in the previous chapter, the light here illuminates the objects themselves. The light seems to make shoes dance (p. 171) and glints off the cobbler's knife blade and off the coins that Howe gives to the man (p. 172). In short, the light now illuminates solid objects instead of casting on the wall the "grotesque" shadows of men thinking. In the space of a chapter, Dos Passos has taken the reader from the world of men's idealism to empirical fact, which is a good deal less pleasant. The trio of thinkers had constructed idealistically symmetrical worlds, but the cobbler with his ghastly, "wheezy, coughing laugh" (p. 172) has the task of dealing with everyday exigencies. The difference between the two worlds—the worlds of philosophic idealism and of empirical reality—is noted by James: "Are not all our theories just remedies and places of escape? And, if philosophy is to be religious, how can she be anything else than a place of escape from the crassness of reality's surface?"[23] James and Dos Passos know that the complex modern world does not permit escape. There is no authorial commentary in chapter 10, but it is obvious that Howe has come to an acceptance of life's pragmatic basis. Like William James, Howe would no doubt "sympathize heartily" with the American writer Morrison I. Swift: "The philosophers are dealing in shades, while those who live and feel know truth."[24] In visiting the old cobbler, Howe confronts reality directly, and in so doing he discovers the core of reality by which his life must be lived. He discovers how to be "alive" in the face of death; that is, as the final two chapters show, Howe has become a pragmatic register of empirical sensations.

John W. Aldridge has written that "the energy that enlivens Dos Passos' best work always has its source in the conflict created by [an aesthetic] sensibility as it takes its revenge upon the established social order for failing to keep the faith."25 And, indeed, as already seen in *Streets of Night,* the aesthetic sensibility is an important consideration in Dos Passos's fiction. His protagonists must deal with reality by applying moral and philosophic values that have a basis in an aesthetic sensibility. Thus Howe criticizes the "phrases" (p. 159) that anesthetize consciousness; his own "old watchwords," on the other hand, have the potential to "consume to ashes all the lies in the world" (pp. 45–46). Obviously though, such bravado belongs to the younger, uninitiated Martin Howe. The protagonist's real mission is not to mouth "watchwords" but to "see" war directly, and what he sees is reported in concrete language; this is what he brings back: "scarlet poppies, and cornflowers, and white daisies, and the red-tiled roofs and white walls of cottages, all against a background of glaucous green fields and hedges" (p. 52). The empirical language of sense impressions here reflects Howe's choice of reality over idealism. His sensibility is moral, philosophic, and aesthetic.

In summary, it is proper to say that the aesthetic values by which the novel is constructed are the same values that Martin Howe assumes through his initiation. In the end, Howe's vision of the world is similar to James's view of the nature of reality and Whitman's regard for the reality of nature. This is indicated by Howe's encounter with the cobbler and by the straight reportorial style that describes Howe's final presence in the novel. To the extent that Howe ceases to be a reflective actor, he has assimilated into—or at least becomes indistinguishable from—the narrator.

Howe has undergone exactly the same transformation as Dos Passos himself in the war, from one sympathetic to acting for change to an aesthetic consciousness that sees and describes reality as it is. This is the necessary precondition for Dos Passos's own art. It is not action that is essential, but a vision that might incite change. Dos Passos writes to his friend McComb in 1918 to explain this:

> No I believe no more in the gospel of energy—One thing the last year has taught me has been to drop my old sentimentalizing over action; action when it is anything at all is a foolish running about, a sheeplike scurrying from the wolves, or a wolfish snarling stalking of the sheep; let us have none of it. A voice of one crying in the wilderness, rather . . . I still believe in that. To turn one's nose to the moon and bay—to blow trumpets and have the walls of Jericho crumble.26

Written while *One Man's Initiation* was being formulated, this letter utilizes the same imagery as the novel (energy, action, sheep, walls of Jericho) and should dispel the notion of those critics such as John Wrenn, who sees Martin Howe as the "one dedicated individual" left to work for the revolution.27 The letter makes clear the distance between Dos Passos's beliefs and those of the thinkers in chapter 9. Howe, like Dos Passos,

One Man's Initiation: 1917

comes to see the moral problem in terms of aesthetic issues. While this approach might serve as a basis for one's moral judgment, it also tends to make the perceiver unfit to act. It is one of the paradoxes implicit in choosing an aesthetic basis for moral insight, and it also accounts for the fact that Dos Passos's protagonists are incapable of success in any great measure. Howe succeeds only in being "alive."

7
Three Soldiers

With the publication of *Three Soldiers* in 1921, John Dos Passos won critical acclaim for the first time. The kudos were well deserved, for in this novel Dos Passos achieves a significant breakthrough in his developing aesthetics by his acute and persistent attention to characterization. Unlike his first published novel, *One Man's Initiation: 1917,* in which Dos Passos created one character and a number of subsidiary silhouettes, *Three Soldiers* manifests several rounded characters, plus a number of well-realized minor figures.

In *Three Soldiers,* Dos Passos used three protagonists, who represent three examples of the diverse American experience: John Andrews, from rural Virginia, stands for the educated upper classes; from rural Indiana, Chrisfield is the native country youth; and Fuselli, from urban San Francisco, embodies the values of the aspiring middle class. None of these characters benefits from the social or military systems, though Dos Passos does seem to sympathize with each man. To some degree or another, each has a goal but is unable to achieve a sense of order in his life, a fair relationship with the system.

In section 47 of "Song of Myself," Whitman gives an evaluation of his role as model for other writers:

> I am the teacher of athletes;
> He that by me spreads a wider breast than my own, proves
>   the width of my own;
> He most honors my style who learns under it to destroy
>   the teacher.
>   (Ll. 1231–33)

Whitman, here, employs hyperbole to prove a point about the nature of the aesthetic experience: for a writer to "follow" Whitman means that he must develop his own unique voice, his own style. This suggests the paradox that is inherent in Dos Passos's own achievement of his artistic maturity in *Three Soldiers:* he turns once again to his experiences in World War I, but he has finally discovered his own style. The themes are not much different from *One Man's Initiation,* but the fictive density of *Three Soldiers* suggests the author's increased artistic control. To say, however, that Dos Passos establishes his identity as a writer in this novel is not to say that Whitman's influence is not present. Dos Passos does not "destroy the teacher," although the teacher's presence is muted. There are, for example, a number of allusions to Whitman in the novel. In addition, the poet's influence can be detected in three major areas: in an interest in human psychology, in a continuing appreciation of nature, and in what I will call an aesthetics of the word.

There are conscious echoes of Whitman in *Three Soldiers* that suggest the large extent of Dos Passos's debt. At times the allusions are explicit. At one point, for example, Andrews shouts " 'Libertad, Libertad, allons, ma femme!' as Walt Whitman would have said."[1] In addition, Andrews is a throwback to the nineteenth-century romantics; he is a romantic in a period that seems antithetical to the romantic spirit. Instead of being satisfied with reality, he wants "so much more of life than life can give" (p. 329). At one point, after fondly remembering his childhood spent dreaming in his garden, Andrews loses himself in a mystical union with all the other sleepers in his barracks:

> He thought of himself and Chrisfield picking up cigarette butts and the tramp, tramp, tramp of feet on the drill field. Where was the connection? Was this all futile madness? They'd come from such various worlds, all these men sleeping about him, to be united in this. And what did they think of it, all these sleepers? Had they too not had dreams when they were boys? Or had the generations prepared them only for this?
> He thought of himself lying under the crêpe-myrtle bush through the hot, droning afternoon, watching the pale magenta flowers flutter down into the dry grass, and felt, again, wrapped in his warm blankets among all these sleepers, the straining of limbs burning with desire to rush untrammelled through some new keen air. Suddenly darkness overspread his mind. (Pp. 32–33)

This passage suggests the shadowy and mystical world of Whitman's poem "The Sleepers," where the soul "comes from its embower'd garden" (l. 171) to "unite" (l. 180) with all the other sleepers. The garden, the sleepers, the yearning, and the sense of mystical union are details that are shared by the two works. But Whitman's poem ends with a sense of reconciliation and harmony, whereas John Andrews faces only the "darkness" of sleep. Dos Passos was aware not only of his affinities with earlier literature, but also of the insurmountable differences that come with a new age.

One of the striking features of both Whitman's and Dos Passos's art is that they are both intensely interested in the human psyche. Harold Aspiz has recently examined Whitman's interest in phrenology and states that Whitman believed so strongly in the "laws" of phrenology that the pseudoscience influenced the shape of his poetry.[2] Whitman was very much aware that his poetry was "the heart's geography's map."[3] And Whitman, like Dos Passos after him, toyed with the idea of the psychological double in literature.[4]

Part of the appeal that Whitman had for Dos Passos must have sprung from the acuteness with which the earlier poet had examined the human psyche. Of course, Dos Passos lived in a later and very different age. Freud had changed the way that human beings perceived the landscape of the human soul. One knows from *Streets of Night* that Dos Passos had at least a passing acquaintance with Freudian psychology,[5] and of course he was infatuated with the psychology of William James. But at least part of his interest in human psychology in *Three Soldiers* derives from a Whitmanesque sense of nature. That is, as I noted in a previous chapter, for both Dos Passos and Whitman, human psychology was the nexus of nature and human nature. Moreover, both writers realized that the creation of a literary text was an expression of a part of oneself. As Whitman suggests in "Eidolons," a literary text replicates a part of oneself. A close examination of Dos Passos's technique reveals a similar concern.

In his pioneering work, *The Double,* Otto Rank has postulated that the literary double is closely connected with an author's narcissism,[6] and in a more recent study Ralph Tymms has shown that the double is a prevalent motif in romantic and postromantic literature.[7] One can find examples of this motif in Dos Passos's first written novel, *Streets of Night* (his third published novel), where Wenny and Fanshaw may be said to illustrate what Tymms calls doubles "by division."[8] Yet it is in *Three Soldiers,* Dos Passos's first mature work of fiction, that human psychology is examined most thoroughly. In particular, Dos Passos's examination of psychological doubleness is manifested both in the split consciousness of his central character, Andrews, and in other variations on the theme. Written from Dos Passos's own experiences in World War I, *Three Soldiers* reveals the author's perceptive insights into the consequences of war and his appreciation and use of the literary convention of the double.

In *Three Soldiers* Dos Passos's characterization seems to devolve from the author's obsession with traumatized consciousness. Although such an interest was apparent in Dos Passos before the war, one might presume that the tremendous pressure inherent in the mechanized nature of life in the military would no doubt have exacerbated this predisposition. Freud says that the everyday soldier was prone to neuroses due to the very nature of combat:

The conflict is between the soldier's old peaceful ego and his new warlike one, and it becomes acute as soon as the peace-ego realizes what danger it runs of losing its life owing to the rashness of its newly formed, parasitic double. It would be equally true to say that the old ego is protecting itself from a mortal danger by taking flight into a traumatic neurosis or that it is defending itself against the new ego which it sees is threatening its life.[9]

As shall be seen, whether war related or not, John Dos Passos's concern with the psychic split manifests itself in the characterization of John Andrews, the protagonist in *Three Soldiers,* but it also operates on another, more pervasive, level as well, informing the very texture of the fiction.

An important image in *Three Soldiers,* one that illustrates the theme of the split consciousness, can be traced to the beginning of Dos Passos's literary career, to a brief note in his college diary. There he makes a notation for a writing project (presumably a short story) entitled "The Man in the Mirror": "Walking through a hall between two mirrors—he sees hisselves [*sic*] down the long arcade but alien people gibbering and making faces at him."[10] This image would seem to be an expression of something fundamental to Dos Passos's emotional life, for he employs something very much like it a number of years later in *Three Soldiers:*

> The major's office was a large white-painted room, with elaborate mouldings and mirrors in all four walls, so that while Andrews waited, cap in hand, to go up to the desk, he could see the small round major with his pink face and bald head repeated to infinity in two directions in the grey brilliance of the mirrors. . . . Andrews stepped up to the desk. On both sides of the room a skinny figure in olive-drab, repeated endlessly, stepped up to the endless mahogany desks, which faded into each other in an endless dusty perspective. (P. 339; my ellipses)

It is not merely the physical detail of the dual mirrors that is echoed from the diary; the passage in the novel also emphasizes the alienation that the protagonist feels in the military environment. In addition, both passages seem to symbolize the psychic division of his character. John Andrews's essential condition is a fragmented consciousness.

Critics have frequently noted Dos Passos's *unamiste* intentions in *Three Soldiers,* but clearly John Andrews is the central character. His story takes up half the novel, and Dos Passos obviously sympathizes the most with this character's values and problems. The doubleness that Andrews senses is apparent throughout *Three Soldiers,* frequently exhibiting itself in similar mirror images. For example, when he is seriously wounded, he is peering into a pool of water studying "the outlines of a stained grimacing mask" (p. 193). And he is conscious that the military has forced him to see his life in terms of two antithetical beings. To illustrate this he refers to the mirrors in the major's office:

> He thought of the Major's office that morning, and of his own skinny figure in the mirrors, repeated endlessly, standing helpless and humble before the shining mahogany desk. . . . In those office buildings, with white marble halls full of the clank of officers' heels, in index cards and piles of typewritten papers, his real self, which they had power to kill if they wanted to, was in his name and his number, on lists with millions of other names and other numbers. This sentient body of his, full of possibilities and hopes and desires, was only a pale ghost that depended on the other self, that suffered for it and cringed for it. (P. 347; my ellipses)

Late in the book, when Andrews escapes from the military work brigade by jumping into the water, he experiences this dual state when he at once struggles to survive and notes that "one half of him was thinking how wonderful it would be to drown" (p. 370). In short, Andrews suffers the effects of a fragmented consciousness, and his story is a quest for a solution to his problem.

Later in this chapter I shall examine more particularly Dos Passos's elaboration of Andrews's peculiar psychological condition in connection with the theme of the double. But perhaps more important than the convention itself, there are other ramifications that Dos Passos uses to good advantage in *Three Soldiers*. Unlike the paradigmatic case of the double—say, Poe's William Wilson—Dos Passos's doubles for the most part are not involved in a plot that is centered around one character who shadows another, the one essentially embodying the nether side of the other's troubled consciousness. One might say that Dos Passos—perhaps suffering the anxiety of influence—attenuates the convention and in doing so makes it into a supple and extremely useful tool. In *Three Soldiers* his characters for the most part are not true doubles but might be called reciprocal characters—characters who share a common psychological locus, but who represent diverse, sometimes contrasting attributes. Unlike Poe, who used two characters, Dos Passos discovered that this technique allowed him to effect a pervasive influence on the shape of the text, influencing the characterization of both his three major figures and his minor figures. As in the double, the similarities and differences of the reciprocal character result from the author's acknowledgment of complex psychological forces.

There can be little doubt that reciprocal characters are crucial to the book's design, and they are quite essential to an understanding of the novel. An example can be seen in the portrayal of two minor figures, Antoinette and her older sister. Antoinette is young and relatively attractive, except for "ugly yellow teeth" (p. 141). Her shoulders and breasts reveal "strong curves," and her forearms and face are tanned "golden brown" (p. 140). When she is not smiling, her face is even "beautiful" (p. 142). In contrast, her older sister has "sallow and wrinkled" skin (p. 142), a fact that startles Chrisfield when he quickly turns and mistakenly embraces her instead of Antoinette (p. 144).

Dos Passos also contrasts another two women: Jeanne and Genevieve, Andrews's two lovers. The former is simple, lowerclass, warmhearted, sexual, and receptive. Genevieve possesses the opposite characteristics: sophisticated, aristocratic, cold, sexually aloof, and condescending.

An examination of a minor but highly symbolic character will serve to suggest some of the more important facets of John Andrews's character. When Andrews is taken to Paris by Henslowe, they visit a bar called the Butte, and there Andrews sees a "lame boy" in the company of a girl "who was with him and who never took her eyes off his face, leaning on his crutch all the while" (p. 232). The boy is a model of independence in that he is self-employed in "making toys" for "Noah's Arks" (p. 236). Later in the evening, after having left the bar, Andrews thinks he sees them on the foggy street, but he is mistaken. Inexplicably, Andrews can't forget the boy and girl. Some months later, he does see the boy again, but Andrews is surprised this time because the boy is alone: "Yes," says the boy in response to Andrews's question, "I am always alone" (p. 329).

In a number of ways, the boy parallels Andrews. Just as the boy is afflicted with a "withered leg" (p. 235), so too Andrews suffers a leg wound and spends the last third of the novel recovering. In creating toys, the boy, like Andrews, is an artist, though he manages to be self-sufficient whereas Andrews is not. It is not surprising that the boy's situation appeals to Andrews:

> What a wonderful life that would be to live up here in a small room that would overlook the great rosy grey expanse of the city, to have some absurd work like that to live on, and to spend all your spare time working and going to concerts. . . . A quiet mellow existence. . . . Think of my life beside it. Slaving in that iron, metallic, brazen New York to write ineptitudes about music in the Sunday papers. (P. 236)

Finally, the boy and his girl at first present an idyllic picture of love and are then separated; such is also the case with Andrews and Genevieve. Andrews is madly in love with her, and then she deserts him. At this point, Andrews unconsciously echoes the lame boy's sentiments on love: "Yet people were always alone, really; however much they loved each other, there could be no real union" (p. 425). Because his actions foreshadow the fate of the protagonist, the boy serves as an alter ego for Andrews.

References to the lame boy take up only a small part of this moderately long novel, but the other manifold uses of reciprocal characters account for the bulk of the book. As I said, the three main characters are representative types of the American experience. The differences among these three main characters, of course, are obvious, and it would be repetitive of existing scholarship to examine in extensive detail such factors. But to understand better Fuselli's and Chrisfield's roles in the novel, it is necessary to point out what critics have failed to see: Andrews shares with the two other characters fundamental, compelling elements that suggest that the three soldiers are developed from a single psychological locus.

There are minor characters in *Three Soldiers* who succeed, but it is safe to say that no one character that Dos Passos cares about benefits from the social or military systems. This is especially apparent in the failures of Fuselli, Chrisfield, and Andrews. Dos Passos does seem to sympathize with each man, though each is markedly flawed. To some degree or another, each has a goal but is unable to achieve a sense of order in his life. In this regard, four parallels between Fuselli and Andrews are revealing and obviously intentional.

First, both characters perceive the movies in very similar terms. Fuselli, for example, takes the propaganda movies as literal reportage; he is moved by the sight of "jolly soldiers in khaki marching into towns, pursuing terrified Huns across potato fields, saving Belgian milk-maids against picturesque backgrounds" (p. 57). Though Andrews is too sophisticated to be deceived by the propaganda, he also is affected by the movies just like the others are: "Andrews felt blind hatred stirring like something that had a life of its own in the young men about him. He was lost in it, carried away in it, as in a stampede of wild cattle" (p. 27). That Andrews can regain his perspective, whereas Fuselli has none to regain, suggests that in this respect the two are foils, with Fuselli assuming one of the traditional roles of the double, embodying undesirable qualities.

A second parallel can be found in the imagery that Dos Passos uses to characterize the situation of each man. Fuselli started out in the military with some hope for success, though he is constantly thwarted, finding reality radically different from his dreams. Going to Europe aboard ship, he is "in one of the lowest of three tiers of bunks" (p. 43). It is as if he were in a "dark pit" (p. 44). His situation deteriorates from then on. Andrews's case is described in nearly identical imagery. In the last part of the novel, when he is with a work battalion, Andrews feels like "a man looking at the stars from the bottom of a pit" (p. 362). Furthermore, like Fuselli, Andrews sleeps in a "dark, airless bunk, in the lowest of three tiers" (p. 367). These parallels seem too close to be fortuitous.

There is a third parallel between Fuselli and Andrews that suggests that the two characters are both rooted in a single vision that antecedes "character." As he does not do with other figures in *Three Soldiers,* Dos Passos repeatedly calls attention to a trait common to both Fuselli and

Andrews: both are acutely aware of a sense of yearning, of unquenched desire. Fuselli at one point feels "a flush of desire all over him" (p. 39), and the word "desire" is frequently associated with him. Similarly, Andrews's frequent daydreaming of the queen of Sheba makes him feel within reach of "all the fiery imaginings of his desire" (p. 204). Though Andrews's and Fuselli's perceptions are ultimately of a different order, there is a basic erotic motive in each character.

A fourth major similarity that Dos Passos emphasizes is a peculiar likeness that strongly suggests the reciprocal nature of Fuselli and Andrews. This similarity devolves from their shared erotic motive: for both characters, sexuality and failure are inexplicably but inextricably connected. Fuselli, for example, loses his girl Yvonne to his top sergeant, and on the evening he sees the two rendezvous for a tryst, he also discovers that his unit's corporal is back from the hospital, an event that effectively subverts Fuselli's chances for a much-desired promotion (p. 110). That sexual failure and the failure to win promotion should be presented in such proximity suggests that the two may be connected in some way that is not necessarily explainable by logic or by the quotidian experiences of the average person. This connection between sexuality and failure is reinforced when Dos Passos relates Fuselli's ultimate fate. Late in the novel, Fuselli reappears, reduced in rank, working permanent KP, and one of the principal causes of his bad luck within the promotional system is that he has contracted a veneral disease (p. 302).

To observe this pattern in Fuselli's life is to identify a central concern in the novel and also to see that Fuselli shares certain unmistakable and important characteristics with Andrews. Though the connection is relatively muted, the latter's failures are also linked with sexuality. For example, when Andrews sleeps with Jeanne, he is discovered by his friend Walters. As a result, he feels a "passionate disgust towards himself and Jeanne and Walters" (p. 332). This sexual guilt is followed shortly afterward with a slip in Andrews's judgment: he goes AWOL to the country with Genevieve and is captured by the MPs. Furthermore, the novel's conclusion is marked by his dual failure to win Genevieve and to finish his symphony. Genevieve suggests that Andrews cannot be "a great composer and a deserter too in the year 1919" (p. 430). She says this before, in fact, the reader discovers that Andrews will not be a great composer. There is no obvious logic to her statement; there is no reason why Genevieve should know the statement to be true—and the reader might completely ignore it if it were not for the fact that it is an exact description of the book's conclusion. But what Genevieve should have said is "you can't be my lover and a deserter too in the year 1919," for when she discovers Andrews's military status, she then decides that she will have nothing to do with him. This hypothetical statement does make sense in terms of the immediate situation, in terms of the working out of the plot, and in terms of the unstated determinism under which Dos Passos's three major characters work out their destinies: the failure in love, as in the related failure in work, has its unexplainable roots in an inability to live up to an accepted standard. Guilt in both work and love are intertwined and mutually sustaining. Like Fuselli, Andrews is incapable of worldly success.

Andrews and Fuselli, while sharing fundamental attributes, are very different characters, of course. Fuselli clearly embodies numerous undesirable qualities and thus serves as a foil to the generally admirable Andrews. To choose only one difference from many that have led critics to contrast these two figures, one notes that each character has the opportunity to reflect on one of Dos Passos's major concerns, language. For Fuselli, the way the military uses language evokes in him a "strange excitement": "These phrases 'entrainment,' 'order of march,' had a business-like sound" (p. 35). But when Andrews contemplates similar abstract language ("detachment, battalion, commanding officer"), he deems the words "silly," "pompous" and "efficient" (p. 421).

Chrisfield also is a projection of Andrews, and here the parallel is not only much more obvious but in some important respects also much more complex. As in the case with Fuselli, the similarities are compelling. There is a fundamental question, for example, as to why two seemingly disparate characters, Chrisfield and Andrews, should be the close friends they are. Why do they shadow each other for a good part of the book? Chrisfield is "like me," says Andrews, in that both are in "a hurry to get overseas" (p. 29). But since that feeling is shared by almost all the soldiers, the comparison is gratuitous. On the other hand, one objective condition that both share is that they desert from the Army, as Chrisfield pointedly states: "God damn! That's funny that you an' me should both do it, Andy" (p. 390). This statement serves in no way to advance the dialogue or the action; it sits inertly on the page and like the previous quotation sounds forced. It is a grand pronouncement without significance—at least no overt significance. The real purpose behind the remark is to force the reader to see the two characters as possessing very similar traits. But to understand the real point of identification between the two men, one must realize that both Chrisfield and Andrews grapple with the same problem: the subordination of the self to the organization, with special emphasis on the military system of rank. Thus Andrews is needlessly humiliated by an officer (p. 25), and there is an implicit sense of ironic injustice when he meets another Harvard man, Bleezer, who has not graduated yet but who holds a military position superior to Andrews's, the rank of lieutenant (p. 258). Similarly, as the novel proceeds, Chrisfield's rising sense of impotence finds an objective foil of the crescendo of promotions given to

Sergeant Anderson. "First you was a corporal, then you was a sergeant, and now you're a lootenant," says Chrisfield, just before murdering him (p. 188).

These similarities between Andrews and Chrisfield seem to be overshadowed by their contrasting qualities. Thus Andrews's central fault is that he is "tame" (p. 168); Chrisfield, on the other hand, readily admits that he must have "a bit of the devil in me" (p. 158). Yet while these two descriptions reveal surface dissimilarities, they also point to a single origin for the two characters. In fact, though Chrisfield and Andrews are not pure doubles, they do possess qualities that show that Dos Passos was aware of the literary convention of the double. Freud's remark that is used earlier in this chapter serves as a paradigm for discussing Chrisfield and Andrews: because of the war, the ego is refracted into two entities, the violent and the civilized. Otto Rank states explicitly the reason why this is necessary: "The most prominent symptom of the forms which the double takes is a powerful consciousness of guilt which forces the hero no longer to accept the responsibility for certain actions of his ego, but to place it upon another ego, a double. . . ."[11] Chrisfield's irrational actions become clearer when he is seen as a double of Andrews. He acts out his frustrations toward the military hierarchy while Andrews only *feels*.

Dos Passos gives one other attenuated form of the traditional double when he introduces the character of Sergeant Anderson. By naming Chrisfield's adversary Anderson, Dos Passos is suggesting that Chrisfield and Andrews share a bond closer and deadlier than friendship. Indeed, Chrisfield fits exactly Ralph Tymms's description of one form of the double; he "represents elements in a man's complex nature" which "are normally suppressed by the conscious mind."[12] As has been suggested, he embodies the unsocial and murderous impulses that are not appropriate to his reciprocal figure, Andrews. To see the extent to which this is so, one has merely to look at a most obvious illustration, Chrisfield's dream of killing Anderson:

> He dreamed he was home in Indiana, but instead of his mother cooking at the stove in the kitchen, there was the Frenchwoman who had stood in the farmhouse door, and near her stood a lieutenant with a little red book in his hand. He was eating cornbread and syrup off a broken plate. . . . Suddenly he stopped eating and started swearing, shouting at the top of his lungs: "You goddam . . ." he started, but he couldn't seem to think of anything more to say. "You goddam . . ." he started again. The lieutenant looked towards him, wrinkling his black eyebrows that met across his nose. He was Sergeant Anderson. Chris drew his knife and ran at him, but it was Andy his bunkie he had run his knife into. He threw his arms round Andy's body, crying hot tears. . . . He woke up. (P. 137; only first ellipses are added)

If Chrisfield's murderous impulses are dangerous to Anderson, then on a symbolic level, as the dream suggests, they are dangerous to Andrews as well. Chrisfield's acting out of his murderous hatred in the dream, the releasing of his id impulses, is not only destructive but self-destructive—as the consequences of his later actual murder of Anderson makes abundantly clear. In the dream life, the differentiation between the characters of Chrisfield, Anderson, and Andrews breaks down. There are not three characters here; there is only one, though refracted through the narcissistic ego. Why this is necessary is described by Rank, who sees the flight from the double as a veiled form of suicide:

> The suicidal person is unable to eliminate by direct self-destruction the fear of death resulting from the threat to his narcissism. To be sure, he seizes upon the only possible way out, suicide, but he is incapable of carrying it out other than by way of the phantom of a feared and hated double, because he loves and esteems his ego too highly to give it pain or to transform the idea of his destruction into the deed.[13]

Both Anderson and Chrisfield then are—to the limited degree that Dos Passos uses the convention—doubles of Andrews. At one point, a character asks Andrews, "Did you say your name was Anderson?" (p. 227). Dos Passos here seems to be consciously working on the level of psychological symbolism in inviting the reader to see these two characters—and by extension a number of other characters as well—as doubles.

How Chrisfield and Anderson relate to Andrews is best seen in the conflict in part 3, chapter 3 when Chrisfield threatens Anderson, and the latter, using his superior rank, puts Chrisfield under arrest (p. 161). Just as Chrisfield embodies asocial impulses, Anderson represents the socially acceptable behavior. Andrews must reject the unsocial, violently criminal behavior of Chrisfield, but he must also reject conformity to the system, as represented by Anderson. Andrews truly is "the man in the mirror": he stands between Chrisfield on the one hand and Anderson on the other. Both are images of himself, distorted projections of his deepest fears, failure and success, a familiar tension in Dos Passos's work.[14] Andrews must, like Anderson, "arrest" Chrisfield, and like Chrisfield, Andrews feels the need to destroy the system and its representatives. Both Chrisfield and Anderson illustrate Andrews's internal conflicts, and their actions highlight his impotence. He can be like neither of them, but his actions, too, are suicidal; he is capable only of withdrawing from the problem, deserting the military to write music in the country. And he does so under the certainty of failure: in going AWOL and in being careless in the unauthorized absence, he insures that his symphony will never be completed. And this is the real mystery of Dos Passos's art: his protagonists, like doubles of himself, seek aesthetic solutions to moral, economic, and social problems. Those solutions, though aesthetic, are nevertheless real and important.

Due largely to the advances in human psychology in the early twentieth century, John Dos Passos had many more sophisticated insights into the problem of the literary representation of character than were available to Walt Whitman. Still, one can say that Whitman's and Dos Passos's worlds were largely generated from an intense regard for the dimensions of the human psyche. Both authors were aware of the many facets of the fragmented consciousness. And for both authors, this fragmentation needed healing. In *Three Soldiers,* Dos Passos turned once again to nature to find a basis for his faith in man.

I have already examined how Dos Passos's earlier novels reflect a strong belief in the efficacy of nature. Dos Passos here is drawing on the long and pervasive American literary tradition that identifies nature as a source of value, and as I pointed out in the foregoing chapter on *Streets of Night,* it is Whitman himself that Dos Passos identified as the chief spokesman for nature. Wenny's death, to repeat, is not an occasion for mourning but is an apotheosis of sorts, and Dos Passos uses Whitman's "When Lilacs Last in the Dooryard Bloom'd" to stress that when death is seen within the context of the wholeness of nature, an efficacious reconciliation is possible. In *Three Soldiers,* nature again is the answer to the problem of a troubled consciousness, that of John Andrews. To state that Andrews's consciousness is fragmented is to imply at the same time the obverse: there exists for the author (in theory at least) an ideal state of wholeness. This contrast—the fragmented versus the whole—reveals itself in counterpointing images that are widely used in Dos Passos's early fiction—nature versus the inorganic.

Imagery of the machine and of the inorganic is used repeatedly, and its central purpose is to suggest the conditions where life is negated. It is a critical commonplace in discussing *Three Soldiers,* for example, to note that the titles of the six main parts of the novel emphasize the dominance of Andrews's life by the military machine (for example, "Machines," "Rust," and so on). Descriptive passages also abound that emphasize the machinelike quality of military life. The payroll clerks, for example, "pushed the money into the soldier's hands with a rough jerk and pronounced the names as if they were machines clicking" (p. 333). A lieutenant speaks "in short shrill periods, chopping off the ends of his words as if with a hatchet" (p. 99). A sergeant's hand snaps "to salute like a block signal" (p. 10). Andrews feels like an "automaton" (p. 277), and Fuselli, who does not have the inner resources needed to cope with the deadening routine, is utterly "lost in the vast machine" (p. 63). A catalog of additional images could be adduced to show Dos Passos's insistence on portraying life in the military as subordinate to cold, inhuman forces.

In the counterpoint to the inorganic, in the celebration of nature, Dos Passos once again discovers a redeeming value. Only in the title of part 5, "The World Outside," does Dos Passos not use an image of mechanism. In this section of the novel, John Andrews enjoys a relatively free existence, and the title should be interpreted not merely as "the world outside the military." It is also the outside world, that is, nature. Dos Passos seems to have taken great care—as he did in *Streets of Night* and *One Man's Initiation*—to structure the novel on the natural cycle, using mythic values of the seasons. Thus the novel covers two years. Part 1 begins in the autumn, the time of decay, when the "three soldiers" enter the military. In part 3, the first spring, the novel switches its point of view to Chrisfield and Andrews and their early hopes. At the end of part 3, winter approaching, Chrisfield kills Anderson. The onset of winter is detailed in part 4, where Andrews's second "decay" is suggested by his severe wounding. Part 5, spring, deals with the recovery of Andrews and his exuberance in being assigned to the school battalion in Paris. Part 6, the final section, telescopes a good deal of time and takes Andrews through a prolific period of creative vitality (summer) and his eventual arrest by MPs in late summer or autumn. As this brief schema suggests, the mythic value of the seasons reinforces the mood of the action.

Besides providing a framework, nature plays other roles in *Three Soldiers*. At times, Dos Passos indulges in elaborate—sometimes overlong—scene painting. For example, in part 2, entitled "Machines," Chrisfield and Andrews escape for a while from the regimen and take a walk:

> On both sides of the road were fields of ripe wheat, golden under the sun. In the distance . . . low green hills . . . blue, pale yellow . . . ripe grain . . . a thick clump of trees or a screen of poplars . . . long smooth hills . . . hedgerows . . . blue cornflowers and poppies. . . . The bees droning in the big dull purple cloverheads and in the gold hearts of the daisies. (P. 153; my ellipses)

Nature, however, is not merely a setting, but an objective reality that mirrors the natural organic state of man. It is an objective reality that is both nonthreatening and a remnant of the premechanistic age. Not surprisingly, Dos Passos also uses such imagery to suggest the close identification between man and the objective world. For example, at one point Andrews contrasts his present slavery in the military with his youth dreaming in his garden (p. 199). Another time, he recognizes an affinity between his own life and the natural world when he feels "his blood grumble and swell in his veins as the new life was grumbling and swelling in the sticky buds of the trees" (p. 314). One spring, Andrews feels in his own breathing "the faint premonition of the stirring of life in the cold earth" (p. 260). And when he and Genevieve are at her country estate, his love seems to find a parallel in the "sappy richness of vegetation" (p. 410).

The sea is the most important natural image because it characterizes Andrews's aspirations. When he is caught by the MPs and assigned to a work battalion, he is engaged in unloading cement bags from a barge. He notices "the black water speeding seawards" (p. 370). He escapes by jumping into the river, is picked up by an anarchist boatman and "goes seawards"—at least out of the city to the countryside. The escape is made symbolic by the previous accumulation of sea images. Early in the novel, after reading Flaubert, Andrews's "mind was full of intangible floating glow, like the ocean on a warm night" (p. 208). Andrews conceives of absolute freedom as a harmonious plasticity of free consciousness: "somewhere, beyond everything, he was conscious of the great free rhythm of the sea" (p. 347). Most important, this image of freedom is associated with his own art: the beauty of his music is like the "great rhythm of the sea" (p. 334). At one point, his music is a "great wave" that has a "rhythm" like a "flowing river" (p. 348). Thus his escape to the countryside by way of the river has a symbolic appropriateness. Water suggests baptism, or at least a rejuvenation.

It might be said that the similarities pointed out thus far between Whitman and Dos Passos are striking if only that they reveal the extent to which the twentieth-century author is predisposed to a romantic viewpoint in the tradition of Whitman. But the fundamental aesthetic concerns of each author are also very similar. To understand the profound effect that Whitman had on the young Dos Passos, one has only to see the extent to which these two authors' aesthetics mirror each other both in methodology and in meaning. *Three Soldiers* records Dos Passos's discovery of his life's work, and it is useful to compare Dos Passos's awareness of his developing aesthetic with the poem that records Whitman's similar discovery, "Out of the Cradle Endlessly Rocking."

The problematic center in "Out of the Cradle"—as it is in *Three Soldiers*—is the protagonist's search for a way to heal his fragmented consciousness. To the boy in Whitman's poem, the newly aroused and "bursting" soul, the problem is stated in terms of "questions" (l. 144) that need answering. There is some "clew" (l. 162), a "word" (l. 164) that will in a sense restore him to equilibrium. It must be a "word final, superior to all" (l. 171) to answer the boy's nascent, teleological groping. Just as in *Three Soldiers,* the solution to life's troubles is associated with the sea. For Whitman, the answer comes from the sea waves lapping the shore: "death" (l. 178). By centering his attention on one vital word—death—the poet is exploring the fecund nature of paradox. On one level, death will release the boy from his new burden, the sweet-hell within. Death is simply the end of yearning. But on another level, finding the word is not an end at all. The knowledge of death is made possible through language, in particular through the word "death." That language, in turn, allows the poet to transcend the very limitations of his suffering and demise by casting his experiences into a permanent form. The poem itself becomes a "living" record of the poet's consciousness impinging upon reality. Through language, he becomes aware of death, which in turn leads him to transcend death through language in poetry.

Concerning the foregoing argument, a number of generalizations might be made, generalizations that pertain as well to Dos Passos's own art. First, in isolating a single word with a broad range of aesthetic and philosophic implications, Whitman also chooses a word that is a nexus for two realms of experience—the Me and the Not Me, the real and the ideal, the concrete and the abstract. As Rohn Friedman has demonstrated, Whitman's art constitutes a "search for a unifying relation between the subjective and the objective orders of reality."[15] This leads to a second generalization: Whitman's search for the "word" in "Out of the Cradle" is in fact a metaphor for the poet's task, a search for every word that will reflect accurately the experience of the poet confronting reality. The search for the "word" exfoliates into a search for all language. Thus, rather than being abstract or ideal, Whitman's language and art illustrate what F. O. Matthiessen has called Whitman's "material ideality."[16]

For Dos Passos, too, one word in particular comes to take on a meaning that has a peculiar resonance, a word that is used as literal description but that through incremental repetition becomes a key word in the aesthetics of the novel. Indeed, to understand its significance for *Three Soldiers* is to better understand Dos Passos's intentions in his later (and even his earlier) works, for although the word "gesture" is not emphasized in later works, the aesthetic principle embodied in this term stands at the heart of Dos Passos's thought and art.[17] To understand the importance of this word, one has merely to turn to a book of essays that Dos Passos published only six months after *Three Soldiers, Rosinante to the Road Again*. It would not be surprising if these essays would deal at least tangentially with important issues that also arise in the novel. As a matter of fact, like the war novel, this book examines as its overriding concern a single issue: the aesthetic implications of the "gesture." *Rosinante* begins with a sketch in which the central character, Telemachus, watches Pastora Imperio dance. Although he watches intently, "only the victorious culminating instant of the gesture was blurred to him." He leaves the hall "aching for memory of it."[18] The rest of the book tells of his adventures on the road in Spain and of his futile attempt to regain the memory of her "gesture."

What actually does Dos Passos mean here by "gesture"? The simple dictionary definition notes that it is a bodily motion that expresses an interior state or attitude, and that is the way that Dos Passos uses it—except that he also gives the word a large metaphysical and aesthetic burden by employing it so extensively. A good understanding of the word can be gained by noting another similar term used in *Rosinante, lo castizo.* This, Dos Passos says, is "the essence of the local, of the regional." Furthermore, it refers not to the "empty shell of traditional observances but to the very core and gesture of them." *Lo castizo,* like the gesture, deals with a quality, but it is not something merely abstract. It is inextricably linked with the physical; it "means all that is salty, savourous of the red and yellow hills. . . ."[19] It is, in short, a bonding of the twofold nature of reality: matter and essence. Similarly, the gesture is a significant event that unites the internal state with external action, which embodies in a transitory moment a hypostatic bonding of the physical and the spiritual. Thus Dos Passos twice associates gesture with "essence."[20] It is something antithetical to "machine movements."[21] The gesture, then, should not be seen only in terms of its simple definition, but as a crucial element in defining his aesthetics.

In *Three Soldiers,* the word "gesture" has much the same purpose as it does in the more analytical essays of *Rosinante to the Road Again.* It is often used by the narrator to describe actions by diverse characters, to suggest an essential truth, the moment at which the concrete action and the spiritual life of a character are melded inextricably. Thus Henslowe tells a story "in his drawling voice, with gestures" (p. 235). A waiter empties a bottle of wine with "a tragic gesture" (p. 237). Aubrey speaks of the coming revolution as "the first great gesture towards a newer and better world" (p. 297). Andrews thinks of Genevieve as having "passionately-restrained gestures" (p. 338). A flower woman ties up flowers with "a deft abstracted gesture" (p. 342). Rosaline, the anarchist's daughter, "Pulled the coverlet round Andrews with an awkward gesture" (p. 375). Slippery, a character in the Paris underworld, hands Andrews money with "an offhand gesture" (p. 405). In most cases, the word "gesture" is modified by a descriptive adjective, and the situations in which the word is used can be humorous, serious, or inconsequential, but in every case, the description suggests something about the intangible qualities of a subjective state.

Andrews too is preoccupied with making gestures. But whereas the narrator's observations of gestures typically involve the commonplace activities of everyday existence, John Andrews's "gesture" aims toward the sublime and is an act that would relieve the soldiers from acting like "machines," would "free them all for life and freedom and joy" (p. 331). Again the discussion in *Rosinante* proves useful. Telemachus wishes to "catch that gesture, formulate it, do it." It must be "made permanent."[22] This is exactly Andrews's intention. He wonders if there is "no outlet, no gesture of expression" for the things he feels (p. 341), and he laments, "what's the use of just seeing and feeling things if you can't express them?" (p. 234). The implication is that his symphony—if he could ever complete it—would be such a gesture. The novel traces (just as does "Out of the Cradle") the protagonist's growing awareness of his real purpose in life—to be an artist. At first, the topic is "arbeit und rhythmus" (work and rhythm), the tangible and the evanescent. Although Andrews is temporarily sidetracked to a purely sensual subject, "The Queen of Sheba," he finds his true subject in "the Body and Soul of John Brown." Again, like the word "gesture" and Whitman's word "death," the title of his composition points toward the dual nature of Dos Passos's concern, the body and the soul, the concrete as it expresses subjective truths. Thus a symphony can be a gesture—just as surely as a novel can be. In this regard, one final parallel can be made between *Rosinante* and *Three Soldiers*. Telemachus fails to recapture the "gesture" just as Andrew fails to make his gesture in his symphony. Yet both books are themselves gestures that deal with the essentially evanescent nature of Dos Passos's subject.

Dos Passos's examination of this theme—language as gesture—is a significant intuition concerning the nature of the aesthetic experience, and it is a prescient postulation of modern aesthetic theory. Twenty years later, R. P. Blackmur would make an identical claim for language. "When the language of words most succeeds," he notes, "it *becomes* gesture in its words."[23] Furthermore, "the highest use of language cannot be made without incorporating some such quality of gesture within it."[24] Finally, in his definition of "gesture," Blackmur identifies the possibilities of language in terms very similar to Dos Passos's musings in *Rosinante* and *Three Soldiers:*

> Gesture, in language, is the outward and dramatic play of inward and imaged meaning. It is that play of meaningfulness among words which cannot be defined in the formulas in the dictionary, but which is defined in their use together; gesture is that meaningfulness which is moving, in every sense of that word: what moves the words and what moves us.[25]

In short, Dos Passos himself strives for a language that will give "much more of life than life can give."

Thus far, the discussion of the gesture has been somewhat schematic. The idea can be further elucidated by reference to pragmatism, for the word's metaphysical implications presuppose a theory of mind and of that mind's relationship to objective reality. In this regard, Dos Passos's ideas are similar to the pragmatized consciousness as outlined in William James's *Principles of Psychology*. Even in his psychology text, James was reacting against the rationalists and emphasizing empirical reality. Thus he sees a "spiritualistic" interpretation of mind as incompatible with modern scientific knowledge.[26] His approach is strictly empirical, emphasizing that the "nervous system is well understood to-day to be nothing but a machine for receiving impressions and discharging reactions preservative to the individual and his kind."[27] Idealistic demands do not have a priority over the immediate facts of empirical reality.

John Andrews, like Martin Howe, is initiated into a world of harsh empirical reality, and his survival depends to a large extent on a pragmatic awareness. Thus before the war, Andrews had been as much an idealist as the characters in Dos Passos's first war novel: Chenier, Lully, and Dubois. The enlistment in the military changes all that: "In a week the great structure of his romantic world, so full of many colors and harmonies, that had survived school and college and the buffeting of making a living in New York, had fallen in dust about him. He was utterly in the void" (p. 32). Like Howe, Andrews is reduced to a primal condition of consciousness without preconceptions. *Three Soldiers* might be said to take up where *One Man's Initiation* concluded. The latter book stops with Howe as a mere reflector of reality, his illusions destroyed; *Three Soldiers* charts Andrews's groping for and partial attainment of a reintegrative viewpoint consistent with his newfound condition.

As is usual in Dos Passos's fiction, two antithetical conditions devolve upon his protagonist. On the one hand, he is a product of modern pessimism. "Men had become ant-like," he realizes. There could be no individuals in the vein of the "strong figures" of the past, men like Michelangelo and da Vinci (p. 343). The military presents the perfect example of this declension of human scale. The soldiers' "faces were cowed into the same expression, their thoughts were the same" (p. 272). On the other hand, Andrews is deeply committed to being like those heroes from the past who "had given themselves smilingly for the integrity of their thoughts" (p. 207). He is conscious of "everything that made him an individual apart from his fellows" (pp. 207–8). "He must keep his will power" (p. 31), and he wants, over all else, "dominion over himself" (p. 207). He rejects his former dream life and wants "to build himself a new foundation" (p. 200), something solid. It is a "thread" (p. 31) or a "fabric of his life" rebuilt from "real things" (p. 31). The most convincing image signifying his change from dreamer to realist is given when he notes that "his mind seemed to have become a hard meaningless core" (p. 21). As my earlier discussion of the "core" intimates, this suggests some irreducible reality, without any metaphysical preconditions. A more positive variation of this basic image occurs when Andrews imagines an aesthetic response to his situation: "a rhythm began pushing its way through the hard core of his mind, leavening it, making it fluid" (p. 22). Here then is the critical center of Dos Passos's world: a response to his world with a pragmatized consciousness, the "core," without illusions, registering reality. In the middle of the novel, at the point he is wounded, Andrews makes a critical decision: "He would give up this cowardly cringing before external things" (p. 199). The refocusing of his consciousness here onto "external things" is the first step in healing his scarred dualistic nature. Neither ideals nor the harsh reality of empirical facts will have dominion over him. His pragmatized consciousness centers the significance of life in the core of his being, in the self's perceptions of reality, in the act that binds, like the gesture, the real and the ideal.

If his previous life seems like "a dream read in a novel," his awakened consciousness sees life directly as "a raw, fantastic world" (p. 31). Like Wenny in *Streets of Night* Andrews is "dazzled by the gorgeousness of everything" (p. 352). This new attitude is inextricably linked with the use of language. Thus Andrews notes that the greater part of humanity is and always has been taken in by "shams"—"gigantic phrases that floated like gaudy kites high above mankind." Such devotion to abstraction is typified by the "unworldliness" of the idealists: Democritus, Socrates, Epicurus, Christ (p. 211). Even the present day is afflicted with this attention to the unreal at the expense of the real. Andrews shares a hospital ward with a young man who, with his father, ran an undertaking establishment. The two of them, Andrews meditates, "lived by pretending things they didn't feel, by swathing reality with all manner of crêpe and trumpery. For those people no one ever died, they passed away, they deceased" (p. 207). Andrews, on the other hand, is wary of using "just rhetoric" (p. 241). A true use of language has to do with naming things rightly, of being worldly but suggesting the evanescent, of being concrete but recognizing the overwhelming importance of the ineffable qualities of human nature.

The issue under discussion—the mind's relationship with objective reality—can be clarified by reference once more to James's *Psychology*. In a chapter entitled "Psychology and Philosophy," James discusses "the relation of states of mind to their 'objects.' "[28] He examines the "sensational" and the "non-sensational" states of mind. Should the sensation of "blue," he asks, be described as a "quality of our feeling" (conscious state) or as "our feeling of a quality" (objective reality)? That is, is it part of the mind or part of reality? Whereas sensations are "self-sufficient," conceptional states present themselves immediately as referring beyond themselves. "Blue," substantively considered, is a word; but it is a word with *meaning,* James stresses. By conceptualizing, the mind reflects the same objective/subjective dualism. Thus, the content of the thought (objective state) is the word blue; the object of the thought (conscious state) is the quality blue. But whether one is speaking of the sensational or the nonsensational states of mind, "object and conscious state seem to be different ways of considering one and the same fact." This last statement is at the heart of

James's pragmatic philosophy. The objective and subjective realms meet in the act of perception; they are "one and the same fact."

It should be obvious at this point that Dos Passos's concept of the "gesture" is an elaboration of this same psychological/philosophical problem. Dos Passos's theory of language reflects the synthesizing quality of pragmatic thought. Andrews's task is the sensing through real life the transcendent possibilities that the mundane has to offer. His sense perceptions—and by extension the words used to describe them—become the nexus that heals the metaphysical dualism that has been Western man's burden since Descartes. Through his senses, Andrews's free imaginative life melds both with concrete reality and with the evanescent quality of that reality—just as the essence can reveal itself through the gesture and as the transcendental can be suggested by concrete language. A passage that deals with Andrews's aesthetic response to life describes this:

> He was free now of the imaginings of his desire, to loll all day at café tables watching the tables move in changing patterns before him, to fill his mind and body with a reverberation of all the rhythms of men and women moving in the frieze of life before his eyes; no more like wooden automatons knowing only the motions of the drill manual, but supple and varied, full of force and tragedy. (P. 289)

Andrews's "mind and body" feel the "reverberation" of the "rhythms." In this and other such transitory moments, Andrews experiences a holistic satisfaction that momentarily, at least, assuages the fragmented consciousness.

This ideal personal response is mirrored in the product of Andrews's emotions, his music, which also embodies a holistic state. In composing his symphony, John Andrews feels "his mind and body becoming as if fluid, and supple, trembling" (p. 425). Like his subject, "The Body and Soul of John Brown," Andrews's "mind and body" here reflect a harmonious whole, an aesthetic ideal, that is transitory in life but "formulated" in art. The final evaluation of Andrews must be made in light of this aesthetic standard. He must be judged by his intentions rather than by his accomplishments. Thus the unfinished symphony may reflect personal failure, but it is symbolic of Dos Passos's private aesthetic: paradoxically, material failure is a prerequisite for moral triumph. The wind blowing away leaves of Andrews's composition suggests that life does have significance even if the world is too crass to notice. If Dos Passos succeeds in his intention in *Three Soldiers*, he does so by utilizing the same aesthetic terms that John Andrews himself formulates and advocates: an awareness of nature's central importance provides the novel's formal framework, and the narrator's pragmatic concerns determine the body of the book.

If there is an aesthetic ideal toward which Andrews is working, it is represented by the "rabbit man," who is self-employed making toy animals. These rabbits have the air of "organic completeness" (p. 287), and as the rabbit man says, they are made "d'après la nature" (p. 288). When Genevieve tells Andrews that the music should be written in the countryside "when the sap is rising in the trees," he concurs by invoking the sentiments of the rabbit man: "D'après nature" (p. 337). Thus the subject of Andrews's symphony is the monotony of military life, but the implied aesthetic is a holism that will at once deal with the harsh realities of military life and at the same time invoke, in contrast, the full range of human emotions that that life inhibits. Thus he hears "feet tramping in unison" and "unconsciously" begins working: "He must make it into music; he must fix it in himself, so that he could make it into music, and write it down, so that orchestras could play it and make the ears of multitudes feel it, make their flesh tingle with it" (p. 22). Like a dancer's gesture, even military life has an "essence" that the artist can perceive, appreciate, and formulate in art.

In many of Dos Passos's novels, the climax of the plot is often less effective than the symbolism that is used to illuminate the ending. This is certainly true of *Three Soldiers*. The final chapter presents Andrews as a dreamer, an idealist who is fulfilling his only possible destiny. Andrews is a modern-day Don Quixote, and to emphasize this point, Dos Passos repeatedly mentions the scenic backdrop of windmills against which the final action of the book takes place.[29] Dos Passos knew *Don Quixote* well, and in *Rosinante* he quotes approvingly of a passage from Unamuno, who like Dos Passos admired the misguided idealist. "What is the new mission of Don Quixote in this world?" asks Unamuno:

> To cry, to cry in the wilderness. For the wilderness hears although men do not hear, and one day will turn into a sonorous wood, and that solitary voice that spreads in the desert like seed will sprout into a gigantic cedar that will sing with a hundred thousand tongues an eternal hosanna to the Lord of life and death.[30]

Dos Passos saw his own role as writer in just these terms, "A voice of one crying in the wilderness." No doubt, he wished himself to be an artist who was an effective instrument in effecting change. The picture the reader receives of John Andrews, though, is quite different. When he is at his best, Andrews is a pragmatist who is in touch with reality. But he also has the residuum of his old stubborn idealism. Thus, he never fully integrates his self into the requirements of reality. He is writing a musical composition whose only audience is nature.

8
Manhattan Transfer

Manhattan Transfer, which was published in 1925, ends with Jimmy Herf turning his back on the city and fleeing to an indeterminate place. In taking this action, Herf is reenacting a mythic pattern endemic to American literature. Natty Bumppo, for example, invariably chooses to live in the purity of the wilderness rather than to tolerate the corruption of civilization. Thoreau chooses a temporary stay at Walden Pond for similar reasons. When Huck lights out for the "territory," the reader feels that he will have to go, like Herf, "pretty far" before he finds happiness. And no less than Ishmael, who alone escapes the wicked city-state of the *Pequod,* Jimmy Herf by fleeing is in a position to tell of a community that has lost track of honest means and valuable ends. Dos Passos tells the tale for Herf, and although the novel does not allude to Cooper, Thoreau, Twain, or Melville, *Manhattan Transfer,* like Dos Passos's earlier novels, is strongly marked by other American traditions.

To better understand the values that are implicit in *Manhattan Transfer,* it is useful to look first at a passage initially published in 1921 and later incorporated into *Orient Express,* which appeared in 1927. In a section entitled "Bees," Dos Passos gives an account of a new school program in Russia. The "secretary of the commission for schools" tells of the plan:

> All education is to be by work, nothing without actual touch; he spread his hands, that were angular tortured painful hands, wide, and closed them with a gesture of laying hold onto some slippery reality. The words he used, too, were concrete, dug out of the soil. —From the very first, work. . . . In summer in the fields, the children must cultivate gardens, raise rabbits, bees, chickens, learn how to take care of cattle. They must go into the forests and learn about trees. Everything they must learn by touch. . . . [my ellipsis] For in our republic every man must be able to attend to his wants himself. That will be the primary education. You see, nothing by theory, everything by practice. . . . [my ellipsis] You see, merit will be according to work, not by theories or examinations. And all through there will be instruction in music and gymnastics and the theater; the arts must be open to anyone who wants to work in them. But most important will be nature; the young children must be all the

time in the fields and forests, among the orchards where there are bees. . . . It is in the little children that our hope lies. . . . among orchards where there are bees.[1]

Whether or not this is an exact quotation from a Russian official (one might presume that it is accurate), it is clear that the sentiments expressed here are heartily endorsed by Dos Passos and are, indeed, representative of the author's own calendar of values: a pragmatic approach to life (an emphasis on touch and work rather than on theory), self-sufficiency (illustrated best by bees), and "most important," a knowledge of and harmony with nature (gardens, fields, orchards, forests). Significantly, the description of the official's speech suggests how Dos Passos himself believes that language itself is affected by one's environment: "concrete, dug out of the soil." Unlike this idealized vision of society, *Manhattan Transfer* presents a very different and disturbing picture. In this novel, there are few children; the adults are, for the most part, unpragmatic (in its true Jamesian sense); they are also *dependent* on the established capitalistic system and out of harmony with nature. The last fact, perhaps, accounts for their widespread abuse of language. Nature, though, is "most important" in this novel too, and Dos Passos uses it in four ways: as a formal framework, as an object of characters' ideals, as a common element in counterpointing scenes, and as a basic, pervasive image pattern.

In one respect, *Manhattan Transfer* remains a puzzle to critics, for the novel, like *One Man's Initiation,* gives the illusion of formlessness. Blanche Gelfant has stated that for *Manhattan Transfer* "the technical problem inherent in Dos Passos' subject was to find a formal framework to express an interpretation and a moral judgment of the times." Thus one of the ways he structured the novel, Gelfant notes, is by employing a "circular movement": the book both opens and closes with a scene at the ferry slip.[2] John Wrenn, on the other hand, notes that "superficially the form is chaotic," and resorting to metaphor to solve the problem, states that the "apparent chaos of the whirlwind itself provides the form and the action."[3] Craig Carver takes a different approach. He identifies newspaper headlines mentioned in the novel and concludes that such references "led at least indirectly to the creation of a chronological framework composed of the dated fragments from newspaper sources and upon which all the other fragments of the novel could be positioned."[4] Each of these views has merit, but there is, in fact, a more solid framing device that Dos Passos employs.

Section 1 of *Manhattan Transfer,* the first written, does not have a tightly knit structural pattern, and one might deduce that by the time Dos Passos came to see the overall design of this novel, he did not go back and change that section to make it conform in every instance to his overall scheme. But sections 2 and 3 do show Dos Passos's tight control over the ordering of events, and, except loosely speaking, that order is not the chronology of history. This is most obvious in section 2. Here, the sequence of identifiable historical dates and their page references in the novel are as follows: November 1913 (p. 138), March 1913 (p. 162), June 1906 (p. 169), June 1914 (p. 183), and July 1914 (p. 222).[5] It is possible that the notorious murder of Stanford White (June 1906) is not meant to be contemporaneous with the action of the scene in which it is mentioned, though I believe that it is meant to be. Nevertheless, even by deleting that date, the chronology is still confused with the occurrence of the ambassador's visit (November 1913) coming in the text before the death of Pierpont Morgan (March 1913). Furthermore, Carver identifies the newspaper source for the ambassador's visit (which I take to be accurate) and notes that the visit occurred in November;[6] but the event as reported in the novel obviously takes place in the summer (see p. 137). Clearly, in using these historical references, Dos Passos's primary concern is with providing a historical perspective, a sociological "depth" to the fictional events, rather than with establishing a "solid framework."

The structure of *Manhattan Transfer* resulted from Dos Passos's continuing appreciation of nature—appreciation that he had already frequently associated with Walt Whitman. Waldo Frank, who would later become one of Dos Passos's acquaintances, also admired the nineteenth-century American poet, and he too affirmed the importance of nature. In his book *Our America,* published in 1919, Frank states that "the New Yorker has no power with which to meet the speaking solitudes of Nature."[7] Frank captures succinctly the twentieth-century intellectual's feeling that man has lost touch with something important. Whitman himself constantly invokes Nature as a positive force and always interprets the term broadly: it was not merely physical nature but the organic, spiritual continuum that linked man with his place. So in "Democratic Vistas" he notes that Nature has "invisible roots" that have to do with "the profoundest meanings" of a particular "place, race, or nationality." It is the author's task, he continues, "to absorb and again effuse" this spirit.[8] And this is what Dos Passos does with the place, race, and nationality represented by New York. He constantly reminds the reader that his characters are out of touch with nature and with their own human natures. Jimmy Herf, for example, knows that man's natural spirit is repressed in the urban environment. With one eye on Whitman's "The Sleepers," perhaps, he echoes a Whitmanesque statement about the human condition, about the people "in all the pigeonhole bedrooms, tangled sleepers twisted and strangled like the roots of potbound plants" (pp. 235–36). The characters' problems are a manifestation of a deformed human nature, but as I shall demonstrate, Dos Passos takes pains to note that organic nature is an abiding presence and a solid standard by which human shortcomings can be measured and judged.

Dos Passos knits together the loosely connected vignettes (which range over twenty-five years) by using a mythic structure of the seasonal cycle, the same cycle that plays such a dominant role in his three previous novels. In the notebook draft of section 3 of *Manhattan Transfer,* Dos Passos marked in the margins a progression of seasons that parallels the progression of the plot. In historical time, the events in sections 2 and 3 run from around 1913 to 1925. Cutting across this run of years, however, is the mythic time of a well-ordered single season: summer, fall, winter, spring. Indeed, a close reading of the novel finds these seasonal references (there are at least forty-three of them) unobtrusively embedded in the text.[9] Citing only a few of these will suggest this consistently developed pattern. On page 137, the women wear "summer dresses"; on page 254 there is "a tang of fall in the wind"; on page 333, the time is a "sparkling winter afternoon"; and the novel ends in May (p. 401). Section 1 does not present such an orderly arrangement, but three of the scenes that Jimmy Herf appears in do suggest the seasons and do follow this same pattern: summer (p. 72), fall (p. 96), and spring (p. 113). Since (as I will argue) this is Herf's novel, this pattern too is significant, for after his mother's death in the spring, which ends section 1, Jimmy Herf undergoes in sections 2 and 3 an emotional cycle that leads to his rebirth in the spring, the novel's close. Presently, however, it is important to note only that Dos Passos meant nature in its largest sense to provide a structure for the novel: the historical time of twenty-five years is enveloped in the mythic time of two seasonal cycles.

Nature is also developed as a positive force in the novel by characters who are able to envision an ideal society. It is true that Bud Korpenning's agrarian existence before coming to the city is marked with strife, but when honest characters in the novel dream of an ideal order, it usually has to do with nature. Thus early in the novel, a young, honest, and engaging Gus McNeil knows that "this here livin in the city's no good" (p. 46). He dreams of "movin West" to "be a wheatfarmer and have a big farmhouse an barns an pigs an horses an cows an chickens" (p. 47). And Jimmy Herf regrets having attended Columbia University (the name suggests America's origin, but is also symbolic of twentieth-century America, as the context makes clear); instead, he wishes that he had gone to the real "Columbia"—"Bogota and the Orinoco and all that sort of thing" (p. 174). "All that sort of thing," of course, stands for a country less "civilized," closer to nature, than the United States is. But not everyone's dream necessitates moving out. The visionary architect Specker had plans for a city that does not divorce nature from the urban landscape. He envisioned an organic "communal building," a skyscraper "seventyfive stories high stepped back in terraces with a sort of hanging garden on every floor" (p. 170). This ability to envision a harmonious order results, one may believe, from man's essential desire for an organic relationship to his world—to nature and to other truly human natures.

A third way in which nature serves as a standard of value in contrast to the sterility of modern America is best seen in Dos Passos's use of counterpointing scenes, one set of which involves Ellen riding trains. In the scene that gives the novel its title, Ellen, who will prove to be frigid, and Oglethorpe, who will prove to be homosexual, ride the train to their honeymoon in Atlantic City. The event is reported through Ellen's consciousness: "the wheels rumbled in her head, saying Man-hattan Tran-sfer Man-hattan Tran-sfer." The scene is generally dismal: "brown marshes . . . black windows of factories . . . puddly streets . . . a rusty steamboat . . ." (p. 116; my ellipses). The other train scene involving Ellen is again a trip with her lover, this time Jimmy Herf. But this trip takes place in Europe, a place that Jimmy thinks of as a "green park" (p. 192), and is reported through his consciousness. Late in the novel, he fondly remembers their idyllic journey as they left Avignon:

> Diddledeump, going south, Diddledeump, going south, sing the wheels over the rails down the valley of the Rhone. . . . Glubglub glubglub from the bushes, from the silverdripping poplars along the track. . . . Deedledeump, going south. Gasp of nightingale along the track among the silverdripping poplars. The insane cloudy night of moonlight smells of gardens garlic rivers freshdunged field roses. Gasp of nightingales. (P. 301; my ellipses)

The two scenes have in common the train ride and the multisyllabic sounds coming from the wheels. But in this latter scene the mishyphenated "Man-hattan Tran-sfer" (which jars the reader) is replaced by the lighthearted "Diddledeump." The contrast between the two scenes reveals something about Jimmy's and Ellen's characters: he enjoys a harmonious relationship with nature, at least through his memory, while she is alienated.

Another set of contrasting scenes involving Ellen and Jimmy is to much the same purpose. Having abandoned Oglethorpe, Ellen checks into a hotel feeling ebullient at first, then terrified: "she felt hungry and alone. The bed was a raft on which she was marooned alone, always alone, afloat on a growling ocean" (p. 168). Dos Passos is not using nature in this instance (nor in the previous scene where Ellen rides the train with Oglethorpe) as an antagonistic force. Rather it serves as an expressionistic image to note how far Ellen is divorced from her own natural self. In a counterpointing scene, Jimmy as a child daydreams in bed to escape the unhappy news of his mother's stroke:

The surf thundered loud on the barrier reef. . . . Jack was swimming fast through the calm blue waters of the lagoon, stood in the sun on the yellow beach shaking the briny drops off him, opened his nostrils wide to the smell of breadfruit roasting beside his solitary campfire. Birds of bright plumage shrieked and tittered from the tall ferny tops of the coconut palms. (Pp. 97–98; my ellipsis)

The language and the details are from a typical boy's adventure story, but the important point here is what the daydream reveals about Herf. Like Ellen, Jimmy pictures himself alone in a natural environment, but he enjoys a peaceful harmony with nature—the water is calm, a lagoon protectively encloses him, nature feeds him and gives him pleasant, exotic things to look at. Since nature plays such a positive role for Jimmy, it is appropriate that when later in life he uses a natural image to describe Ellen—"the deep woods of her hair" (p. 330)—he at the same time acknowledges to himself his love for her. It is the only time in the novel that the word "love" is used sincerely. This image from nature reflects both on Herf's honest emotion and on Ellen's inability to reciprocate. Nature in all these instances serves as a standard by which the reader can measure the relative fulfillment of the character's human nature.

A fourth way by which Dos Passos repeatedly reminds the reader of man's vitiated organic nature is through flower imagery. There are simply scores of references to flowers in this urban novel. Nellie McNeil, for example, has a "purse with pansies burned on the back" (p. 73), and she wears a hat decorated with "red poppies" (p. 72). An unidentified girl wears a "flowered bonnet" (p. 19), and Stan Emery, a "small flowered straw hat" (p. 245). Ruth Prynne has a straw hat with "red poppies" (p. 155). These and numerous other such references do not simply satisfy Dos Passos's love of minute detail; they also suggest the abiding presence of nature—with which the characters are out of touch.

Flower imagery is especially apparent in the characterization of Ellen. She is repeatedly associated with roses. As in the earlier novels, Dos Passos uses roses here to signify an innate capacity for love—both eros and agape. This capacity is something that Ellen possessed early in her life but loses as she grows older, as she becomes a success in the city. Thus Ed Thatcher brings roses to his wife when Ellen is born (pp. 5, 7)—but as is made clear as the novel progresses, the roses and the father's love belong to Ellen, not Susie. As a little girl, Ellen dances in front of her father on a carpet with a red rose pattern (p. 17). Later, when she is a success on stage, she brings her father roses (p. 198). Her romantic affair with Stan takes place in a bedroom that contains roses (p. 151), and Jimmy's fond memory of Ellen and himself in Europe is associated with nature and specifically roses (p. 301). But Ellen comes to lose her sense of organic integrity as she rises in her profession. Her dinner with George Baldwin, which begins yet another unsatisfactory romance and marriage, takes place with "rusty red and yellow roses" on the table—roses that are "faded" (p. 219). Later, he sends her "coppery" colored roses, "Gold of Ophir" as the clerk describes them (pp. 279–80). One is led to believe here that an organic commodity (roses) perceived as inorganic (copper and gold) is a debased currency and as artificial as the pattern of "silveryshiny roses" on the Merivales' wallpaper (p. 99). Finally, Ellen is a hit in *Peach Blossoms* (p. 134) and then a smashing success in *The Zinnia Girl* (p. 243). But her fame is gained at the expense of her natural self, and the shows' titles suggest that slow transmogrification that she has undergone in the novel, from "rose girl" to zinnia girl, a change that marks the declension of her own organic self.

The flower imagery is given a final irrefutable meaning in the very last section of the novel. When Jimmy escapes from New York City, he takes the ferry and shares the ride across the river with a relic from the old city of New York, a horse and wagon. This "brokendown springwagon" is loaded with flowers. Jimmy finds it "unexpectedly merry, stacked with pots of scarlet and pink geraniums, carnations, alyssum, forced roses, blue lobelia. A rich smell of maytime earth comes from it, of wet flowerpots and greenhouses" (p. 403). Although Jimmy wants to ask the driver where he is going with the flowers, he resists. But the unasked rhetorical question doesn't need answering; the reader understands intuitively that the driver leaving the city with his flowers is as symbolic an act as Jimmy Herf's flight. The wagonload of flowers serves as an objective correlative to the natural harmony that Jimmy Herf is in the process of recapturing.

Readers were quick to catch Dos Passos's portrayal of urban sordidness in *Manhattan Transfer,* but it is important to note that the author also had a keen awareness of and concern for natural beauty, and in this, his first great novel, he uses nature in manifold ways to remind the reader that an ideal order does in fact exist, even within the sordidness of New York.

While nature may be the ideal, the reality of the city shows a very different reality. And behind the sordidness is Dos Passos's peculiar cosmogony. The metaphysical basis of the fictional reality of *Manhattan Transfer* rests on a dialectic, much like Jimmy Herf's "doublefaced word . . . Success Failure" (p. 303). This dialectic can be seen operating in one of the novel's image patterns, the vortex. One part of this image is the pellmell movement and sense of vertigo that affects most of the characters in the novel. Thus Ellen, on being told of Stan's marriage to Pearline, hears and feels "the clatter of plates spouted spiraling louder and louder about her" (p. 245). Stan immolates himself in the middle of the "revolving kitchen" (p. 253). Upon appearing before the judge to be sentenced, Francie feels the courtroom "going round and round . . . all going round and round . . . going round and round until she thought she would throw up" (pp. 390–91). Similarly, Baldwin characterizes life in New York as a process of going "round and round in a squirrel cage" (p. 220). When Jimmy dances with Ellen, people "rotated densely about them" (p. 228). When he gets drunk, "the room would start going around him solemnly and methodically" (p. 345). When he is down on his luck, he stands in "Columbus Circle" (p. 370), and the physical circle here is symbolic on a larger level, of his and America's predicament: the endless circularity without progress of American culture. Finally, the fate that Jimmy must avoid is the "revolving doors" of the business world (p. 120). All of these images reflect feverish activity without redeeming results.

The motion of the vortex has its dialectical opposite: if the vortex suggests the feverish activity, it also suggests the quiet center, the attainment of which seems to offer satisfaction, relief from anxiety. Thus Bud, escaping from the law, repeatedly asks directions to "the center of things" (pp. 4, 24, 25), and Ellen uses a similar image in talking with one of her many male companions (p. 267). Also, she perceives her job on Mr. Harpsicourt's periodical as making "every reader feel Johnny on the spot in the center of things" (p. 368). She better than most understands why it is a much-sought-after feeling and why in Manhattan it is only an illusion. The "center of things" should be in every person as an organic wholeness, but this condition is not attainable in Manhattan. Over fifty years before, Whitman had recognized this problem in America: because of commercialism, he said, "never was there, perhaps, more hollowness at heart than at present."[10] Things have not changed much by Dos Passos's time; most of his characters are like Ellen, "all hollow inside" (p. 375). Thus Goldwiser, for one, knows of the vitiated life and courts Ellen to get "that old feelin back" again (p. 204). Even Jimmy Herf, whose brain seems an "empty chamber" (p. 303), suffers this sense of incompleteness. He at least recognizes that the quest for material possessions provides him with "no organic sensation" (p. 384). He comes to know that man cut off from the organic, from feeling, from nature, will not find relief, regardless of the illusions generated by slick magazine editors and spokesmen for culture.

The basis for characterization in *Manhattan Transfer* lies in a similar metaphysical dichotomy. Reality is both physical and spiritual. This contrast leads to a number of variations: external versus the internal; material versus the spiritual; and form versus content. How this principle applies to the characters in the novel is suggested by the clear and forceful analysis of human nature that is given by Martin Schiff. Undoubtedly a spokesman for Dos Passos's own views, Schiff contrasts a person's "personality" to a real aspect of himself, the "work" he does (p. 360), and he counterpoints people's "pretense" to "real souls" (p. 361). His ruminations on man's basic nature, "the black pit of the soul of man" (p. 361), lead him to the metaphor of a room, "windowpane" outside, "deep black inside" (p. 361).

The one positive element here is a distinction—an important one—between employment and "work." As Schiff notes, in modern New York, real work is not valued as much as personality. Bud Korpenning, for one, finds this out early when someone tells him that "it's looks that count in this city" (p. 5).

There are, roughly speaking, two kinds of characters in *Manhattan Transfer:* those who succeed financially and those who fail. To his credit, Joe Harland is one of the latter. He succeeded once, of course, but the major obstacle that inhibits his getting along is that his heart is too good to accomplish much in a world that is devoted to crass, materialistic manipulation of abstractions. His major role in the novel seems to be to serve as an example to Jimmy Herf of the pitfalls of modern business society, especially as it is exemplified by the Merivales. Harland's end is much too inevitable for the reader to take pleasure in Dos Passos's slow and methodical plotting of Harland's decline, but one scene that depicts Harland's rise and fall is interesting for the light it sheds on his condition and on the novel's themes.

The short tale (pp. 144–48) has the force of a parable, and a close reading of the incident reveals the heart of Dos Passos's concerns in *Manhattan Transfer.* A writer, "a dirty blackguard," Harland tells some people in a bar, fictionalized Harland's early business career and entitled the book "Secret of Success." Joe as a young man speculated in the stock market and because of his astounding success came to be known as the "Wizard of Wall Street." The reason for his unusual luck, he says, was "a blue silk crocheted necktie that my mother made for me when I was a little boy." When he wore the necktie he made money; when he didn't, he lost. The tie, needless to say, became rather worn. He subsequently fell in love with a woman, and to prove his love he gave her the tie. Seeing it to be an old tie and thinking the gift a joke, she "threw it in the fire." Joe never made money again. To Joe, this is "only another illustration" of what has been his—and many other characters'—reiterated excuse: "the peculiar predominance of luck." But the crutch of "luck," one feels, is not something to which Dos Passos himself gives much credence. There are other answers.

Joe Harland's story invites a symbolic interpretation. The "Story of Success" is in many ways the novel *Manhattan Transfer* itself. Thus the denigration of the writer as a "blackguard" is consistent with Dos Passos's persistent need to belittle his own occupation. Note, for example, that Martin Schiff, Dos Passos's spokesman, states that Jimmy Herf is "a useless fardel on society. . . . The artist is a fardel" (p. 361). This is an ironic statement, of course; the self-belittlement actually points to aggrandizement of the writer's trade, the only honest living that can be imagined in the novel, though Dos Passos is too modest to endorse himself or his trade outright. In fact, Jimmy Herf's career in *Manhattan Transfer*, as suggested previously, prepares him to be the writer who will eventually tell the story of Manhattan, though Dos Passos neatly refuses to make that identification explicit. Jimmy never does become Ishmael "escaped alone to tell thee."

There is a more important aspect to Joe Harland's story, and this involves the passage of time and the differences between the generations. Joe's mother worked with her hands and crocheted the necktie; in contrast, Joe is passive and is fed the ticker tape. Most importantly, his job does not entail a task that is concrete, self-evident, and immediately meaningful; rather, he has the job of manipulating symbols, abstractions. Clearly, Joe's life is several removes from the more natural world of his mother.

Another important aspect of his story has to do with sexuality. Joe's squandering of his inheritance by giving the tie to a woman fits the common paradigm of Dos Passos's fiction: man seduced and ruined by a sorceress. The woman is an irresistible lure whose fire, sexuality, ruins man's hope for success. The connection between failure and sexuality is never explicit or causally linked in Dos Passos's fiction, but it is there nevertheless. (Note, for obvious examples, Andrew King's sexual temptation before death and John Andrews's sexual indulgence before desertion.)

Harland's squandering of his fortune, the handmade tie, is very much like Faulkner's treatment of the same theme in "The Bear." There, Ike McCaslin's legacy is "a Thing, possessing weight to the hand and bulk to the eye and even audible: a silver cup filled with gold pieces."[11] Over the years, Beauchamp occasionally borrows from it, leaving, ultimately, a tin coffee pot and worthless scraps of paper, IOUs. Faulkner's symbol actually works better—it is a realistic detail that figures in the plot—yet Dos Passos's tale of the tie, though it requires the unrealistic surface explanation of "luck," is exact in pinpointing the cause of modern man's failure: concrete, meaningful labor has been replaced by an unhealthy regard for abstraction.

Standing in contrast to Harland, Ellen Thatcher represents the other kind of character, the "Success." Dos Passos admired Henry James's ability to portray realistic women characters,[12] and some of Dos Passos's own women are sympathetically drawn and realistic. Ellen Thatcher is a good example. Despite her flaws, she is a woman that Dos Passos obviously empathizes with. As the flower imagery makes clear, she too—like Joe Harland—has squandered her inheritance. She gives up her full rich human nature in order to succeed in Manhattan, and figuratively her success kills her. In some respects, the reader sympathizes with her because it is the city exacting its toll on her—rather than her acting volitionally to trade her virtue for success.

As Maxwell Geismar suggests, Ellen is similar to Nancibel Taylor in *Streets of Night*.[13] Both, for example, suffer in their respective fields; both love an irrepressible man—Wenny and Stan; and when the two men die, both women find that they loved the man even more than they had thought. Ellen's sad, too-late comment might just as well have been uttered by Nan: "I guess I don't love anybody for long unless they're dead" (p. 345).

Like all of Dos Passos's major characters, Ellen might be said to suffer the ill effects of a divided consciousness, which contributes much toward making her life intolerable. She seems to suffer character dissociation or a mild form of schizophrenia. This becomes apparent toward the end of the novel. At one point, eating at the Algonquin, she feels acute self-consciousness, and like those hospitalized schizophrenics who sense that they can look down at themselves from the room's ceiling and see themselves in bed, Ellen feels "the smart probing glances of men and women at the tables round about"—as if she could see a "mirror behind her" (p. 368). This division in her personality results in a separation of her intellect from her emotion, and in fact she no longer feels any emotion. She tries to rationalize her impairment, however, interpreting her vice as a virtue. Thus she admires the geometry of the city "laid . . . out in numbers." But like those numbers and like the city, she herself is "cold and emotionless" (p. 373).

Dos Passos goes to great pains to portray Ellen's peculiar lifelessness. She is repeatedly described in terms of the city and of society's mechanical accoutrements. Unlike Daisy Buchanan's voice, which is "full of money" (which for Fitzgerald as for Dos Passos is destructive enough), Ellen's voice is "a tiny flexible sharp metalsaw" (p. 228). She feels another time like "a busted mechanical toy" (p. 400). Most important, she partakes of the mechanical qualities of the city's structures. A fall in her spirits is "like a rollercoaster's into shuddering pits of misery" (p. 153). "Like a lighthouse," she "sits up cold white out of reach . . . Men's hands crawl like bugs on the unbreakable glass. . . . But in deep pitblackness inside something clangs like a fire engine" (p. 182). Even when she is happy, her emotion doesn't bubble up as from a fountain; rather, upon hearing her stage performance praised, the words seem to her "an elevator carrying her up dizzily, up into some stately height where electric light signs cracked scarlet and gold and green" (p. 154). She is slowly becoming hard and mechanical like the city itself.

One final word needs to be said about Ellen as the embodiment of the city. She lacks feeling, it is true; at one point she has an "icy coldness stealing through her like novocaine" (p. 375). But Dos Passos goes beyond describing her anesthetic personality. She becomes through imagery as hard as the buildings surrounding her: "Ellen felt herself sitting with her ankles crossed, rigid as a porcelain figure under her clothes, everything about her seemed to be growing hard and enameled" (p. 375). In this respect, she has become the fulfillment of a prophecy of the city—Sandbourne's interpretation of Specker's architectural vision. Ironically, Sandbourne speaks of this vision to George Baldwin, the man who will eventually acquire Ellen, the woman turned to enamel:

> Do you remember years ago old man Specker used to talk about vitreous and superenameled tile? Well I've been workin on his formula out at Hollis. . . . Imagine this city when all the buildins instead of being dirty gray were ornamented with vivid colors. Imagine bands of scarlet round the entablatures of skyscrapers. Colored tile would revolutionize the whole life of the city. . . . Instead of fallin back on the orders or on gothic or romanesque decorations we could evolve new designs, new colors, new forms. If there was a little color in the town all this hardshell inhibited life'd break down. . . . There'd be more love an less divorce. (P. 257; first ellipsis is mine)

The final fatuous sentiment increases the irony when Ellen becomes the embodiment of men's dreams, a vitreous "porcelaine figure under a bellglass" (p. 300).

Joe Harland, Ellen, and many other characters are intriguing, but I take *Manhattan Transfer* to be primarily Jimmy Herf's story. In light of recent Dos Passos scholarship, this seems to be a daring judgment. Most critics are reluctant to assign to Jimmy the kind of primary value that one usually expects of fictional protagonists. Thus Maxwell Geismar writes that "at the end of the novel, his job pointless, his marriage a disaster, his attempts at social integration blocked, his will paralysed, and his mind again turning into the confused fantasies so familiar to us—returning in short to the original mould of the isolated, nerveless individual—Herf wanders off, a ghost from the past."[14] Likewise, E. D. Lowry states that Herf's final "gesture" is "merely another dead end."[15] Blanche Gelfant also thinks that the novel's resolution shows Jimmy's ineffectual nature.[16] Perhaps it is such widespread agreement that prompts Linda Wagner to see Ellen as the protagonist in *Manhattan Transfer*.[17] But in an excellent article, David Vanderwerken takes a minority position, on which I would like to elaborate.[18] I think that there is overwhelming evidence for seeing Jimmy Herf as the backbone of the novel, as the core of value, as the one character who embodies a redeeming vision and then acts on it.

Jimmy Herf deserves to be called the hero of *Manhattan Transfer* because he is the main spokesman for Dos Passos's moral humanism. Essentially, he comes to embody moral and ethical values that provide a standard by which the action of the novel is to be judged. His values constitute a secular morality in the tradition of Walt Whitman and William James.

Whitman offers a very specific program about what should constitute an

American literature, and a key component of that program is an emphasis on man's spiritual life. It is one of his favorite themes, and he expounds upon it in various essays. In "Democratic Vistas," for example, he states that the literature of the United States should first express the spirit of nature. Furthermore, he says, "the question of Nature, largely consider'd, involves the questions of the esthetic, the emotional, and the religious—and involves happiness."[19] The source of "value" is, quite simply, the individual, "Being": "the object's self, according to its own central idea and purpose, and of growing therefrom and thereto . . . is the lesson of Nature."[20] Sounding much like a poet giving an early version of pragmatism, Whitman says that "identity" is the "hardest basic fact, and only entrance to all facts." In the face of a well-established identity, he says, "creeds, conventions, fall away and become of no account" and are replaced by "the luminousness of real vision."[21] True religion, then, is to be found "in this field of individuality, and is a result that no organization or church can ever achieve."[22] The "religion" he is espousing here is a secular humanism. No doubt, it is because of Whitman's iconoclastic views toward religion and because of his indomitable, optimistic belief in man's ability to envision an ideal life that William James describes this poet as one "of the genuine lineage of the prophets."[23]

In William James one finds similar statements on man's ethical life. James is best remembered as a secular philosopher, but all of his writings in some way recognize the central importance of man's moral nature. If a modern pragmatist asserts that only "facts" exist, he is a hybrid and is not reading his James faithfully. Far from rejecting outright the idealistic school, James defends "rationalistic hypotheses so far as these re-direct you fruitfully into experience,"[24] and he notes that his philosophy can even "be called religious."[25] But it is in *Varieties of Religious Experience,* the book that so deeply impressed Dos Passos, that James examines directly the question of man's subjective religious states ("personal religion") rather than in the "institutional branch" of theology: ecclesiastical organizations and systematic theology.[26] Thus James defines "religion" in terms of "the feelings, acts and experiences of individual men in their solitude, so far as they apprehend themselves to stand in relation to whatever they may consider the divine."[27] Later, he defines religion even more broadly: it is "any total reaction upon life."[28] Furthermore, his study of religion is decidedly influenced by his philosophy; the "pragmatic way of taking religion," he says, is "the deeper way."[29] Even if he is a scientist committed to empirical analyses, at the same time he recognizes that life transcends facts. With the delicate touch of a poet, he avers that "individuality is founded in feeling."[30] As deeply as Whitman, he understands that the primacy of the felt life is compatible with philosophical reflection and moral action.

Just as Whitman and James interpret "religion" in its broadest ethical sense, so too does Dos Passos. Like Whitman and James, he manages to be philosophic, moral, and aesthetic in his examination of human life: in its intentions and its processes, his art impinges upon the realm of morality. Organized religion, Dos Passos states in an essay, is a "backwater" that caters to corrupt political organizations.[31] But at the time when he himself was writing plays, Dos Passos reviewed John Lawson's *Processional* and made the connection between religion and art explicit. "Since religion has failed humanity," he writes, "the theatre is the focus of mass emotion."[32] What is clear here is that Dos Passos sees an aesthetic response to life as a moral experience, an alternative to the vacuum left by religion.

Jimmy Herf is an ethical humanist. Herf recognizes the sterility of New York City, he sees the stifled roots of humanity, and he is aware that his own moral life is in danger by his staying there. His decision to leave the city, therefore, is essentially a moral choice. In Whitman's terms, his action "involves the question of the esthetic, the emotional, and the religious—and involves happiness." He chooses life in its widest sense, and though it is a simple action that he takes, it devolves from Dos Passos's view of Herf as the embodiment of complex human values.

In an excellent article examining the growth of *Manhattan Transfer*, Lois Hughson notes that Dos Passos achieved mastery in his novel because he learned to distance personal emotion by deflecting it away from his protagonist to subsidiary characters. Thus, she notes, the legless man is one version of the sense of frustration that belongs as well to Jimmy Herf.[33] In like manner, but at a considerably more intense level and with only slight displacement, the story of St. Aloysius of Philadelphia, the secular "saint," is also an objectification of Jimmy Herf's own predicament. Coming at the end of the novel, Aloysius's story is brief but essential for an adequate understanding of the novel. Bob Hildebrand tells this tale to Herf:

> Say Herf did you read about the man in Philadelphia who was killed because he wore his straw hat on the fourteenth of May? . . . This man had the temerity to defend his straw hat. Somebody busted it and he started to fight, and in the middle of it one of these streetcorner heroes came up behind him and brained him with a piece of lead pipe . . . he died in the hospital. (P. 401; my ellipses)

Herf responds to this story by saying, "if I was starting a new religion he'd be made a saint" (p. 401). A little later, while waiting for the ferry to take him out of town, Herf expounds further upon the subject: "By gum if I were a painter . . . I'd do Saint Aloysius of Philadelphia with a straw hat on his head instead of a halo and . . . a little me praying at his feet" (p. 403; my ellipses). Herf does homage enough to St. Aloysius by acting in the same spirit: Herf too is idiosyncratic by indulging in an apparently inconsequential act, leaving the city. The Philadelphia saint is an objective parallel to Herf's own condition.

Herf's regard for Aloysius and his desire to paint his picture suggests a frequent theme in Dos Passos's work, what might be called the "hallowedness of the protagonist." This has already been seen explicitly in Dos Passos's treatment of Wenny, but it is present as well in Martin Howe and John Andrews. The protagonists strive for more than life can give, and it isCed Passos's intention to create characters who are cynosures. In an interview that took place late in his life, Dos Passos reflected upon his early attempts at fiction:

> I have always paid a good deal of attention to painting. The period of art I was very much interested in at the time was the thirteenth and fourteenth centuries. Its tableaux with large figures of saints surrounded by a lot of little people just fascinated me. I tried to capture the same effect in words.[34]

Dos Passos is speaking in particular here of the Biographies (the "saints") in the *U.S.A.* trilogy, but in light of Herf's comments on Aloysius, this quotation has an authentic ring that is sometimes missing from authors' old-age reminiscences of their youthful, aesthetic intentions. This passage suggests that it might be useful to look in more detail at the possibility that Herf himself, like Aloysius, is a secular "saint," one who embodies the ethical and aesthetic values of the author and who stands "large" next to all the other "little people" of *Manhattan Transfer.*

It may be nothing more than coincidence, but the change in Jimmy Herf's character is in many ways similar to the condition of the saint's conversion in *The Varieties of Religious Experience.* It is impossible, perhaps it is superfluous, to prove that James provided Dos Passos with the model. Perhaps it is inevitable coincidence—in that the psychic patterns of some writers at a certain period in their careers match in the secular mode of art the same conflicts that saints work out in religious metaphors. Certainly, Dos Passos's treatment of this theme in *Manhattan Transfer* is consistent with his very positive response to James's book (see chapter 3). Both authors examine the moral crisis and resolution pattern of the human psyche. As can be seen in his treatment of Saint Aloysius, Dos Passos is concerned with the way that positive human values can give meaning to life—even if religion in the conventional sense is absent. Thus Herf is similar to the traditional figures that James examines in that he too undergoes a "conversion" from "the divided self" to being one "who lives in his religious centre of personal energy."[35] Moreover, the five main elements that describe the saint's newfound condition are mirrored in Herf's own life: (1) the loss of all worry; (2) the perceiving of new truths;

(3) the objective change that the world often appears to undergo; (4) automatisms; (5) the ecstasy of happiness. James does not present these elements as a sequential, ordered process, nor do they occur to Herf in this ordered arrangement. Yet all of these elements are present, and they all seem to point toward Herf's final action of leaving the city.

The first characteristic that James identifies, the loss of all worry, is summed up by its concomitant attributes of "peace," "harmony," and a "willingness to be."[36] This last phrase is most important and is explained further by James in another part of his text: "The opposition between the men who *have* and the men who *are* is immemorial."[37] Thus the "claims which *things* make," James recognizes, "are corrupters of manhood, mortgages on the soul, and a drag anchor on our progress towards the empyrean."[38] Dos Passos too recognizes this. One of the major strands of the novel is James Merivale's progress toward material success, a strand that is crossed by the counterpointing strand of Herf's "decline." On the novel's last page, Dos Passos emphasizes Herf's freedom from the claims of things by having him buy breakfast with his last quarter: "that leaves him three cents for good luck, or bad for that matter" (p. 404). That Herf is broke suggests his freedom from "mortgages on the soul," but that he is indifferent to the kind of luck that awaits him certainly shows his loss of all worry.

William James's second criterion is "the sense of perceiving truths not known before."[39] Herf actually experiences this epiphany early in the novel, in section 1, when he eats dinner with Uncle Jeff at the club. His uncle offers Jimmy the chance for success, for working "your way up through the firm" (p. 119). This offer forces Jimmy to confront his destiny, and the scene is portrayed symbolically (pp. 119–21). Jimmy leaves the club, "not knowing which way to go." He is faced with the "perpetually revolving doors." He takes a walk to the Battery and finds in Trinity Churchyard "stenographers and officeboys are eating sandwiches among the tombs." He decides that Uncle Jeff and his office "can go plumb to hell." And while he is staring "up the deep gash of Broadway" he is at the same time "facing the wind squarely." This scene plays out in small his final grand decision to choose nature rather than the stultifying life among the "tombs." It will take him a few years to discover his true path, but his immediate decision is his first step, choosing the relatively independent life of a reporter.

The third characteristic is "the objective change which the world often appears to undergo. 'An appearance of newness beautifies every object.'"[40] Jimmy experiences this change in perception whenever the natural order, rather than the man-made environment, becomes the focus of his attention. The first time this happens is right after his mother's funeral. This and similar succeeding scenes mark a cumulative effect on Herf and presumably enable him to make the final correct choice late in the novel. The scene after the funeral, for example, is only one of several that involve death, defeat, or disappointment, but that turn Herf's affections away from the comfortless material world to the ideal harmony of nature. Here his mother's death accentuates Herf's isolation and his helplessness in having to face a mechanistic and uncaring social system, which is symbolized by the steamroller, surfacing a road. Yet before him is a "new road" (p. 112), and in his blood, Herf feels "little worms of May" (p. 112), and suggestive of spring, the trees have "sticky pointed buds" (p. 113). Thus instead of being a time of despair, there seems to be a suggestion that the event marks a renewal in Herf's life. One image in this scene suggests the need for life to continue, to progress: "From a fencepost came the moist whistling of a songsparrow. The minute rusty bird flew ahead, perched on a telegraph wire and sang, and flew ahead to the rim of an abandoned boiler and sang, and flew ahead and sang" (p. 113). Nature here reflects man's condition in a number of ways. It points the way to an ideal sense of harmony and acceptance, and it provides a symbol of the author's task, to sing of Nature's redeeming value.

Nature, then, as it suggests an ideal order is never far from Jimmy Herf's consciousness, and when he actively perceives his environment, there is usually the suggestion that an attractive ideal is possible even if Jimmy doesn't realize it. Thus standing in "Columbus Circle" and "not knowing which way to go" (p. 370), Herf notes that "a smell of rainy pavements mingled with the exhausts of cars and occasionally there was a whiff of wet earth and sprouting grass from the Park" (p. 370). His final change in perspective has already been noted, the "springwagon" loaded with flowers on the ferry; it is a sight that makes Jimmy "unexpectedly merry" (p. 403). This, of course, should not be seen as the "final" revelation, for nothing in Dos Passos's writing suggests that a final ideal is achievable—or even desirable. Like the bird that keeps progressing to various resting places, Herf's progression is without a real end. This attitude of the *evolution* toward a final ideal state is consistent with the pragmatists' advocacy of a melioristic philosophy. As William James states in *Pragmatism,* "Meliorism treats salvation as neither inevitable nor impossible. It treats it as a possibility, which becomes more and more of a probability the more numerous the actual conditions of salvation become."[41] Dos Passos's melioristic pragmatism ought not to be taken by critics as a sign that *no* progress is being made by Herf. He knows that he still has to go "pretty far" (p. 404). But in *Manhattan Transfer,* in true pragmatic fashion, there are no final resting places, merely stages in salvation.

Another of James's criteria is what he calls "automatisms": "unconsciousness, convulsions, visions, involuntary vocal utterances, and suffocation."[42] Significantly, Jimmy is obsessed with a vision. Instead of a religious subject, however, he sees an appropriately secular object of adoration, Ellen:

> All these April nights combing the streets alone a skyscraper has obsessed him, a grooved building jutting up with uncountable bright windows falling onto him out of a scudding sky. . . . Ellie in a gold dress, Ellie made of thin gold foil absolutely lifelike beckoning from every window. And he walks round blocks and blocks looking for the door of the humming tinselwindowed skyscraper, round blocks and blocks and still no door. Every time he closes his eyes the dream has hold of him, every time he stops arguing audibly with himself in pompous reasonable phrases the dream has hold of him. (P. 365)

As shall be seen, Dos Passos elsewhere in the novel introduces the resurrection motif, but here too it seems relevant: Ellen is meant to stand for the false god of materialistic society. Dressed in "thin gold foil," she represents the beautiful illusion that lacks substance. She is safely ensconced in the prime symbol of the materialistic age, the skyscraper. Instead of hanging on a cross, her fate this spring is to inhabit a skyscraper and to appear "absolutely lifelike" even though she is dead—spiritually dead. Her fate is a parody of Christ's crucifixion, which symbolizes the positive obverse, life in death.

The "most characteristic" element in the conversion crisis, James says, is "the ecstasy of happiness."[43] This clearly is what Herf experiences as he is leaving the city by ferry. In the lighted waiting room,

> He sits a long time waiting for a ferry in the seedy ruddylighted waiting room. He sits smoking happily. He cant seem to remember anything, there is no future but the foggy river and the ferry looming big with its lights in a row like a darky's smile. He stands with his hat off at the rail and feels the riverwind in his hair. Perhaps he's gone crazy, perhaps this is amnesia, some disease with a long Greek name, perhaps they'll find him picking dewberries in the Hoboken Tube. He laughs aloud so that the old man who came to open the gates gave him a sudden sidelong look. Cookoo, bats in the belfry, that's what he's saying to himself. Maybe he's right. . . . The only passenger on the ferry, he roams around as if he owned it. My temporary yacht. By Jove these are the doldrums of the night all right, he mutters. He keeps trying to explain his gayety to himself. It's not that I'm drunk. I may be crazy, but I dont think so. (Pp. 402–3; my ellipsis)

Neither drunk nor crazy, he is experiencing the "ecstasy of happiness" over his newfound liberation.

William James notes that the psychological basis of the crisis conversion of the "twice-born character" is "a certain discordancy or heterogeneity in the native temperament of the subject, an incompletely unified moral and intellectual constitution."[44] As already seen, this is true of many of Dos Passos's protagonists, Jimmy Herf included. There are numerous examples of Herf's discordancy: his divorce, for example, and his inability to find lasting satisfaction in his job. The important point here, though, is that Jimmy does experience a spiritual rebirth. This is obvious in the preceding discussion, but Dos Passos also makes Herf's change clear by establishing an implicit parallel between Jimmy and Jesus. Late in the novel, Jimmy says, "But here I am by Jesus Christ almost thirty years old and very anxious to live" (p. 384). The juxtaposition of Christ's name with Jimmy's self-assertion suggests a significant connection: both begin to "live" their spiritual lives at about the same age, thirty. Moreover, Jimmy's rebirth takes place in the spring, and at one point, shortly before he leaves town, he is depicted looking into a bakery window at an "Easter" cake that has "a resurrection banner" on it (p. 359). There can be little doubt that the novel is meant to have a conclusion that is "redeeming" in the widest secular sense of the word and that *Manhattan Transfer* is Jimmy Herf's story.

Dos Passos has very specific ideas as to why modern America is a bankrupt society, as to why redemption is necessary. It is a problem with many ramifications, and a large part of the reason has already been examined in Joe Harland's squandering of his inheritance, substituting the abstract for the concrete. Indeed, the "abstract" is a rubric that might be used to identify all the ills of society. The corresponding solution, of course, which is usually missing, is a pragmatic consciousness in touch with reality. The pattern is inescapable. Gus McNeil, for example, is critically injured because he is not paying attention to what he is doing. And a large part of Bud Korpenning's problem occurs because he consistently and unrealistically daydreams about himself being made an alderman of New York City. Indeed, this daydream is connected with his death, and it is difficult to determine whether he falls from the bridge intentionally or from inattention because of his absentminded daydreams. Similarly, Cassie has such an unrealistic attachment to "this beautiful divine spiwitual thing" (p. 166), romantic love, that she is oblivious to the real concrete danger of becoming pregnant, which is what happens to her (p. 187). The newspaperman who is working on the Goldstein robbery operates from an abstract, erroneous "theory" of the robbers: "he's a college boy and . . . she's a society girl" (p. 367). The attitude of Alice Sheffield is typical of the problem. In speaking to Herf about his courage in giving up his job, she says, "it's wonderful . . . throwing away a career for an ideal" (p. 360). Herf responds to this fatuous statement by excusing himself, going to the men's room, and saying to himself, "Don't talk. . . . What you talk about you never do" (p. 360). Here then is the crux of the problem: action versus talk, concrete reality versus abstraction. Above all, as Herf realizes in this scene, language too is most susceptible to the problem. He even laments, at one of his lowest points in the novel, "If only I still had faith in words" (p. 366).

Herf cannot have faith in words because people permit language to drift away from being a valid sign for reality. One way that Dos Passos emphasizes this fact is by the attention he gives to proper names. On this subject, Iain Colley makes an interesting observation. He notes that Susie Thatcher's neurotic concern over the "labeling" of her baby (p. 7) reveals that she is more interested in abstraction than in the warmth of human realities.[45] This same insight can be applied to the larger social system. Thus, by his use of proper names, Dos Passos shows that his characters are most interested in the shifting surfaces of life. People "have" names (in William James's distinction), but it is questionable whether they "are." Ellen, for example, becomes "Elaine of Lammermoor" (p. 54), Ellie (p. 151), and Helena (p. 340). Even more revealing, the frequent changes in her last name (she is first Thatcher, then Oglethorpe, then Herf, then Baldwin) suggest that she can superficially alter her status but can never achieve an authentic relationship with anyone. Similarly, John Oglethorpe becomes "Jojo" (p. 139). Even "Congo," in some ways a sympathetic figure, frequently changes names. Congo is not his real name (see p. 226), and he becomes Marquis des Coulommiers (p. 300) and then Armand Duval (p. 382). Jimmy Herf too suffers from this linguistic dislocation when he becomes known to Ellen as "Jimps" (p. 329). Thus names are not "concrete, dug out of the soil," but arbitrary fads, pretentions, and illusory surfaces by which characters assume the affectation of identity.

The misapplication of language is examined by Dos Passos in numerous other instances as well. Mr. Harpsicourt, for example, the editor of Ellen's magazine, is one who should be extremely conscious of words as a medium of communication; yet he awkwardly misuses the language. In speaking to Ellen about her ability to make every reader feel "Johnny on the spot in the center of things," he says that "it's a knack that I can prophesy in you more than in any girl" (p. 368). Ellen points out his error, but she is meant to receive very little credit from the reader. The magazine's title, *Manners* (p. 340), suggests that the work she is involved in deals with social surfaces rather than with substance. In casting about for a suitable career, Jimmy Herf finally decides to enter the newspaper profession, and the reader might deduce that he is acting admirably, especially since that occupation employs a medium that Dos Passos is most concerned with: language. But as Craig Carver notes, "The newspaper for Dos Passos was one of the hallmarks of corrupt language and inevitably he identified it with the culture that generated that language."[46] Jimmy certainly has good intentions, but rather than bringing truth to bear upon his job, he is slowly corrupted by his occupation: when he returns from witnessing the bootleggers' fight at Sheepshead Bay, he resorts to telling a false version of the events to a crowd of friends at the Sheffields' (p. 323). And when Herf finally quits his job, the corruption has so infected his system that he is described in terms of abstract language. Herf expressionistically imagines himself becoming as bloated as the language he has been forced to use: "with every deep breath Herf breathed in rumble and grind and *painted phrases* until he began to *swell,* felt himself stumbling *big* and *vague,* staggering *like a pillar of smoke* above the April streets" (pp. 352–53; my italics).

As has already been suggested, Dos Passos has a program that would rectify the problem of abstractness. His ideal, of course, is a language that is "concrete, dug out of the soil." That Dos Passos would associate language with "soil" suggests that it has its antecedents in nature; but if one is to look for a logical formulation that might explain Dos Passos's own aesthetic intentions, the best place to look is in pragmatic philosophy, where concreteness is oftentimes cited as a virtue.

In analyzing the subjective emotional life in *Varieties of Religious Experience,* William James focuses his attention on the subjective experience as a whole. Unlike his *Psychology,* which mainly examines the consciousness and its relationship with external reality, his examination of the mystical religious experience probes "objective reality" as it might be present within consciousness. Even this partakes of man's dual nature. "The world of our experience," he notes, "consists at all times of two parts, an objective and a subjective part":

> The objective part is the sum total of whatsoever at any given time we may be thinking of, the subjective part is the inner "state" in which the thinking comes to pass. What we think of may be enormous,—the cosmic times and spaces, for example,—whereas the inner state may be the most fugitive and paltry activity of mind. Yet the cosmic objects, so far as the experience yields them, are but ideal pictures of something whose existence we do not inwardly possess but only point at outwardly, while the inner state is our very experience itself; its reality and that of our experience are one.[47]

Man's inner "experience" in James's view is one part of solid reality; his thoughts may or may not be true, real. The "ideal picture" may or may not be true and, insofar as they are incapable of pragmatic verification and not part of one's immediate experience itself, may very well prove to be false. In the subjective field, he is arguing, there are certain levels of abstraction about which it is useless to argue from a pragmatic basis. Nevertheless, the subjective field does hold "reality," most of which is true, and much of which one may suppose to be true even if unverifiable:

> All our attitudes, moral, practical, or emotional, as well as religious, are due to the "objects" of our consciousness, the things which we believe

to exist, whether really or ideally, along with ourselves. Such objects may be present to our senses, or they may be present only to our thought. In either case they elicit from us a *reaction;* and the reaction due to things of thought is notoriously in many cases as strong as that due to sensible presence. It may be even stronger.[48]

James describes how man's subjective state might be considered pragmatically, as real experience:

A conscious field *plus* its object as felt or thought of *plus* an attitude towards the object *plus* the sense of a self to whom the attitude belongs—such a concrete bit of personal experience may be a small bit but it is a solid bit as long as it lasts; not hollow, not a mere abstract element of experience, such as the "object" is when taken all alone.[49]

His true subject, then, is the way that the mind engages "reality" directly, which is also his concern in his other major books: *Psychology, Pragmatism,* and *Essays in Radical Empiricism.* As this study has argued, this is also Dos Passos's real concern: not "hollowness" that accompanies ideals, but reality—objective and subjective—as it is directly engaged by the mind. Language as an object of contemplation is itself one form of reality—when that language is used pragmatically.

In an excellent essay on *Manhattan Transfer,* E. D. Lowry, though he does not mention pragmatism, gives a perceptive analysis of Dos Passos's metaphysical concerns: "Reality is seen as a single, organic continuum in which the private world of feeling 'overlaps' and interacts with the public world of objective fact."[50] Lowry also notes that Dos Passos's "literary technique" is "based upon the dual unity of thought and emotion, subjectivity and objectivity, freedom and order, precision and indeterminacy."[51] One cannot give a better definition of pragmatic metaphysics. Other critics have similarly defined Dos Passos's aesthetics and philosophy. Lois Hughson states that Dos Passos's literary method consists of "the exploitation of the immediate moment at the expense of a sense of either memory or expectation. The characters are isolated in a present time . . . and brilliantly evoked in sights, sounds, and smells."[52] Whereas Dos Passos's characters are unpragmatic, concerned with the abstract surfaces of life, the author himself employs a pragmatic technique. As Sinclair Lewis noted long ago, in *Manhattan Transfer* Dos Passos "has given the panorama, the sense, the smell, the sound, the soul, of New York."[53] The soul is present, but it is evoked through the concrete reality.

Like a good pragmatist, Dos Passos believed that the subjective field could contain "objective" elements. Language is the best example of this. On the one hand, language is itself part of objective reality, but it can also exist within the subjective field as an object of man's thought. As a matter of fact, it is through language that man is enabled to meld his deepest subjective feelings and the objects of his thought. Man can find words that link inextricably his emotions and factual reality. On a purely descriptive level, Dos Passos shows that he is concerned with depicting the fictional "reality as concretely and pragmatically as possible." The aesthetics that underpins the language of *Manhattan Transfer* implies what I will call Dos Passos's theory of identity (which is not to be confused with Whitman's theory of Identity, Personality, and so on). In short, there is a basic assumption on Dos Passos's part that language "mirrors" reality, forms a bond of identity with reality, when that language is used pragmatically. I have already shown that in *Three Soldiers* Dos Passos was experimenting with such a theory of language. There he used language concretely to mirror reality. In his treatment of the "gesture," he postulated an aesthetic theory that encompassed within a verbal texture the full range of reality: from the hardest facts to the evanescent and ethereal. In *Manhattan Transfer,* Dos Passos refines even further his technical virtuosity in using language. He achieves high art in this novel because of the increased technical skills at his disposal, and those skills find outlet in numerous avenues in which Dos Passos experiments with the manifold implications of identity, which is Dos Passos's effort to regain his—and the readers'— "faith in words."

Dos Passos achieves an identity between words and reality by using language as pragmatically as possible. So his descriptions of characters tend to be impressionistic, yet use precise imagistic language. Lapland Matty, for example, is described as a "little yellow man" who has "fireblue eyes" and "a face like a toad, large mouth, protruding eyes and thick closecropped black hair" (p. 93). Color figures frequently in this description: "smoke, purple chocolatecolor fleshpink climbed into light" (p. 125). Color, of course, is "concrete," but in pragmatic psychological theory it is more than an inert fact. "Each color-feeling is a 'specific energy,'"[54] William James says. That is, the perception of color produces a feeling. Furthermore, "every possible feeling produces a movement," and "the movement is a movement of the entire organism, and of each and all its parts."[55] Using color in particular, but all concrete language, is one way in which the author engages the organism of the reader with reality. The writing of the novel becomes a visceral as well as an emotional and intellectual experience for the author, and the reading of the novel reproduces in the audience visceral, emotional, and intellectual responses.

Dos Passos also achieves an immediacy for the reader by presenting scenes dramatically—frequently avoiding use of proper names until the scene is otherwise set in the reader's mind. He even goes so far as to sacrifice initial clarity so that the reader will be forced to look harder at the scene as it is presented. Therefore, unlike the characters, who depend so much on proper names to give themselves identity, Dos Passos himself begins scene after scene with indefinite pronouns. Notice these examples from the randomly selected section 3, chapter 1:

—In the dark of the stoop in front of the tenement door, he reaches for her hand and drags her to him. (P. 274)
—The baby with tiny shut purplishpink face and fists lay asleep on the berth. (P. 275)
—Nobody said anything while they ate the soup. (P. 282)
—Two stout men and a lean man sit at the table by a window. (P. 287)

The pronouns do not refer to obscure, nor to the central, characters. In every case, the reader is in doubt as to who is being described until he reads further. Dos Passos wants the reader to concentrate on the physical details, the pragmatic reality, of the situation instead of on preconceived notions.

A second way in which identity is used is in the reporting of historical events. Thus the appropriation of headlines ties the novel into the continuum of the reader's social reality. A novel such as *Manhattan Transfer,* filled with historical references, gives a new twist to Henry James's aesthetic goal "solidity of specification." The murder of Juares, and the death of Pierpont Morgan, the Battle of Mukden—these and other historical references serve to create an illusion of reality about the events of the novel; they force the narrative texture toward the factual and real. This creates the illusion that the fictive language is the factual language of history.

Yet another way that identity works is by Dos Passos's fictionalizing of historical events. The factual event helps blur the distinction between fact and artistic creation as used in the novel. When Phil Sandbourne mentions the shooting death of Stanford White, the architect, Dos Passos's readers would no doubt have been familiar with the case, one of the most sensational scandals in the history of New York City. In her book about New York, Susan Lyman notes that the murder took place at Madison Square Garden, a building that White designed: "The Garden, too, was a landmark, and famous in city annals as well, for it was at the Madison Square Garden Roof that Stanford White met his death in 1906, shot by Harry K. Thaw, the millionaire husband of the actress Evelyn Nesbit."[56] Since the Thaw murder trial and the news of his subsequent confinement made headlines for years after the event, it is not unlikely that many of Dos Passos's readers would have seen the parallels between Evelyn and Ellen Thatcher. Both the real woman and Dos Passos's heroine became stars on Broadway. Like Ellen's, Evelyn's two musicals had titles with floral motifs, *Floradora* and *The Wild Rose,* and the latter is suggestive of the roses that Dos Passos associates with Ellen.[57] Moreover, both women are involved in love triangles that cause their lovers to pull guns: Harry Thaw, Evelyn's husband, killed White, and George Baldwin draws his gun on Ellen herself in a similar fit of jealousy (p. 229). The historical event here gives an air of reality to the fictional event.

Allusions to biblical events serve the same purpose. The mad prophet-tramp who tells the two scared boys of God's impending vengeance predicts that God will take seven seconds, not seven minutes, to destroy New York because "There's more wickedness in one block in New York City than there was in a square mile in Nineveh" (p. 381). The chapter headings also suggest the parallel between the fictional and the biblical worlds: "One More River to Jordan," "Rejoicing City That Dwelt Carelessly," and "The Burthen of Nineveh." The purpose of these allusions is clear: to heighten the reader's response to the fictional events.

Another way in which Dos Passos uses language as identity is in the chapter headings. The headings often refer not to an incident within that chapter but to an element within another chapter and might with more justification be said to belong there. "Revolving Doors," for example, is a significant title because Herf's earlier monologue on the subject makes it a symbol for the business world (p. 120). "Tracks" (section 1, chapter 4) seems most appropriate in describing Gus McNeil's encounter with the train, an encounter that comes somewhat earlier (p. 48). "Rollercoaster" (section 2, chapter 7) finds an objective parallel in the prose poem that introduces the preceding chapter (p. 237). These and other chapter headings serve to create and reinforce the various levels of meaning: chapter headings, objective event in the novel, symbolic statement.

Another way that Dos Passos uses identity is by replicating details in diverse scenes. So the saint from Philadelphia is hit with a "lead pipe" (p. 401) just as Cardinale uses a piece of pipe on hijackers (p. 320). Ruth tells of Jojo's brandishing a "revolver, a little nickel one" (p. 155), apparently because of a lover's quarrel, and Baldwin later uses a "nickel" handgun in a similar argument (p. 229). When Jimmy Herf imagines that he is being deported (p. 353), that imaginary event is given a greater emotional impact by having been preceded by a scene involving deportations (pp. 289–90).

Thus the aesthetics of identity works in manifold ways: in gaining an impressionistic and dramatic immediacy, in assimilating historical events into the text, in doubling the historic with the fictional event, in appropriating biblical allusions, in using symbolic chapter headings, and in replicating specific details. In all of these instances, Dos Passos is intensely aware that language mirrors some important facet of reality. In all cases, the fictional reality is pictured as grim and lean on lasting values. It all adds up to a fictional reality where a good man is hard to find.

Among all of the characters in *Manhattan Transfer,* Jimmy Herf stands out as possessing a unique set of values. As mentioned, though, he too is implicated in their sins and must redeem himself. At one point Herf's mother calls the young Jimmy "My little dreamer" (p. 81). Thus even early in the novel, Herf is implicated in the central problem that plagues the others. The solution for him is to find experience that is connected with nature and words that are "concrete, dug out of the soil." The solution, a symbolic one, is also implicit in a scene from his childhood. He is so happy to return to New York, his home, that he tells a fellow passenger on the boat that "I could fall down and kiss the ground" (p. 68). When he grows older, Jimmy does in fact do that. Ellen tells him of her heroic decision to have Stan's baby, even though Stan is dead. To Jimmy, this decision seems an affirmation of some unstated transcendent value. If abortions are life-negating, a childbirth is an affirmation of woman's natural role, of a human being's organic relation to the natural world. Ellen leaves Jimmy standing in the street. Instead of being jealous over Ellen's decision (which she later reverses), Jimmy "dropped on his knees and kissed the step where she had stood" (p. 266). It is a melodramatic act, but there is no doubt that the reader is to think that it is sincere and representative of the deeply felt values that Herf implicitly advocates: man in touch with the ground, with the natural cycle of life, man intimately connected with the environment.

That Jimmy is well on his way to living by these values is suggested in the final image of Herf on his way out of the city: "Then he walks on, taking pleasure in breathing, in the beat of his blood, in the tread of his feet on the pavement, between rows of otherworldly frame houses" (p. 404). Here, finally, is a man exulting in his own physical being, a man who is in touch with himself. The houses are "otherworldly" because of the fog, but they are symbolically "otherworldly" because Jimmy's final decision to leave is a search for a world "other" than houses; it is a search for an existence in which man can foster and appreciate his own human nature by establishing a harmonious relationship with the natural world.

9
The *U.S.A.* Trilogy

With the publication of *The Big Money* in 1936, John Dos Passos completed what has generally been acclaimed as his masterpiece, the *U.S.A.* trilogy. While this work is far superior to anything he had written previously, it also shares with Dos Passos's earlier novels a number of familiar elements: technical innovation, a fierce concern for the individual, and a dire need to confront social issues. The trilogy achieves greatness, one might argue, because it represents a watershed in Dos Passos's career. In the earlier novels, he had to work out the technical problems of writing fiction and to achieve his distinctive voice, while in many of the books that appeared after the *U.S.A.* trilogy he seemed to lose the creative vitality that permitted him to surprise his readers, his characters, and himself. In *U.S.A.*, then, he achieves a critical mass, where vision and technique fuse, and the result is an innovative work of fiction that is at times unpredictable, at times seeming to possess an unstable quality, but at no time dull.

A major element in *U.S.A.* is the sense of despair that derives from a perception of life as multitudinous and incomprehensible. The text illustrates a major theme of pragmatic metaphysics: a pluralistic universe with no overarching unity. Indeed, an examination of Dos Passos's novels in the order of their publication reveals the gradual "unstiffening" (James's term for the effects of applying pragmatic principles) of his fictional cosmology: one man's initiation, three soldiers' ordeals, three characters' frustrations in *Streets of Night*, the half dozen or so major figures of *Manhattan Transfer*, and the dozen major narrative strands of *U.S.A.* Furthermore, the cast of supporting characters grows at an even more explosive rate, from the relatively few people who make up the war novel to the cast of hundreds in the trilogy. Dos Passos was pragmatic from the beginning of his writing career, but this brief survey suggests that the logical implications of pragmatic thought developed as his career progressed, culminating with explosive force in the trilogy.

In *Pragmatism,* James includes an essay entitled "The One and the Many," in which he argues the relative merits of pragmatic pluralism versus the "all-enveloping noetic unity" of rationalist philosophy.[1] The unity of reality, he says, can be argued from many different aspects, but in all cases, a pluralistic reading provides a more satisfactory viewpoint, whether the subject is causality, taxonomy, teleology, or any number of other approaches. Speaking again of reality in general, he notes that there is also the temptation to impose an aesthetic unity on events; putting it simply, he says that often "things tell a story." For the purpose of this study, one might apply these comments on aesthetic unity to Dos Passos's fictional world as well, for James's response to the rationalists is emphatic and to the point: "The world is full of partial stories that run parallel to one another, beginning and ending at odd times. They mutually interlace and interfere at points, but we cannot unify them completely in our minds."[2] Here is the world according to James, and it is very close to the world that Dos Passos sees in *U.S.A.*: numerous partial stories running parallel to one another, at times interlacing and interfering. Being finite and fictive, of course, the trilogy can approach being a unified whole in a way that the philosopher's reality cannot, though the trilogy does in fact give the impression of discontinuity. In these three novels, pragmatic principles—to be discussed later in more detail—form the aesthetic basis for Dos Passos's fragmented structure.

As the previous chapters show, Dos Passos always took great care in structuring his novels. In particular, he applied his conception of nature as an all-encompassing unity, a background against which the finite lives of the characters were drawn and by which they were judged. The trilogy represents the first novel in which Dos Passos does not resort to using nature as the predominant structural device. One might argue that the full implications of Dos Passos's pragmatic and pluralistic world view finally caught up with him and that he could no longer justify interpreting nature as "an all-encompassing noetic unity." Part of the power of the individual lives in the trilogy seems to come from the lessening impact of nature, though as will be seen, it is not absent as a force in these books.

Any number of elements might be said to contribute to the structure of *U.S.A.* Arnold Hoffman, for example, points out that the reappearance of Doc Bingham at the trilogy's close brings the novel full circle.[3] Barbara Foley takes a different viewpoint and argues that "history provides the frame for *U.S.A.*"[4] Although this last view seems attractive enough, I find it less satisfying than other readings. I would argue that history in *U.S.A.* serves the same purpose as it does in *Manhattan Transfer:* it is an important factor that determines the quality of the characters' lives and explains their predicaments, but, except loosely, it can hardly be said to provide the novel's structure. It would be more proper to say that Dos Passos *de*structures history for the convenience of his characterization. For example, as Foley notes, Charley Anderson lives a fictive life that does

The *U.S.A.* Trilogy

not depend on the structure of an objective history: he grows old, withers, and dies, though the chronology would dictate that he is barely more than twenty-five.[5] Also, in the historical chronology, the life of the typical character in the trilogy often begins at a historical point that is *before* the historical time-frame that ended the previous narrative. The frequency with which this happens has the effect of *diminishing* the sense of a coherent historical framework. Furthermore, I would argue that history as Foley perceives it is one of those "all-encompassing noetic" unities that neither Dos Passos nor James would feel comfortable with.[6] In *U.S.A.* Dos Passos is less concerned with building unified overviews than he is with examining the effect of an individual's collision with discrete historical events.

Foley argues that in *The Forty-Second Parallel* "the shaping power of the plot derives from history itself, and not from the principles of form inherent in any mode of fictional narrative."[7] The structure, I would argue, devolves not from a historical "overview," nor from a traditional conception of plot, but derives, nevertheless, from formalistic considerations. Dos Passos uses reciprocal characters for the trilogy's structure, a technique that he used in a more limited fashion in all of the previous novels. In *Manhattan Transfer*, for example, Dos Passos created reciprocal characters in "Jimmy" Herf and "James" Merivale, who represented two sides of that "double-edged coin: Failure Success." In *U.S.A.*, however, the device is used with considerably more sophistication and more clearly for structural purposes. Instead of being based on success and failure, the reciprocal characters can be classed as two kinds of people: Muckers and Rover Boys. The terms come from Camera Eye (7).[8]

To understand better these two terms, it is useful to examine a remark that Dos Passos makes in his autobiography. He writes of his youthful attempts to classify people:

> I was trying to divide all humanity into the useful people like cooks and farmhands and woodworkers and architects and engineers, who were always building up mankind, and the destructive people like politicians and bankers and college presidents and national propagandists, who spread illusions and caused wars and destroyed civilization as fast as the producers built it up. Black was black and white was white. Producers were good, exploiters were evil. Myself and my friends I classed with the producers.[9]

Dos Passos here gently mocks his youthful naïveté, but also identifies the basic conflict in his work that this study has noted from the first: Dos Passos sides with the useful producers, the workers (the pragmatists), and opposes the propagandists, who spread illusions (the rationalists). One can put the same argument in terms of Camera Eye (7): it is the Muckers, who "put . . . write . . . do" things (the distasteful—yet strangely appealing—"bohunk and polak kids"), versus the "clean young American Rover Boys," who are more concerned with the refined (they work not directly with their hands, but with tools), with the abstract (they "cut figure eights on the ice"), and with the idealized (they are "Deerslayers . . . Achilles Ajax Agamemnon"). In point of fact, Dos Passos isn't clear as to the group with which to associate himself: he skates with the Rovers (though he falls down[10]), but his sympathies are consistently with the outcast, the Vag. No doubt this conflict is one source of the power in his fiction.

In an interview someone once asked of Dos Passos this question concerning the trilogy: "Did you intend at any point to have one character or set of characters somehow typify each of the volumes?" Dos Passos responded, "Yes, that's about right. I think I did have that in mind."[11] In fact, the structure of the trilogy derives from the use of reciprocating characters: Muckers and Rovers. To show that Dos Passos actually did "have this in mind," one merely has to look at the following example of autograph notes for the trilogy (as cited in Ludington's biography):

> This is all in the career of Amory Savage,
> The man who climbed to fame and
> fortune via the Red Cross
> --
> Then the career of the man who didn't make
> good by the same method.[12]

Here is Dos Passos's plan to contrast Savage the Rover Boy with an as yet unidentified Mucker.

This pattern is also evident in the text itself. Of the twenty narratives in *The Forty-Second Parallel,* all but one deal with the four central characters of that volume. Of the fifteen narratives in *1919,* all but one deal with the four central characters of that volume. Of the seventeen narratives in *The Big Money,* all seventeen deal with the four central characters of that volume. Furthermore, in each volume these four characters can be divided conveniently: two male and two female. But most important, if one is willing to concede that Muckerism and Roverism have more to do with philosophy than with social status or pedigree, each volume has its equal share of Rovers and Muckers, one of each sex:

		Male	*Female*
42P	Rover	Moorehouse	Eleanor
	Mucker	Mac	Janey
1919	Rover	Dick Savage	Eveline
	Mucker	Joe	Daughter
BM	Rover	Dick Savage	Margo
	Mucker	Charley	Mary French

Even the odd narrative strands in the first two volumes (Charley Anderson and Ben Compton) are not superfluous to this structure, for they both serve as "hinges" to the last volume, in which the two characters reappear. These two are, one might say, the two residual Muckers, who taking the place of Mac and Joe carry over the male Mucker line to the final volume.

Mac, Joe, and Charley all qualify as Muckers because of their propensity to experience things firsthand. (It is to Charley's credit that he cannot sustain his success in the speculative world of the Rovers and is indeed expelled from their milieu.) Likewise, Janey (however much she comes to mouth Moorehouse's platitudes) is a worker, a *useful* person, as is Mary French. Daughter, whose birth would seem to align her with the Rovers, actually is a Mucker, a pragmatist who deals directly with experience, who, for example, wants her brother's death attributable to *someone* rather than to the abstraction of the military system (II, p. 282). Furthermore, she can appreciate her sexuality, whereas Savage, Eveline, and the other Rovers suffer serious problems in this regard.

The Rovers are easier to spot. Moorehouse and Savage peddle abstractions under the name of public relations; that is, they lie. Eleanor and Eveline are in a similar line, selling appearances to the clients of their interior decorating business. Finally, Margo, by birth a Mucker, rises by her own fortitude to the role of Rover. As an actress, she too is involved in high-class hucksterism: creating illusions and pandering her physical features to the public at the expense of her integrity. Clearly, Margo is not necessarily a loser, for this scheme of Rovers and Muckers has nothing to do with winners or losers: there are no winners in *U.S.A.* The most that can be said is that Dos Passos reserves most of his bitter edge for the Rovers (Savage, Moorehouse, Eveline, Eleanor, and Margo) and sympathizes most with the Muckers (Mac, Joe, Janey, Daughter, Charley, and Mary French).

This method of structuring his fiction suggests a shift in Dos Passos's thinking: a holistic vision of nature is now less important than a regard for empirical reality. The increased emphasis on pragmatic epistemology suggests that Dos Passos was increasingly preoccupied with the disintegration and fragmentation of modern life. In *Manhattan Transfer,* Dos Passos could invoke the overarching, holistic, mythic value of nature as a time frame, but in *U.S.A.* time has become fragmented, and nature no longer seems so accessible to man. The best illustration of this new view of fragmented time can be seen in the fact that Dos Passos adopted four separate and distinct modes of constructing the trilogy: Biographies, Newsreels, Camera Eye, and Narratives. The four modes reflect the fragmented epistemology that rules Dos Passos's cosmology, especially since each method utilizes a distinctly different use of time.[13]

Time appears most objectively in the Biographies. One can trace through the Biography of "Meester Veelson," for example, an unwavering chronological order from first lines ("The year that Buchanan was elected president Thomas Woodrow Wilson was born") to the last ("In 1924 on February 3rd he died"). In between those two historically verifiable, scrupulously reported facts, Dos Passos strings similar chronological dates: "In 1870 . . . At twenty-nine he married . . . In 1909 . . . and in 1910 . . . at the Jackson Day dinner . . . on December 4th, 1918 . . . January 18, 1919 . . . On April 7th . . . on April 9th. . . ." Clustered around the events, of course, are the more important thematic concerns of Wilson's life, but the time frame is a succession of identifiable temporal events.

In spite of their historicity, even the Biographies are sometimes subject to the fragmentation of time. "Tin Lizzie," the biography of Henry Ford, provides a good example. It begins not with Ford's birth but with a journalist's comment written in 1900—then moves back to 1879 (when Ford was sixteen), then to 1898, back to "the late eighties," to 1898 again, back to the 1880s (when Ford was "in his early twenties"), then to 1900, to 1903, to 1909, to 1919, to 1913, and so on. Here is objective time stressed repeatedly, but even verifiable temporal succession cannot serve as a basis for coherence. The implied narrator of the piece reflects a fragmented consciousness and has discovered, one might presume, a more effective organizing principle based on tempo, on the principle of contrast, on rhetorical effectiveness.

Thus, even if it is fragmented, chronological time is most apparent in the Biographies. If the mythic time of nature is suggested at all, it does not provide structure or even suggest the timeless dimension of reality. Rather it is to portray the pitiful life of someone like Isadora Duncan, who is in some respects "like Walt Whitman" (III, p. 157). Although she tries to embody the aspirations of America, to give free play to the potential of human nature, she stands wholly within the grasp of modern industrialized social structure: she leads "the Greek life of nature in a flutter of unpaid bills" (III, p. 156). Or if one of Dos Passos's heroes does manage to give satisfactory expression to human aspirations, he will be without honor "in his own country," as is Frank Lloyd Wright, whose "blueprints, as once Walt Whitman's words, stir the young men" (III, p. 433). Here then are figures who strive for the heroic, whose visions are derived from nature, but whose lives are bound by the inexorable demands of a mechanized society.

The Newsreels are also roughly chronological. The first Newsreel, for example, emphasizes the beginning of the new century, and the final Newsreel heralds Black Friday, the stockmarket crash of 1929. Though Dos Passos uses headlines from real events, the use of time here is oblique. Dos Passos is just as much interested in the historical flavor of the event (the "collective atmosphere of the given period," to use Cowley's phrase[14]) as he is of the more objective date. Even though objectively verifiable events are referred to, the Newsreels stress the inexorable march of a society's progress with its attendant ills. Though the final effect of the Newsreels is not objective (Dos Passos's use of montage will be discussed shortly), each discrete headline itself is objective, and time as a historical framework is suggested only obliquely.

This objective time scheme of the Newsreels is also antithetical to the mythic value of nature. In these sections, nature has lost its primitive force. If it is treated at all, it appears on stage as a minor character overshadowed by the protean and immense figure of progress:

> At the time only twenty years ago when the site of the Bay of Biscayne Bank was a farmer's hitchingyard and that of the First National Bank a public barbecue ground the ground here where this ultramodern hotel and club stands was isolated primeval forest. My father and myself were clearing little vegetable patches round it and I was peddling vegetables at the hotel Royal Palm, then a magnificent hotel set in a wild frontier. Even eight years ago I was growing tomatoes. (III, p. 277)

Or nature is a quaint curiosity that has been tamed alike by the industrialized city and by a rhetoric that diminishes its real significance by trite romanticizing:

> The stranger first coming to Detroit if he be interested in the busy economic side of modern life will find a marvelous industrial beehive; if he be a lover of nature he will take notice of a site made forever remarkable by the waters of the noble strait that gives the city its name; if he be a student of romance and history he will discover legends and records as entertaining and as instructive as the continent can supply. (III, p. 285).

Although objective time is relatively predominant in the Newsreels—as it is even more so in the Biographies—it would be improper to suggest that this conception of time should be equated with the trilogy's structure, as it is only one pattern that must share the duties with yet another pattern.

In the Camera Eye, Dos Passos removes himself one step further from objective history. Chronological history is still identifiable, but the emphasis is on the stream of consciousness of the author, on how objective reality—whether of worldwide significance or of the personal—affects his development. Of course, the Camera Eye is bound by time; the first Camera Eye begins by examining the author as a young boy at the turn of the century and subsequent segments progress along with the drift of thirty years' historical events. But an important distinction needs to be made. In chronological time—say, in the context of the Treaty of Versailles—the Camera Eye is insignificant. On the other hand, the Camera

Eye is outside of chronological time: the physical, intellectual, and moral growth of the Camera Eye is meaningful insofar as it is not time-bound, insofar as it points toward a transcendence of time and insofar as it is part of and spokesman for a system of values that is antithetical to the historical process.

To what extent does the Camera Eye embody a vision that tends toward—even if it does not confirm—the mythic value of nature? Part of the reason that *U.S.A.* is the watershed work in the Dos Passos canon is that it seems to reflect a spiritual crisis in the author's life. Whereas the earlier novels could espouse a solid faith in the kind of nature that Dos Passos associated with Whitman, *U.S.A.* is an agonizing search for the validity of such a view—and such faith is by no means any longer certain. In Camera Eye (1), the young protagonist treads "on too many grassblades the poor hurt green tongues shrink under your feet" (I, p. 5). They are "bright anxious grassblades" quite different from the reassuring cosmic symbols portrayed in *Leaves of Grass*.[15] In *Streets of Night,* as already seen, Dos Passos could accept those Whitmanesque tongues of grass as reassuring symbols; in *U.S.A.* he cannot. From the opening Camera Eye, then, there is a certain amount of skepticism concerning the mythic value of nature. Later in the trilogy this skepticism becomes more pointed when Dos Passos ponders—without attaining a solution—"the course of history and what leverage might pry the owners loose from power and bring back (I too Walt Whitman) our storybook democracy" (III, p. 150). Clearly, the Whitmanesque values in the trilogy threaten to be no more than a "noetic unity" without any possibility of pragmatic application.

The Camera Eye represents that last resort of romantic individualism. Like Whitman's poetry, the Camera Eye presents the individual as cynosure. Its form, of course, re-creates the illusion of pure consciousness. It is the pure, undifferentiated part of human nature that connects the observer with nature—both through the act of perception, melding perceiver with perceived, and through its physical factness: the consciousness, the subconsciousness, and the mind as pure matter are part of nature. The Camera Eye is a manifestation of the pragmatized "core" of being, the reality of which Dos Passos devoted his early career to attaining. In addition, the Camera Eye makes clear through its central metaphors that the critical problem facing the protagonist deals with this very question: nature as an active powerful force in men's lives. In the crucial Camera Eye (50), which deals with the Sacco and Vanzetti affair and in which the beliefs of the author are crystallized, the following passage occurs:

> all right we are two nations
> America our nation has been beaten by strangers who have bought the

laws and fenced off the meadows and cut down the woods for pulp and turned our pleasant cities into slums and sweated the wealth out of our people and when they want to they hire the executioner to throw the switch. (III, pp. 462–63)

Sacco and Vanzetti will die, and this dire fact bears out Dos Passos's belief that the declension of values in American history—from the true to the false—is complete. This declension is illustrated by the metaphor of man's relationship to the soil. A mythic, holistic unity is replaced by division in nature ("fenced off the meadows"), by a destruction of nature ("cut down the woods"), and by a separation of man from his own human nature ("pleasant cities into slums"). When Charles Walcutt argues that Dos Passos is misreading American history in this passage, the critic has mistaken the significance of Dos Passos's statement.[16] In this passage, Dos Passos is not dealing with historical time but with the mythic time he associated with the American landscape. The passage represents a statement about the values that he fears after all may be applicable only to a "storybook" democracy.

In the Camera Eye, then, there is an implicit ideal of transcendence. There is the timeless mythic dimension of nature versus the differentiation of time and space that the growth of American society demands. "Life in our changing industrial world," Dos Passos would write later, "has become so cut up into specialized departments and vocabularies, and has become so hard to understand and to see as a whole."[17] In the case of Sacco and Vanzetti, Dos Passos has found his symbol for this tragic state of America. Americans have lost their ability to see as a whole in a way that Dos Passos believed Sacco still could. Writing in *In All Countries,* Dos Passos notes of Nicola Sacco: "He loved the earth and people, he wanted them to walk straight over the free hills, not to stagger bowed under the ordained machinery of industry; he worried mornings working in his garden at the lethargy of the working people."[18] Unlike the American born, who "couldn't get back the seed they sowed" in the earth, Italian immigrants "start truck gardens in back lots, and by skillful gardening and drudgery bring forth fiftyfold."[19] Undoubtedly, there is some exaggeration here and the passage is thus poor sociology, but it is effective as the myth that Dos Passos needs to propagate: man can realize an ideal relationship with the soil. In his essay on Sacco, the last view that Dos Passos has of the immigrant, Sacco is incarcerated but looks out of the room's window at the "unfenced sky."[20] For Dos Passos, the throwing of the switch, the execution of Sacco and Vanzetti, has sundered the world into two halves, and nature, a valid enough ideal, seems lost forever to America. This attitude, new in the *U.S.A.* trilogy, accounts for the unusual treatment of time in the fourth and final mode, the Narratives.

It has already been noted that the cumulative effect of the successive Narratives suggests the fragmentation of the modern world. This is not only because the action switches from the Narrative of one character to another, but also because time itself is discontinuous between the Narratives. Thus the Narrative of Daughter ends sometime in 1919 (II, p. 418), and the next Narrative, that of Ben Compton, begins somewhere near the start of the century (II, p. 423). Furthermore, there is no uniform pattern of time *within* the Narratives: one scene might take up several pages only to be followed by a page that quickly summarizes a number of months in the character's life. All of this works against the reader maintaining a coherent sense of time. But there is a more fundamental consideration to be noted. The differences in the way that each of the four narrative modes treat time are critical. The Biographies are strung on the line of specific months and years. The Newsreels depend on the objective headlines, which suggest the passage of historical time. The Camera Eye is even further removed from the objectification of the years—and as I have shown actually tends toward a mythic time, only to question whether it is a useful, workable mythos. In the Narratives, the basic structural device is—in a limited sense—historical time, for clearly identifiable historical events impinge on the characters' lives. But the basic structural device from page to page, from one experience to another, is the familiar mythic time frame of the natural cycle. Specific years are not referred to (except obliquely), but months and seasons chart the characters' progress. Thus Mac's fourth Narrative begins in spring (I, p. 61), goes through summer and fall (I, p. 71), and ends in November (I, pp. 79–80). The seasons are referred to as often as they were for Jimmy Herf. But for Mac—and all the characters in *U.S.A.*—there is a critical difference. Whereas the references to the seasons had a significance for Herf and other early Dos Passos protagonists, in *U.S.A.* seasons have no significance. The characters are alone, completely cut off from meaning, within a natural cycle that confers no value on their lives.

By stressing repeatedly the progression of characters' lives within the natural cycle, Dos Passos suggests the link between the characters and nature. Indeed, oftentimes, Dos Passos makes explicit the fundamental connection between a character and the landscape. There are numerous examples that show this. As an instance, in *1919,* Joe Williams, alone on nightwatch, feels an affinity for the land as his ship approaches the shore:

> The sky was blue as a bowl of curdled milk with a waned scrap of moon bobbing up from time to time. It was honeysuckle, sure enough, and manured garden patches and moist foliage like walking past the open door of a florist's in winter. It made him feel soft and funny inside like he had a girl standing right beside him on the bridge. (II, pp. 55–56)

Similarly, Mac feels the "little breezes that smelt unexpectedly of flowers. The girls looked terribly pretty and their skirts blew in the wind and Fainy felt spring blood pumping hot in him, he wanted to kiss and to roll on the ground . . ." (I, p. 19). Eleanor feels a different response though the source is the same; she hates the first few days of spring: "They made the lines come out on her face, made everything seem to crumble about her, there seemed to be no firm footing any more" (I, p. 355). The character might be in tune with nature or alienated from it, but there is no escaping its effects. Man, quite simply, is a part of nature. Nature, though, is in no way redemptive; rather, nature suggests man's biological fate: he grows, he reproduces, and he dies. For the first time in his fiction, Dos Passos achieves a purely naturalistic vision.

It is fair to say that Dos Passos's naturalistic vision was influenced to some extent by Theodore Dreiser, who bears some comparison with Dos Passos. One of the most effective scenes in American literary naturalism occurs in Dreiser's *The Financier*. Frank Cowperwood as a young boy frequently passes a fish market and on one occasion stops to watch the unusual creatures that are placed in the window aquarium, a squid and a lobster. These, the reader is told, are to play out a struggle that will profoundly affect the way Frank perceives the world:

> The lobster, it appeared from the talk of idle bystanders, was offered no food, as the squid was considered his rightful prey. He lay at the bottom of the clear glass tank on the yellow sand, apparently seeing nothing . . . but apparently they were never off the body of the squid. The latter . . . moved in torpedo fashion; but his movements were apparently never out of the eyes of his enemy, for by degrees small portions of his body began to disappear, snapped off by the relentless claws of his pursuer. . . . Fascinated by the drama, young Cowperwood came daily to watch.[21]

The lobster finally gets the squid, and this incident made "a great impression" on Frank. He uses it to generalize about the way life on earth is organized, and, one is to presume, it affects the way he perceives the rest of his life and determines the way he will live.

Dos Passos's debt to Dreiser has been noted repeatedly. He even inscribed for Drieser a copy of *U.S.A.* with the following note: "Dear Dreiser—Just wanted you to know that I still feel that if it hadn't been for your pioneer work none of us would have gotten our stuff written or published."[22] Dos Passos, here, is paying homage to Dreiser for enlarging the boundaries of fictional discourse. After Dreiser, the subject of sexuality, say, was met with greater tolerance, and Dos Passos's own work clearly benefited from Dreiser's example. But Dos Passos's work also continued the naturalistic vein that had been mined by the earlier writer. All of the characters in *U.S.A.*, for example, can be seen as continuing the naturalistic tradition, but the story of Mac, the Narrative that opens the trilogy, seems to owe something in particular to Dreiser. Mac's introduction to the world of free capitalistic enterprise is given in a scene that is similar to that of the lobster and the squid. Here, Mac passes a taxidermist's on his way to an interview with Doc Bingham, his future employer:

> There was a golden pheasant, stuffed, in a taxidermist's; above it hung a big flat greenish fish with a sawtoothed bill from which dangled a label:
> *SAWFISH (pristis perrotetti)*
> Habitat Gulf and Florida waters. Frequents shallow bays and inlets.
> Maybe he wouldn't go at all. In the back of the window was a lynx and on the other side a bobtailed cat, each on its limb of a tree. Suddenly he caught his breath. He'd be late. He went tearing off down the block. (I, p. 30)

Mac clearly is in the world of predators. In writing of Bartolomeo Vanzetti, Dos Passos speaks to this issue: "He shares the hope that has grown up in Latin countries of the Mediterranean basin that somehow men's predatory instincts, incarnate in the capitalist system, can be canalized into other channels."[23] By gaining employment with Bingham, Mac is thrust into the predacious world of American capitalism, very much the same world that Frank Cowperwood enters.

It is possible that Dos Passos was influenced by the particularly memorable scene in Dreiser's book, but even if he was not, Dos Passos's scene is clearly naturalistic. If Dos Passos is suffering the anxiety of influence—whether in regard to a particular scene or to the philosophy of naturalism in general—he certainly puts a great deal of distance between himself and Dreiser. Both Cowperwood and Mac face similar situations, but Cowperwood is thoughtful and able to generalize about the significance of the contest. Mac, on the other hand, seems only to intuit that the predators in the natural world relate to his own circumstances. Furthermore, instead of the relatively common sight of a lobster and squid brought from Delaware Bay, Mac must confront a species that is relatively exotic. Also, nature is not seen firsthand in Dos Passos's story; it is rather reconstructed by man—by a taxidermist, a specialist—and is given a taxonomic classification in Latin, which further suggests man's distance from a mythic holism.

Mac's career is a particularly apt introduction to the world of *U.S.A.*, for his life spans two decades of immense changes in American society. He begins as a kid in Middletown, a name suggestive of the American mean, and a place where there are still indications of a simpler life: the whale-oil soap (I, p. 6) suggests the barest origins of American capitalism. He ends up in Mexico during the time that the revolution was affecting that country. In between those two periods, he flirts with communism, joins the I.W.W., marries a woman intent on upward mobility, and finally deserts her to go to Mexico with the intention of joining the revolution. But Mac is not a thinking animal; he intuits the justice of various causes but he can never adjust his life to their truth. In the end, he is seduced by creature comforts and stays in Mexico in relative happiness, though he has lost his belief in revolution. His life illustrates Dos Passos's purpose in portraying "man's struggle for life against the strangling institutions he himself creates."[24] Mac's fate, better than the ending of most of the characters in the trilogy, might be attributed to two factors. First, Mac creates a life for himself outside of institutions; his anarchistic nature finds satisfaction in the individual task of running a bookstore. Second, he ends up in Mexico, that is, outside of the United States, the place where the "strangling institutions" are most apparent. In a sense, he is one of the most lucky characters in *U.S.A.*, having escaped the natural order—such as it has become: a naturalistic, predatory world of capitalists.

Doc Bingham is a second character who deals with the American inheritance, and Mac's mentor is treated harshly by Dos Passos. Bingham appears early in *The Forty-Second Parallel,* and he too harks back to a simpler America. Selling goods to the sparsely settled inhabitants of the countryside, Bingham seems a mythic figure from the American past. He changes appearances to suit the needs of the moment: he is an agnostic (I, p. 32), a pantheist (I, p. 43), an admirer of Luther (I, p. 51), or a peddler of Boccaccio's *Decameron* (I, p. 41). His chief aim, however, is to seduce the women he finds in the farmhouses. He is the original confidence man, the living proof (to adapt Daniel Hoffman's phrase) that "rebirth and metamorphosis are bywords of American life."[25]

Though his lineage can be traced to the archetypal American confidence man and though he seems a harmless codger, his appearance in *The Big Money* shows that even the quaint though duplicitous man of nature can become transmogrified by capitalist big business. Suitably, he becomes an outright spokesman for nature and in this regard inverts the values that Dos Passos knew to be America's true, though squandered, legacy. Thus he sells "nature's remedies, herbs and simples culled in the wilderness" (III, p. 499). He lives "by nature's law" eating "only a few nuts and vegetables" (III, p. 498). Though he claims to be one of the "farming folk" (III, pp. 499–500)—that is, close to nature and its values—Bingham reflects Dos Passos's growing disillusionment with the possibility of the redeeming value of nature. When Bingham talks Savage into taking him to a burlesque show because he wants to see "the human form divine" (III, p. 502), the suggestion is that natural man has lost all contact with divinity, whether theological or natural. Dos Passos emphasizes this by having Dick Savage look up to see "a series of bare jiggling female legs spotted from an occasional vaccination" (III, p. 501). Man is cut off from nature, no matter how much Bingham's rhetoric tries to convince people otherwise, and the vaccination marks are meant to symbolize at once man as civilized, as vulnerable to natural disorders, and as imperfect and bound to time.

Moorehouse is a third character who confronts the meaning of mythic time, and he too fails to recognize its importance. In the narrative of Moorehouse, Dos Passos deals most directly with the theme of America's squandered inheritance. The natural landscape and its concomitant mythos have been America's legacy, and J. Ward Moorehouse, born on the fourth of July, seems naturally suited to "ward," to guard these values. But as previously seen, Dos Passos uses the metaphor of "fencing off," dividing the landscape, to suggest the declension of values in America, and the name Ward (suggesting also the district or division of a city) and the character's early career in real estate pointedly align this character with the subversion of natural values. Even his last name, Moorehouse, is consistent with a character who plays an active role in furthering materialistic progress. So Moorehouse learns from Mr. Hillyard (the name again is equivocal, suggesting both nature wild and divided) that "the owner of real estate links himself by indissoluble bonds to the growth of his city or nation" (I, p. 205). This specious statement actually subverts any real meaning that nature might possess, but it appeals to Moorehouse. Sounding like a cross between Doc Bingham and Ralph Waldo Emerson, Moorehouse as a budding young real estate man writes a pamphlet to boost the market value of land in Ocean City, Maryland, and in it notes that "the tonic breath of the pines brings relief to the asthmatic and the consumptive" (I, p. 185). In fact, the real consequences of economic growth are witnessed but unappreciated by Moorehouse when he first enters Pittsburgh by train:

> Through the window he could see black hills powdered with snow, an occasional coaltipple, rows of gray shacks all alike, a riverbed scarred with minedumps and slagheaps, purple lacing of trees along the hill's edge cut sharp against a red sun; then against the hill, bright and red as the sun, a blob of flame from a smelter. (I, pp. 205–6)

Instead of Eden, a place for rejuvenation, America has become a wasteland, where an ugly red furnace fire is a literal equivalent of the sun as seen through Pittsburgh's haze.

With the loss of nature as a viable frame of reference, Dos Passos's intentions, his aesthetic stance, one might say, did not change dramatically. He continues his argument with the existing social system, an argument that lasted his entire career. In an early essay on the Spanish novelist Baroja, Dos Passos notes approvingly the Spanish author's dictum that a member of the middle class can play only a "destructive" role in the reorganization of society. The "great mission" of the intellectual, Dos Passos explains, "is to put the acid test to existing institutions, and to strip the veils off them."[26] In an interview almost fifty years later, Dos Passos expresses a similar sentiment. He suggests that his own art is that of a satirist and states that "the satirist's complaint about society is always that it doesn't measure up to a fairly high ideal he has."[27] The first remark deals with the artist's intention, the second, with something anterior to intention, but they complement each other: the writer's role is to expose the shortcomings of society. To do that, however, he must possess a firmly established moral viewpoint. Obviously, Dos Passos's *U.S.A.* is essentially a moral judgment of American culture even if nature is no longer the primary ethical standard of value.

Dos Passos's fundamental belief in a standard of value is suggested by advice he gives to the *New Masses* magazine in 1926: "I'd like to see a magazine full of introspection and doubt that would be like a piece of litmus paper to test things by."[28] He uses a similar metaphor in *U.S.A.* to suggest the continual testing of personal values: "peeling the onion of doubt" (III, p. 150). Doubt, then isn't a negative quality, but it is a necessary and positive virtue: doubt, he says in *U.S.A.* is "the whetstone of understanding" (III, p. 150). It permits the cultivation of a personal ethos, free from the restraints of society and, based solely on the personal vision, allows the artist to evaluate the culture from a unique point of view. "The average factory worker or clerk or college professor," Dos Passos says, "is only dimly aware of what kind of society he is living in. It is the business of the writer to tell him."[29]

This need for a moral framework is a subject to which Dos Passos returns in a more systematic fashion in his appreciation of F. Scott Fitzgerald's fiction, "A Note on Fitzgerald," which was published in *The Crack-Up*, shortly after *U.S.A.* appeared. "Great" literature, Dos Passos says in the article, is accomplished by establishing a "frame of reference for common humanity." Furthermore, it requires "secure standards of judgment that can only be called ethical." Whereas society's standards are often "temporary," the essential quality of any "powerful work of the imagination" is an "unshakable moral attitude towards the world we live in," and this "firmly anchored ethical standard is something that American writing has been struggling towards for half a century." In addition, Dos Passos credits Fitzgerald with creating in his fiction a "frame of reference" in which "acts and gestures can be described on a broad and to a certain degree passionlessly impersonal terrain of common humanity."[30] This essay may illumine Fitzgerald's work, but it also provides a coherent expression of Dos Passos's own aesthetic ideals: the artist must assume a clearly defined ethical standard by which to test the social values of his culture.

With the absence of nature as a viable alternative, can one identify in the trilogy a basis on which to "firmly anchor" an "unshakable moral attitude towards the world we live in"?—one of the prerequisites for great literature. Dos Passos, I believe, provides an ethical "frame of reference" for his trilogy in the Camera Eye. I agree with John W. Aldridge that these autobiographical sections constitute the "moral center" of the trilogy,[31] but why, exactly, this is so must be answered by a closer examination of the form of the Camera Eye and of its thematic content.

In his diary in 1917, Dos Passos describes his relation to the world: "the stream of sensation flows by—I suck it up like a sponge."[32] The theme of the artist as passive observer of the world is frequent in Dos Passos's writings, and most often he uses the metaphor of the camera to describe that experience, most obviously in the naming of the Camera Eye. The protagonist in these sections is usually portrayed as passive, and this is a fitting quality for the artist, for he must, Dos Passos notes elsewhere, "record the fleeting world the way the motion picture film recorded it."[33] The emphasis of such a technique in its purest form falls on the direct, unmediated experience and illustrates a more general tenet of Dos Passos's aesthetics: he attempts to present his fictive world "always as seen by some individual's eyes, heard by some individual's ears, felt through some individual's nerves and tissues."[34] Thus, unalloyed sense impressions are the basis of an individual's experience, and it is the role of the artist to "record" these sensations—as experienced by himself—for future use. It should be obvious that a pragmatic attitude serves as a basic epistemological foundation for the Camera Eye. According to William James, "thoughts in the concrete are made of the same stuff as things are."[35] The stream of consciousness is a concrete experience, a bond between the self and empirical reality.

The camera metaphor is particularly appropriate to suggest Dos Passos's pragmatic bias. The lens and film insure a lesser amount of distortion than any other means of reporting, and Dos Passos usually employs the metaphor without qualification. But qualifications are needed even for the camera, let alone for the eye. For instance, it is important where the camera is aimed. More importantly, Dos Passos is aware that even a human's eye is automatically subject to numerous distortions caused by religious, economic, and traditional influences, as well as by an individual's idiosyncrasies.[36] But in an essay on George Grosz's etchings, Dos Passos stresses the positive aspects of vision. The eyes, he says, are "an accurate stereoscopic camera," and the process whereby the image is recorded on the brain does indeed entail "a certain amount of unconscious selection." Yet the "subjective distortion and elimination" have a highly personal result. "Seeing," Dos Passos rather startlingly concludes, "is a process of imagination."[37] The implication is that the artist cultivates a unique way of seeing, which allows him to transmit to the reader what Dos Passos elsewhere calls an "intense sense of reality"[38]—not generalities or abstractions, but the most essential pragmatic reality, reported directly as it is seen. One might say that the seer captures the very gesture of life.

A pragmatic attitude not only influences the form of the Camera Eye, but it also lies at the heart of its thematic concerns. As David Vanderwerken has admirably illustrated, Dos Passos's real theme is the "old words," which were used to found the republic but which subsequently became meaningless.[39] Vanderwerken's argument reveals the fundamental issue of the trilogy: the misuse of language. I concur with his reading, with the exception of his position on Dos Passos's historical allusions. As John Diggins has pointed out, there seems to be a curious lacuna in Dos Passos's historical studies: Dos Passos "failed to sustain a consistent standard of historical judgment that would morally bind the present to the past." The result, Diggins concludes, is that Dos Passos "was hard pressed to demonstrate that the fundamental structure of the past was so economically and culturally the same as the present that we can learn anything from the Founding Fathers."[40] But in the trilogy, I would suggest, Dos Passos is not asking the reader to recapture the "structure of the past," nor is he trying to supervene the passage of years to recapture the "old words," an image that should not be taken as literal. Dos Passos's real interest is with recapturing the *process* by which words are given meaning; he found that process in the pragmatic method.

As the central metaphor of the Camera Eye makes clear, the writer has a moral duty to redeem language by making it as close to empirical reality as possible: "you hunch alone from the upsidedown image on the retina painstakingly out of color shape words" (III, p. 196). Significantly, words here are not arbitrary labels, but are "shaped" from the direct sensation of "color" (metonymy for any sensuous—thus empirical—experience). The final step in this process of seeing is "to intersect word with word to dovetail clause with clause" (III, p. 436). This highly elaborate metaphor suggests the melding of the artist's language with reality through the application of pragmatic principles. Most important, there is for Dos Passos no doubt as to the *moral* quality of the result, which is "unshakably . . . the truth" (III, p. 436). In Dos Passos's trilogy, the aesthetic standard, the true use of words, is also the ethical anchor to which the moral life must be grounded. The stream of consciousness of the Camera Eye, with its emphasis on accurate reporting of direct sensation, is an illustration of this basic tenet. Thus, in these autobiographical sections, activity and belief, form and content, merge. The result is that Dos Passos builds an ethical frame of reference that serves as the standard by which other characters and events in the trilogy can be evaluated.

The pragmatic basis of the Newsreels, the second narrative mode, is evident in two ways. First, the Newsreels are compilations of empirical data; they are in a sense artifacts from a historical period: newspaper clippings and songs. They do not provide the coherent overview, but they are the material that a future archaeologist will examine in order to reconstruct the history of the period.[41] In this respect, they are inert, though very real, facts. Yet even the casual reader recognizes that they are more than random assortments; one can sense the author's guiding intelligence in the placement of the data. Thus, critics have generally recognized that the guiding principle in the Newsreels is montage. In an interview, Dos Passos once stated explicitly the importance of this element in his work:

> The whole method is based on contrast. That is what I was saying about what they call montage in the movies. It is a method of getting an effect by using contrasting scenes, contrasting styles. The whole effort was to sort of give another dimension by bringing in things that were going on at the same time as the actual narrative.[42]

I would argue that there is something pragmatic—even radically empirical—about this technique, and though Dos Passos may have encountered montage in Eisenstein's films, his own pragmatic predisposition made its use appealing in this trilogy.

Montage is a particularly apt technique for a writer with a pragmatic aesthetics. One of the problems that James recognized in empirical philosophy is that it is an epistemology that emphasizes the discrete particle and that distrusts theories that attempt arbitrarily to find unity in a pluralistic universe. Rejecting the rationalist's theory of a comprehensive unity, yet recognizing that relationships between discrete data do exist, James developed a *radical* empiricism:

> According to my view, experience as a whole is a process in time, whereby innumerable particular terms lapse and are superseded by others that follow upon them by transitions which, whether disjunctive or conjunctive in content, are themselves experiences, and must in general be accounted at least as real as the terms which they relate.[43]

Whereas empiricism normally stresses the disjunctive nature of reality, "radical empiricism," James contends, "takes conjunctive relations at their face-value, holding them to be as real as the terms united by them."[44]

If the Newsreels present empirical data, the headlines, the relationship of the data through montage is a conjunctive relationship—even if it be a thematic relationship—and that relationship is as much a part of empirical reality as the data itself. The use of montage in the Newsreels, for example, often invites the reader to see the unstated connection between discrete data: "four men in Evanston fined for killing birds/WILSON WILL FORCE DRAFT" (I, p. 351). The reader is encouraged to relate these two headlines and to ask why the larger tyranny goes unpunished. Furthermore, these juxtaposed headlines suggest the inequality of power in America, the lack of a consistent—and thus democratic—evaluation of men's actions. Montage is an effective tool throughout the trilogy, though the radically empirical nature of the technique is most apparent in the Newsreels.

There is emphasis on pragmatic values in the Biographies as well. For example, Frank Lloyd Wright's role as spokesman for nature is a good deal obscured by America's failure to recognize the value of nature. He is, then, as noted previously, without honor in his own country, and thus his true value is obscured. Yet the complementary pragmatic value of his work is apparent and is heralded by Dos Passos as a fundamental virtue. Wright's architecture, Dos Passos notes, is an organic product "a new clean construction, from the ground up, based on uses and needs" (III, p. 431). "From the ground," of course, suggests its affinity with the concrete, even with nature, but the real source of value is that the architecture is useful; it works in harmony with the needs of mankind. A building based on pragmatic uses actually betters the lives of its inhabitants: "building a building is building the lives of the workers and dwellers in the building" (III, p. 432).

In general, these kinds of pragmatic principles are an index to the villains and heroes, the Rovers and Muckers, of the Biographies. In his early notes for *U.S.A.*, Dos Passos included this comment: "Idea of the great/interesting people/people who do things."[45] Edison is clearly one of these people. The inventor "never worried," Dos Passos says, about "philosophical concepts" (I, p. 301). He is pragmatic in that "whenever he read about anything he went down cellar and tried it out" (I, p. 297). Similarly, John Reed used words, but he "was a westerner and words meant what they said" (II, p. 15). "Meester Veelson," on the other hand, used words without regard for their pragmatic value. He "made the world safe for democracy and the New Freedom," the author says, but at the same time Wilson was "talking to save his faith in words . . . (if anybody disagreed he was a crook or a red)" (II, p. 249). The closer a character is to concrete reality—whether through actions or words—the more favorably Dos Passos characterizes him.

Finally, in the Narratives also, pragmatic principles are vitally important. Dos Passos once stated that the Camera Eye drained off his subjective feelings so that he might be completely "objective" in the narrative sections of *U.S.A.*[46] This suggests a complete disjunction between these two important components of the trilogy. On another occasion, he states that the aim of a writer was "to see clearly and to express clearly what he sees."[47] One might argue that in the Camera Eye the emphasis is on "seeing," while in the Narratives the emphasis is on "expressing." That is, the Narratives are an application of the aesthetic theory examined through the metaphors in the Camera Eye. This theory is an attempt to transmit what is seen in an effective way, to rebuild the "ruined words." One might say that if the Camera Eye represents the raw "recording" of sensuous experience, then the Narratives represent that same recording process—with the benefit of the artist's detailed and expert editing—preserving the artist's sense of reality for the future.[48] This search for a frame of reference appears early in Dos Passos's career. It is obvious in Wenny's search for "the word" and later, in *Three Soldiers,* in the pursuit of the "gesture." What I termed the theory of identity in *Manhattan Transfer* only continues this search for an aesthetic standard, which appears in *U.S.A.* as behavioristic writing: the method of "generating the insides of characters by external description."[49] Dos Passos's evaluation of e. e. cummings's play *him* suggests the tenor of his own aesthetic goals: the author tries to "generate feelings and ideas rather than put them immediately up to the understanding, and . . . express sensations rather than to tell about them."[50] That is, descriptive words are "shaped" directly from the reality the artist sees. Those words which the artist chooses are not labels but are intrinsically related to a character's internal state. The writer's role, Dos Passos says, consists of "absorbing and arranging certain sequences of words out of the lives of the people round him."[51] Thus, while the character's actions and beliefs may contrast with and be judged by the aesthetics of the Camera Eye, the creation of the characters in the Narratives is the result of the same aesthetic principles that are expressed in the Camera Eye; the behavioristic theory is pragmatic.

A good illustration of the connection between behaviorism and pragmatism can be seen in the passage where Janey tells Alice about meeting Mr. Barrow:

> Alice wanted to go to sleep, but Janey chattered like a magpie about Mr. Barrow and labor troubles and J. Ward Moorehouse and what a fine man he was, and so kind and friendly and had such interesting ideas for collaboration between capital and labor, and spoke so familiarly about what the President thought and what Andrew Carnegie thought and what the Rockefeller interests of Mr. Schick or Senator LaFollette intended, and had such handsome boyish blue eyes, and was so nice, and the silver teaservice, and how young he looked in spite of his prematurely gray hair, and the open fire and the silver cocktail shaker and the crystal glasses. (I, p. 292)

First, the concreteness of this passage reconstructs in words as exactly as possible empirical reality: "blue eyes . . . silver teaservice . . . gray hair

... fire ... silver cocktail shaker and the crystal glasses." Second, even the parts of this passage that are abstract gain the illusion of concreteness by virtue of their likeness to speech: the reader's interest shifts from the scene described by Janey to the act of Janey speaking, an empirical fact. The *content* of this language—like all of Dos Passos's behavioristic dialogue—deflects away from abstract mental process and toward the superficial aspects of the speech act, even to the point of cliché ("chattered like a magpie"). Generally, this method results in characters whose major qualities are revealed through their perception of things, through activities (speaking, walking, doing), or through a consciousness that lacks depth or fineness. The characters are sum totals of empirical data.

Besides serving as the epistemological basis for the behavioristic method, pragmatism is also a thematic concern in the Narratives. In spite of Charley Anderson's eventual involvement in high finance, for example, his whole life illustrates his role as a Mucker, as one with an essentially pragmatic bias. Born and raised in the Midwest, Charley works in his brother's automobile garage: he "washed cars and drained transmissions and relined brakes" (I, p. 373). He then has a variety of jobs utilizing his mechanical skills: as a ride operator in an amusement park (I, p. 379) and as a "machinist's assistant" in a railroad's shop (I, p. 380). He gets various odd jobs and focuses his attention on going into engineering (I, p. 410). When he engages a number of people in conversation and the talk turns to social injustice, Charley can only say, "It's too deep for me" (I, p. 412). He is essentially a mechanic, a doer, not a thinker.

In the war, Charley is an aviator, though his narrative is not taken up in the second volume of the trilogy; when his story resumes in *The Big Money,* it is fair to say that Dos Passos is drawing on the mythos of the flier in assigning him this wartime occupation. Eric Leed admirably summarizes the aviator's estate:

> The mystique of the flier and of flying was one of the most obvious contributions of the war to the fantasies of the 1920s and 1930s. The flier was engaged in individual rather than collective combat. He was identifiable rather than anonymous. The flier, like heroes such as T. E. Lawrence, fought preindustrial war with modern technology and inherited the values—nobility, honor, vision and visibility—that had formerly surrounded the heavily armored cavalryman but that had been lost by the infantryman.[52]

Several elements are important. Aside from garnering glamor and heroic stature, Charley Anderson engages in a highly individualistic activity that at the same time demands manipulation of a machine. Furthermore, Charley's life of pragmatic activity contrasts with other people's war activities. Moorehouse and his group, for example, are involved in creating illusions, in affecting public opinion. Charley, on the other hand, makes a positive, firsthand contribution to the war effort.

After the war, Charley starts working in industry as a mechanic, but in the inexplicable drift of events, Charley is gradually absorbed into the role of management. Dos Passos's own comments to a friend after the First World War accurately reflect the problem that Charley is facing: "If you want to take up manufacturing, for gods sake take up the scientific end of it. You want to be a brain that creates; not a parasite living off other people's brains, off other people's work."[53] The work Charley is absorbed into is one of specialization and compartmentalization, one where (as Merritt tells him) they have "got to have a separate corporation" for their starter and a "separate production plant" (III, p. 212). Charley does become a "parasite" but not through his own preferences. He is the man with the "knowhow" (III, p. 229). He continually laments his separation from the contact with work, hates being "glued to a desk" (III, p. 201), and seems most at home with "a streak of grease on his nose" (III, p. 201). Since his proclivity is to do work firsthand, his coworker must continually remind him to leave the "routine work" to others (III, p. 202). His final allegiance is to the empirical world of engines, not to the speculative world of theory: "I wish I was still tinkerin' with that damn motor and didn't have to worry about money all the time" (III, p. 310).

One of the best examples of a Rover is Richard Savage. Dos Passos treats Dick's early life with sympathy; especially noteworthy is Dick's early moral objections to the war. But Dos Passos seems to distinguish between Dick's original moral conviction and his later idealism, which, as Dos Passos knows, is easily susceptible to distortion. In fact, his idealism does lead him astray. The critical change in Dick's life occurs when the ambulance service returns him to Paris to be shipped home. In Paris, Dick decides to desert to Spain, a symbol for moral—and pragmatic—values.[54] Dick buys a compass to direct himself to "the Spanish border" (II, p. 211). His plan is naive, is treated ironically, yet generates some sympathy in the reader:

> he was so busy building a daydream of himself living in a sunscorched Spanish town, sending out flaming poems and manifestoes, calling young men to revolt against their butchers, poems that would be published by secret presses all over the world. (II, p. 211)

Part of the ambiguity of this passage results from Dos Passos's own hatred of war. Dick's intention is noble enough; Dos Passos would undoubtedly agree with the sentiments. But it is a "daydream," and since it is never made real by positive action, it is an example of the runaway, abstract thought for which the concreteness of the Camera Eye serves as a corrective. Dick does not go to Spain. Instead, he leaves for America, and on the boat trip, he finds the compass in his pocket and guiltily drops it into the sea. This act serves as an effective, if heavy-handed, symbol of Savage's loss of moral "direction." His life had been a dropping by degrees from a pragmatic application of his ideas. This act represents a significant, irreversible, missed opportunity.

The next time Savage appears in the book, he is an officer; ironically, he is now a member of the hierarchy of "butchers" against whom he had idealistically wanted to revolt. Savage spends his service time in Paris drinking and whoring, meets his future mentor, Moorehouse, and quickly learns the image-building attributes of the printed word. When Elizabeth Trent, his jilted and pregnant mistress, dies in a plane crash (an incident potentially damaging to Savage's career), Dick tells Eleanor Stoddard, "most of the correspondents know me and did their best to kill that story" (II, p. 462). Immediately after this, Miss Williams tells Savage that Moorehouse's interview with the press will "make the front pages" (II, p. 463). The juxtaposition of these two completely unrelated—but thematically complementing—events and the fact that the newspapers distort reality in both cases demonstrate dramatically the failure of the written word to be pragmatic, to reflect reality.

Savage's participation in Moorehouse's interview with the newsmen is not the first association he has with the perversion of the word. When Dick is at Harvard, he enters a prize competition run by the *Literary Digest,* submitting a group of sonnets called *Morituri Te Salutant*. The editors, however, after awarding Dick the prize, "wrote back that they would prefer a note of hope in the last sestet. Dick put in the note of hope and sent the hundred dollars to Mother . . ." (II, p. 96). The suggestion is that in a poem of this kind the words that call up the emotion of hope are interchangeable with those which create the emotion of despair. That is, the words have no intrinsic relation to the felt experience represented in the poem. Dos Passos emphasizes this and parodies Savage's lack of respect for the pragmatic application of words by repeating the trite phrase: the editors want "a note of hope"; Dick gives them "a note of hope." In Savage's world, words have no intrinsic value, but can be interchanged freely. And this disjunction between word and thing, between word and emotion, stands in direct contrast to the pragmatic "shaping" of language in both the form and the thematic content of the Camera Eye sections.

This theme of abstract words divorced from immediate experience runs throughout Dick Savage's career. At the end of *The Big Money,* when Dick is a middle-aged public-relations man, he has completely assimilated his role as surrogate for Moorehouse: "When J. W. smiled Dick smiled too" (III, p. 480). The values to which they both give lip-service are summed up by J. W. when he says, "selfservice, independence, individualism is the word I gave the boys in the beginning. . . . [I]t's going to be a campaign for Americanism . . ." (III, p. 494). It is surely doubtful whether a PR firm can give these qualities to Americans, yet, ironically, "selfservice, independence, individualism" are the very characteristics that even Dick himself lacks in his role of yes-man to Moorehouse. And Moorehouse too lacks them in his role as "yes-man" to the established capitalistic system.

The degree to which Dick has assimilated the values of his mentor is suggested by his speech in defense of Moorehouse, which is a cliché-ridden analysis of American culture:

> Now we may like the way American business does things or we may not like it, but it's a historical fact like the Himalaya Mountains and no amount of kidding's going to change it. It's only through public relations work that business is protected from wildeyed cranks and demagogues who are always ready to throw a monkeywrench into the industrial machine. (III, p. 513)

The unreality of Savage's abstract language, a fatuous attempt to find a "historical" order, is consistent with his failure to ground his personal life in a meaningful way in reality, for "his life was a shambles" (III, p. 483). Thus Savage falls into the error that, as Dos Passos knew, awaits even well-educated and consciously literate men: "he is likely to apply the label before he has really observed the object."[55] This is the problem then: to see reality directly and to name the thing as it really is. This is the nature of the problem that the characters must face and that Dos Passos himself solved with so much precision in writing *U.S.A.*

The early drift of John Dos Passos's career is reflected in the scope of the *U.S.A.* trilogy, as if those three volumes—covering American history between 1900 and 1930—represent an attempt by the mature artist to account as well for his aesthetic development, from his early romantic faith in the redeeming power of nature to a naturalistic despair. Of course, even by the time he wrote the first volume of the trilogy that faith is no longer possible. Written by an older Dos Passos, *The Forty-Second Parallel* can do no more than use America's agrarian past as a tableau wherein comic characters such as Bingham or pitiful figures such as Mac traverse the natural landscape. One might say that if these characters cannot recognize nature's significance, they at least do not diminish its integrity or its value. Furthermore, by the time of *The Big Money,* nature has been largely appropriated and disfigured by industry.

In "Vag," the trilogy's coda, Dos Passos focuses for one last time on the result of America's squandered legacy. Here, the nameless businessman and the nameless hobo—a Rover and a Mucker—present a final illustration of the "two nations." Flying west, the businessman is a Rover Boy, one of those theoreticians who exploit modern technology—here, the

The U.S.A. Trilogy

airplane—and thereby separates himself from the soil. His major concern is with the big money. In the man's airborne nausea, Dos Passos found the perfect symbol for modern man's condition: controlling man, separating him from his real legacy, the machine creates an imbalance in the man's physical and spiritual constitution. Indeed, being airborne is itself a fitting symbol for the businessman's devotion to the abstract, to what James defines as the "saltatory" approach to life. The man has a clear view of the American continent, which sublimely unrolls beneath him, but just as Fanshaw *looked* at the landscape and *thought* of English art, the businessman

> thinks contracts, profits, vacationtrips, mighty continent between Atlantic and Pacific, power, wires humming dollars, cities jammed, hills empty, the indiantrail leading into the wagonroad, the macadamed pike, the concrete skyway; trains, planes: history the billiondollar speedup. (III, pp. 560–61)

America has forsaken the hills for the cities and has traveled the long road of progress, from Indian trails to planes. This, unfortunately, is American history.

Vag, the Mucker, is different. Being outside the system may be a harsh fate, yet it also has its cruel advantages. While the businessman in the airplane may be in the presence of the "cool high air" which "smells of sweetgrass" (III, p. 560), he is apparently too preoccupied to notice; Vag, on the other hand, has his feet solidly planted on the ground and knows "the silent grassy smell of the earth" (III, p. 559). Furthermore, although Vag is a reduced version of a human being—so few hopes, so few dreams remaining—he is also, for better or for worse, a part of the landscape: "the wind of cars passing ruffles his hair, slaps grit in his face" (III, p. 559). The fundamental "desires" that are left to him "crawl over his skin like ants" (III, p. 561). He survives within the landscape—survives, one might say, because the landscape survives. This is a familiar theme in Dos Passos's early novels. For Wenny, it meant a godlike transcendence after death. For Jimmy Herf, it meant a similar rebirth in life, accompanied by a new vitality in his walk out of the city. Nature, however sublime, can provide no such miracles, no rebirth, no transcendence for Vag. Nature persists, but man has lost his holistic connection with the soil.

U.S.A., then, is a testament to America's lost inheritance, and the depth of the despair in the trilogy can be measured by Dos Passos's portrayal of a fictional world in which characters are divorced both from the natural world and from a pragmatic use of language. Yet Dos Passos himself seems reluctant to lose touch with either of these values, as if he must offer America one last time his vision of redemptive possibilities; and in the work's last written addition—the preface, published for the first time in the one-volume trilogy in 1938—Dos Passos's hero, "alone" (p. v), walks through the city:

> He must catch the last subway, the streetcar, the bus, run up the gangplanks of all the steamboats, register at all the hotels, work in the cities, answer the wantads, learn the trades, take up the jobs, live in all the boardinghouses, sleep in all the beds. One bed is not enough, one job is not enough, one life is not enough. (P. vi)

Though he has "no job, no woman, no house, no city" (p. vi), his "greedy eyes, greedy ears" (p. v) suggest the potential for success. The mood is optative, and hope does not seem lost.

Although the trilogy itself does not reveal much cause for hope, this preface makes two important points that lie at the heart of Dos Passos's aesthetics. The first is that language as a cultural phenomenon is a spontaneously generated norm that is naturally produced by the indigenous population. For Dos Passos, this "speech of the people" embodies values that can be associated at once with both nature and pragmatism. Earlier in his career he had associated with language the phrase "concrete, dug out of the soil." In the preface to the trilogy he again identifies the normative language as that which both reflects reality pragmatically and derives from nature; through metaphor language becomes reality, becomes nature:

> Only the ears busy to catch the speech are not alone; the ears are caught tight, linked tight by the tendrils of phrased words, the turn of a joke, the singsong fade of a story, the gruff fall of a sentence; linking tendrils of speech twine through the city blocks, spread over pavements, grow out along broad parked avenues, speed with the trucks leaving on their long night runs over roaring highways, whisper down sandy byroads past wornout farms, joining up cities and fillingstations, roundhouses, steamboats, planes groping along airways; words call out on mountain pastures, drift slow down rivers widening to the sea and the hushed beaches. (P. vi)

Here language not only reflects reality and is derived from nature, but it has become the central actor. Unlike the unnamed protagonist of the preface—who is alone, alienated, and mostly powerless—the language *acts:* the "tendrils" of speech "twine . . . spread . . . grow . . . speed . . . whisper . . ." (p. vi).

The second point of the preface, closely associated with the first, is that language *heals.* The trilogy itself presents Dos Passos's vision of the alienated individual in twentieth-century American culture. In the preface the unnamed protagonist also suffers anomie, and nothing he can do will make him less alone—not in walking, joining the military, eating, swimming, riding the train, or canoeing (p. vi). Only in one thing—language—lies his salvation:

in his mother's words telling about longago, in his father's telling about when I was a boy, in the kidding stories of uncles, in the lies the kids told at school, the hired man's yarns, the tall tales the doughboys told after taps. (P. vii)

Language is "the link that tingled in the blood" (p. vii). Here, the unnamed seeker and the author are for all practical purposes indistinguishable, and the last words of the preface summarize Dos Passos's aesthetic intentions: "But mostly U.S.A. is the speech of the people" (p. vii). The various meanings of the initials U.S.A.—trilogy, people, soil, speech, or the sum total of empirical reality related to the American continent—converge in a common locus, language; and the artist, in the tradition of Walt Whitman, has the power to speak in one voice for a pluralistic society. As a final comment on Dos Passos's aesthetic intentions in the preface and in the Camera Eye, it is useful to emphasize Walt Whitman's prescription for the poet: he is "the arbiter of the diverse and he is the key."[56] By presenting a standard of value in language and by showing how America has not lived up to that standard, John Dos Passos has not only challenged America to examine itself but has also suggested a solution to its problems: a pragmatic and "natural" use of language.

As has been shown, John Dos Passos's art as it developed early in his career was profoundly influenced by its American background and in particular by these two broadly influential American tendencies: a deep belief in nature and a pragmatic epistemology. However wide-ranging his reading and eclectic his mind, John Dos Passos nevertheless found in these ideas a fundamental core of value, a system of belief, that provided the frame of reference for his examination of twentieth-century American life. His task involved the epistemological quest of melding the objective and subjective realms. Such an epistemological problem—as this study has shown—lies at the heart of John Dos Passos's fiction. To the degree that his fiction succeeds as aesthetic object, it succeeds in embodying a vision that is also moral and epistemological, a vision that grapples with—and in some measure solves—the problem of subject and object, of self and others.

10
Conclusion

This study has attempted to show that there is a coherence in the early fiction of John Dos Passos. No matter how much Dos Passos's art changed in the years 1912 to 1938—and it changed considerably—there was behind each novel a single, coherent vision of the world. Thus, the diverse terminology in the discussions of an aesthetics of "the word" in *Streets of Night,* of the "gesture" in *Three Soldiers,* and of "behavioristic" writing in the *U.S.A.* trilogy, all reflect a single interest: a writing that manages to capture the essence of reality, a language that melds the objective and subjective realms.

To be sure, with the republication of the *U.S.A.* trilogy as a single volume in 1938, Dos Passos's world view did not change drastically. Indeed the evidence is everywhere that the beliefs that he held early in his career remained a strong force in his later writing. In *Chosen Country,* for example, Jay Pignatelli's odyssey is an account of his finding of his true self. At the end of that book, when his fiancée asks him where he came from, he responds in an idealized portrait of a landscape, man and nature together:

> "God I wish I knew . . . I start from right here. I feel like my grandfather the first day he landed."
> "Where did he land?"
> "I don't know; Charleston I think."
> "But it seemed a wilderness, an untidy wilderness."
> "Still is. But of this wilderness we must carve our home."[1]

After Jay and Lulie's marriage, "They were alone in the green world" (p. 484). The description of the "first morning" of their marriage borders on the sentimental and the lachrymose, but the reader is left to believe that the natural, mythic paradise has indeed been regained. In his last book, *Century's Ebb,* Dos Passos gives Walt Whitman center stage not only by beginning that volume with a biography of the American poet but also by making references to Whitman throughout the volume.[2]

Conclusion   151

An emphasis on pragmatic thought also lasted late into Dos Passos's career. As I have shown in chapter 3, the intense and enthusiastic early reading of William James was well-suited to Dos Passos's pragmatic proclivities and played a large part in solidifying a pragmatic ethos, and he carried that vision of the world throughout his career. As late as 1961, when Dos Passos writes a biography in *Midcentury* about Major General William Frishe Dean, he is still pondering the problem of how idealism often separates itself from reality:

> The Communist indoctrinators were able to appeal to a sort of ignorant idealism that is the dead shell of the protestant ethics our fathers lived by. Idealism without ethics is no compass.[3]

Except for the fact that it is the Communists that are at issue here and not the American political leaders, this comment about war might very well fit into *Three Soldiers* or *One Man's Initiation*. He is here lamenting the loss of a solid pragmatic center.

Again, near the end of his life, in writing *Century's Ebb*, Dos Passos pays tribute to the importance of pragmatic thought. There, he identifies William James, Charles Sanders Peirce, and John Dewey as the founders of pragmatism, though he dwells on Dewey.[4] He chose Dewey, no doubt, because as the title of the essay indicates ("American Pragmatism, 1859–1952"), Dewey was not only the most famous of the three but also the one who spanned the development of America from the time of Walt Whitman to the present. Although the discussion of pragmatic philosophy might just as easily apply to Peirce or James, John Dewey was the one whose life most obviously stood in contrast to the corrupt modern America. Indeed, the failings of society are the same now as they were in Dos Passos's first books, and they are cast in terms of a failure to be truly pragmatic. Just as in *One Man's Initiation,* "Slogans were taking the place of thought" (p. 120). The original honest and useful pragmatic philosophy had in the course of events become perverted so that now it "dribbled away into the doctrine that anything goes" (p. 123).

Thus there is a unity to Dos Passos's career, and its shape involves an appreciation for nature and a pragmatic epistemology, two complementary ways of ordering reality. In the early works, Dos Passos's narrators are at once (and in varying degrees) the aesthetes who hide their sensitive souls from the world and the scientists who dissect the illnesses of the social system.

In this volume, my interest has not been in examining the early books simply because Whitman's and James's influence could be found. Rather, the point is that those two writers confirmed Dos Passos's vital feelings about the world, and by examining his reaction to these authors one can better understand Dos Passos's own aesthetic principles. In short, the early books show an increasing intensity up through the *U.S.A.* trilogy. In the heated cauldron of his creative effort, Dos Passos discovered several vital ingredients in the making of something new and different in the American literary scene. After the trilogy, the same aesthetic principles were still present, but the vital spark that makes creativity was not. Regrettably, literary criticism will not be able to salvage those later works, though I suspect that those books will gain increased interest as the earlier works are given the widespread recognition that they deserve.

An examination of the later works, then, lies outside the scope of this study. The interesting questions that they pose lie in an altogether different area: why are the later works consistently less interesting, less artful, if not less crafted? It is not because Dos Passos's aesthetic principles changed. The critic who attempts to answer the question as to why Dos Passos's art declined must deal with the mystery of art.

As Blanche Gelfant has suggested in an admirable essay, John Dos Passos's life was a search for an identity.[5] He was very conscious of his illegitimate birth. We might remember the amorphous characters in *Manhattan Transfer,* whose names continually shift, and be reminded that Dos Passos's name too changed in his life, from John Roderigo to John Dos Passos. Dos Passos's personal search for an identity seems to be mirrored in his early fiction. One might say that Dos Passos came to his own identity through his fiction. By becoming a writer, he established a sense of his own self. Thus, the maturing of his artistic style in *U.S.A.* coincides with the development of his most mature characterization of himself: in the Camera Eye, Dos Passos shows us a character who has looked back on his own life and has taken the measure of his own self. He shows in that fictive construct that he has achieved his own voice in relation to the events of the twentieth century. And the Camera Eye shows a broad range and a mature depth and a *certainty* about moral, philosophical, social, and aesthetic issues that suggest the achievement of a high order of insight. And the achievement is no mean one. *The Forty-Second Parallel, 1919,* and *The Big Money* (as *Manhattan Transfer* before them) are books that are solid artistic achievements, and they will live. They are the flowering of a burning passion for self-discovery.

What came after is anticlimax.

Notes

Chapter 1. Introduction

1. *Leaves of Grass,* ed. by Harold W. Blodgett and Sculley Bradley (New York: W. W. Norton & Co., Inc., 1965), p. 566. Subsequent references to Whitman's prefaces will be from this volume and will be cited as *Leaves of Grass* (1965).
2. John Dos Passos, interview, "The Art of Fiction XLIV," *Paris Review* 46 (1969): 163.
3. "The Great Tradition" was delivered at the University of Illinois. A recording of the speech is in the archives of the University Library at Illinois.
4. During Dos Passos's undergraduate years, the Harvard Catalogue lists English 33, "The Literary History of America," and English 63, "Emerson." A few other courses offered a bicultural approach (for example, English 69, "English and American Historians").
5. Malcolm Cowley, *Exile's Return* (New York: The New American Library, 1966), p. 27.
6. John Dos Passos, *The Best Times* (New York: The New American Library, 1966), pp. 10–11.
7. Unpublished diary, 1914–1917, John Dos Passos Papers (acc. no. 5950-AC), Manuscripts Department, University of Virginia Library. Used by permission of Mrs. John Dos Passos.
8. Unpublished essay, p. 7, John Dos Passos Papers (acc. no. 5950-AE), Manuscripts Department, University of Virginia Library. Used by permission of Mrs. John Dos Passos.
9. John Dos Passos, "Against American Literature," *New Republic* 8 (14 October 1916): 269–71.
10. Unpublished and undated letter to Arthur McComb in the archives of the American Academy and Institute of Arts and Letters, New York City. Used by permission of Mrs. John Dos Passos.
11. John Dos Passos, *The Fourteenth Chronicle: Letters and Diaries of John Dos Passos,* ed. Townsend Ludington (Boston: Gambit, Inc., 1973), p. 252. Hereafter cited as *Fourteenth Chronicle.*
12. Unpublished diary, 1914–1917, John Dos Passos Papers (acc. no. 5950-AC), Manuscripts Department, University of Virginia Library. Used by permission of Mrs. John Dos Passos.
13. *Fourteenth Chronicle,* pp. 281, 279.
14. So states Arthur Mizener in his introduction to *District of Columbia* (Boston: Houghton, Mifflin, Co., 1952), pp. viii–ix.
15. William Carlos Williams, *In the American Grain* (New York: New Directions, 1933), p. 39.
16. Ralph Barton Perry, *Characteristically American* (New York: Knopf, 1949), p. 5.

Chapter 2. Walt Whitman and John Dos Passos

1. Charles Child Walcutt, *Man's Changing Mask* (Minneapolis: University of Minnesota Press, 1966), p. 303.

2. Manuscript, John Dos Passos Papers (acc. no. 5950-AE) Manuscripts Department, University of Virginia Library. Used by permission of Mrs. John Dos Passos.
3. *Fourteenth Chronicle,* p. 516.
4. Dos Passos, "Against American Literature," p. 270.
5. *Leaves of Grass* (1965), pp. 717–18.
6. *Leaves of Grass* (1965), p. 712.
7. *Leaves of Grass* (1965), p. 710.
8. *Leaves of Grass* (1965), p. 721.
9. *Leaves of Grass* (1965), p. 751.
10. *Leaves of Grass* (1965), p. 569.
11. Walt Whitman, "Democratic Vistas," *Complete Prose Works* (Philadelphia: David McKay, Publisher, 1891), p. 249.
12. Ibid., p. 253.
13. *Leaves of Grass* (Philadelphia: David McKay, 1900), p. 234. All subsequent references to Whitman's poetry will be to this volume, cited in my text by line numbers.
14. *Leaves of Grass* (1965), p. 714.
15. William James, *Essays in Radical Empiricism* (Cambridge: Harvard University Press, 1976), p. 13. Hereafter cited as *Radical Empiricism.*
16. William James, "What Pragmatism Means," *Pragmatism* (Cambridge: Harvard University Press, 1975), p. 28. Hereafter cited as *Pragmatism.*
17. Ibid.
18. James E. Miller, Jr., *A Critical Guide to Leaves of Grass* (Chicago: University of Chicago Press, 1957), p. 4.
19. Quoted in F. O. Matthiessen, *The James Family* (New York: Alfred A. Knopf, 1947), p. 488. It is interesting to note that Gay Wilson Allen sees Whitman as "exploring problems and presenting empirical answers that actually gave a preview of the main course of American philosophy for the next century, for what was this theory of 'Democracy' but the forerunner of William James's 'Pluralism' and John Dewey's 'Pragmatism'?" See Allen's *The Solitary Singer: A Critical Biography of Walt Whitman* (New York: The MacMillan Co., 1955), p. 390. Also, a recent article by Diane Kepner does not mention Whitman's pragmatism per se, but her analysis of the poet's philosophy repeatedly makes clear the pragmatic basis of Whitman's ideas. Kepner says, for example, that Whitman believes that "truth of Being" lies in the "fusion" of both the materialistic and the idealistic viewpoints. See Diane Kepner, "From Spears to Leaves: Walt Whitman's Theory of Nature in 'Song of Myself,'" *American Literature* 51 (May 1979): 185.
20. Bliss Perry, *Walt Whitman* (Boston: Houghton, Mifflin and Company, 1906), p. 278.
21. John Burroughs, *Whitman: A Study* (Boston: Houghton, Mifflin and Company, 1896), p. 169.
22. Ibid., p. 191.
23. Ibid., p. 122.
24. Ibid., p. 76.
25. Ibid., p. 123.
26. John Addington Symonds, *Walt Whitman: A Study* (London: John C. Nimmo, 1893), p. 39.
27. Ibid., p. 40.
28. Ibid., p. 41.
29. Ibid., p. 43.
30. My analysis of Dos Passos's debt to Whitman and my reading of Dos Passos's conception of Nature differ from the argument made by Lois Hughson, which equates Nature with the "golden age" and "myth" (that is, the unattainable). I will argue that Dos Passos was attracted to the mythic dimension of Nature, but that he did not view it

necessarily as an unattainable fantasy. Furthermore, Hughson sees the real and the ideal as discontinuous elements. She notes, for example, that "If democracy is to be saved, then, by getting a literature which will be its soul, it will be saved rhetorically, not actually; in the spirit, not the flesh" (p. 181). I disagree. I think that Dos Passos from the first saw nature as an expression of man's spirit and that he supposed that man could attain a holistic relation with the world. For Walt Whitman, William James, and John Dos Passos, the "body" and the "soul" are one, not just in literature, but in life as well. See Lois Hughson, "In Search of the True America: Dos Passos' Debt to Whitman in *U.S.A.*," *Modern Fiction Studies* 19 (Summer 1973): 179–92. Similarly, Robert Weeks makes many insightful comments about the relationship of Whitman and Dos Passos, but he emphasizes the surface similarities—similarities in technique. Dos Passos's debt to Whitman, I think, resides in a larger generalization. See Weeks's "The Novel as Poem: Whitman's Legacy to Dos Passos," *Modern Fiction Studies* 26 (Autumn 1980): 431–46.

Chapter 3. William James and Dos Passos

1. Diary, 1914–1917, Dos Passos Papers (acc. no. 5950-AC), Manuscripts Department, University of Virginia Library. Used by permission of Mrs. John Dos Passos.
2. *Fourteenth Chronicle,* p. 299.
3. John Dos Passos, *Rosinante to the Road Again* (New York: George H. Doran, 1922), p. 61. Hereafter cited as *Rosinante*.
4. *Fourteenth Chronicle,* p. 134.
5. Diary, 1914–1917, John Dos Passos Papers (5950-AC), Manuscripts Department, University of Virginia Library. Used by permission of Mrs. John Dos Passos.
6. Ibid.
7. Dos Passos, "Art and Baseball," p. 2.
8. Ibid., p. 11.
9. Dos Passos, letter to Frederick Lowe, 27 August 1948, in the collection of the Pennsylvania State University Library. Used by permission of Mrs. John Dos Passos.
10. *Radical Empiricism,* pp. 36–37.
11. William James, *Psychology: Briefer Course* (New York: Henry Holt and Company, 1892), p. 181. Hereafter cited as *Psychology*.
12. *Fourteenth Chronicle,* p. 306.
13. Ibid., p. 94.
14. Letter to Griffen Barry, dated 28 April 1919, John Dos Passos Papers (acc. no. 5950-AA), Manuscripts Department, University of Virginia Library. Used by permission of Mrs. John Dos Passos.
15. *Fourteenth Chronicle,* p. 57.
16. Letter to Arthur McComb, undated, in the archives of the American Academy and Institute of Arts and Letters, New York City. Used by permission of Mrs. John Dos Passos.
17. John Dos Passos, *The Ground We Stand On* (New York: Harcourt, Brace, and Co., 1941), p. 89.
18. *Fourteenth Chronicle,* pp. 397–98.
19. Diary, 1914–1917, John Dos Passos Papers (acc. no. 5950-AC), Manuscripts Department, University of Virginia Library. Used by permission of Mrs. John Dos Passos.
20. *Fourteenth Chronicle,* p. 220.
21. Ibid., p. 193.
22. Ibid., p. 306.
23. Ibid., p. 456.
24. Ibid., p. 464.

25. Ibid., p. 477.
26. Ibid., p. 70.
27. James, *Psychology,* p. 370.
28. John Dos Passos, "What Makes a Novelist," *National Review* 20 (January 1968): 31.
29. William James, *The Meaning of Truth* (Ann Arbor: University of Michigan Press, 1970), p. 216. Hereafter cited as *Truth.*

Chapter 4. The Early Short Stories and *Streets of Night*

1. Travel Diary, 1911, John Dos Passos Papers (acc. no. 5950), Manuscripts Department, University of Virginia Library. Used by permission of Mrs. John Dos Passos.
2. John Dos Passos Papers (acc. no. 5950), Manuscripts Department, University of Virginia Library. Used by permission of Mrs. John Dos Passos. Page references will be cited in the text.
3. John Dos Passos, "Romantic Education," *Harvard Monthly* 61 (October 1915): 1–4. Page references will be cited in the text.
4. John Dos Passos, *Streets of Night* (New York: George H. Doran Company, 1923). Page references will be cited in the text.
5. Dos Passos himself seems to have loved Boston. He writes in 1916, "I've just been on a tremendously long ramble through Boston—I love cities on a rainy night . . . there's a wonderful atmosphere of gaiety & a sort of paganism about which always delights me—I mean in the cheaper parts of the city." See *Fourteenth Chronicle,* p. 39.
6. Blanche Gelfant, "The Search for Identity in the Novels of John Dos Passos," *PMLA* 76 (March 1961): 134.
7. Linda Wagner, *Dos Passos: Artist as American* (Austin: University of Texas Press, 1979), p. 23. John Wrenn also notes Hawthorne's influence. See his *John Dos Passos* (New York: Twayne Publishers, Inc., 1961), pp. 116–21.
8. Nathaniel Hawthorne, *The Blithedale Romance and Fanshawe* (Columbus: Ohio State University Press, 1964), p. 443. Hereafter cited as *Fanshawe.*
9. Ibid., p. 346.
10. Ibid., p. 350.
11. William Carlos Williams, *Selected Essays of William Carlos Williams* (New York: Random House, 1954), p. 137.
12. Ibid., p. 143.
13. Dos Passos, *The Best Times,* p. 17.
14. Samuel Roads, Jr., *The History and Traditions of Marblehead* (Marblehead, Mass.: N. Allen Lindsey & Co., 1897), pp. 500–501.
15. Wagner, *Dos Passos: Artist as American,* p. 25.
16. Ibid.
17. See, for example, ibid.
18. Dos Passos, *The Best Times,* p. 24.
19. It would seem that this passage—as well as the flower symbolism generally—owes much to a book published in 1913, Elizabeth Haig's *The Floral Symbolism of the Great Masters* (London: Keegan Paul, Trench, Trubner & Co., Ltd., 1913). Compare the above passage with Haig's treatment of the story of St. Francis, who, "kneeling in his cell one winter's night, was much troubled by the memory of a fair woman. To overcome the temptation he went out and threw himself among the briars of the wilderness" (p. 75). Dos Passos had the occasion to read this book since it appeared one year before he took Fine Art 9a at Harvard in 1914–15, a course entitled "Art and Culture of Italy in the Middle Ages and the Renaissance."

Notes

20. Diary, 1914–1917, John Dos Passos Papers (acc. no. 5950-AC), Manuscripts Department, University of Virginia Library. Used by permission of Mrs. John Dos Passos.
21. Dos Passos, "Against American Literature," p. 270.
22. In addition to an anthropology course, Dos Passos also took two courses in Greek literature and three courses in Greek philosophy. I would like to thank Mrs. John Dos Passos for graciously allowing me to have access to Dos Passos's college records.
23. Sir James Frazer, *The Golden Bough*, abr. ed. (New York: The Macmillan Company, 1950), p. 390.
24. Ibid.
25. Ibid., p. 391.
26. Ibid., p. 449.
27. Ibid., p. 453.
28. Charles Mills Gayley, *The Classic Myths in English Literature and in Art* (Lexington, Mass.: Xerox College Publishing, 1972), p. 27.
29. Ibid., p. 104.
30. At first glance, Lowell's poem might seem "the long way" to get at the Greek myth, but it is possible that Dos Passos's knowledge of the Greek legends came in part from Charles Gayley's text *The Classic Myths* (noted above), a book widely used in college courses. It was first published in 1893, revised in 1911, and is still frequently used in college courses. In his discussion of Apollo, Gayley quotes in full Lowell's poem "The Shepherd of King Admetus," pp. 105–6. My quotations from Lowell's poem are taken from *The Poetical Works of James Russell Lowell* (Boston: Houghton, Mifflin & Co., 1897), p. 44.
31. Diary, 1914–1917, John Dos Passos Papers (acc. no. 5950-AC), Manuscripts Department, University of Virginia Library. Used by permission of Mrs. John Dos Passos.
32. John Dos Passos, *Three Plays* (New York: Harcourt, Brace and Company, 1934), p. 54.
33. James, *Truth*, pp. 79–80.
34. *Fourteenth Chronicle*, pp. 26–27.
35. James, *Pragmatism*, p. 107.
36. See Dos Passos's letter to Edmund Wilson in *Fourteenth Chronicle*, p. 522.

Chapter 5. *Seven Times Round the Walls of Jericho*

1. *Fourteenth Chronicle*, p. 178.
2. *Seven Times Round the Walls of Jericho*, unpublished novel, typescript, John Dos Passos Papers (acc. no. 5950-Q), University of Virginia, part I, page 5. Used by permission of Mrs. John Dos Passos. Subsequent references to this work will be cited within the text in parentheses. Parts one, two and three will be cited by Roman numeral, followed by the page number. In the case of part two, references noted by part and page refer to chapters 1 to 17. References noted by part, chapter, and page are to chapters 21 through 23, which have separate pagination, pp. 1–18.
3. *Fourteenth Chronicle*, p. 119.
4. Ibid., p. 177.
5. Ibid. In his outline, Dos Passos here notes the "Vita nova feeling."
6. Ibid.
7. Ibid., p. 119.
8. Dos Passos's fondness for using the literary double is apparent here. A more obvious example of this is in the contrasting characterizations of James Clough and Julius Conelly. Though they share the same initials, Julius Conelly and James Clough contrast in their relative pragmatism, their creativity, and their sexual freedom. For Dos Passos's more refined use of this technique, see the later discussion of *Three Soldiers*.
9. *Fourteenth Chronicle*, p. 328.

Chapter 6. *One Man's Initiation: 1917*

1. John Dos Passos, *One Man's Initiation: 1917* (Ithaca: Cornell University Press, 1969). Page references will be cited parenthetically within the text.
2. Eric J. Leed, *No Man's Land: Combat and Identity in World War I* (Cambridge: Cambridge University Press, 1979), p. 1.
3. Ibid., p. 22.
4. *Fourteenth Chronicle*, p. 88.
5. Susanne K. Langer, for example, describes prose fiction as being in the "mnemonic mode." See her *Feeling and Form: A Theory of Art* (New York: Charles Scribner's Sons, 1953), p. 291.
6. Iain Colley uses this term to describe Dos Passos's novel. See his *Dos Passos and the Fiction of Despair* (Totowa, N.J.: Rowman and Littlefield, 1978), p. 30.
7. Ibid., p. 27.
8. Robert G. Davis, *John Dos Passos*, University of Minnesota Pamphlets on American Writers, no. 20 (Minneapolis: University of Minnesota Press, 1962), p. 10.
9. Wagner, *Dos Passos: Artist as American*, pp. 11, 14.
10. John W. Aldridge, *After the Lost Generation* (New York: McGraw-Hill, 1951), p. 64.
11. In his college diary (1915), Dos Passos writes of a planned novel that would explore an "unromantic account of the influence of nature, of surroundings on an uncultured mind." Diary, 1914–1917, John Dos Passos Papers (acc. no. 5950-AC), Manuscripts Department, University of Virginia Library. Used by permission of Mrs. John Dos Passos.
12. John D. Brantley, *The Fiction of John Dos Passos* (The Hague: Mouton, 1968), p. 20.
13. *Leaves of Grass* (1965), p. 717.
14. Ibid.
15. Dos Passos, *The Best Times*, p. 44.
16. *Fourteenth Chronicle*, p. 284.
17. James, *Pragmatism*, p. 97.
18. Dos Passos, *The Best Times*, p. 44.
19. This letter is quoted in Dos Passos's introduction to *One Man's Initiation*, p. 23.
20. James, *Pragmatism*, p. 108.
21. See, for example, James's conciliatory treatment of the role of belief in traditional religions, *Pragmatism*, pp. 40–43.
22. Just one month after *One Man's Initiation* was published, Dos Passos writes a letter (which I noted briefly in chapter 3) to Rumsey Marvin mentioning Plato and "ideas" and using shadow imagery: "As for ideas I wonder if they are anything more than the pale shadows of gestures. . . . As for Plato—I recently reread the Symposium and except for the skill of his style I think he's an utter windbag" (*Fourteenth Chronicle*, p. 306).
23. James, *Pragmatism*, p. 23.
24. Quoted in ibid., p. 22.
25. Aldridge, *After the Lost Generation*, p. 65.
26. Melvin Landsberg, *Dos Passos' Path to U.S.A.: A Political Biography, 1912–1936* (Boulder: Colorado Associated University Presses, 1972), pp. 57–58.
27. John H. Wrenn, *John Dos Passos* (New York: Twayne Publishers, Inc., 1961), p. 120.

Chapter 7. *Three Soldiers*

1. John Dos Passos, *Three Soldiers* (New York: George H. Doran Co., 1921), p. 279. Subsequent references to this edition will be cited parenthetically in the text.
2. Harold Aspiz, *Walt Whitman and the Body Beautiful* (Urbana: University of Illinois Press, 1980), chap. 4.

3. Quoted in ibid., p. 134.

4. It should be noted, of course, that Dos Passos had many possible models. It is a well-documented fact that Dos Passos read widely in literature that uses the double. His wide reading in Poe could account for this interest in the double. In addition, in college Dos Passos read Dostoyevsky's *The Brothers Karamazov* and was quite impressed with the Russian novelist. See *Fourteenth Chronicle*, pp. 9, 28, 35. It is more than likely that in addition to Whitman, Poe and Dostoyevsky also contributed much to Dos Passos's conception of the double.

5. See chapter 5 in *Streets of Night* for a discussion of Freud and psychoanalysis.

6. Otto Rank, *The Double: A Psychoanalytic Study*, trans. and ed. Harry Tucker, Jr. (Chapel Hill: University of North Carolina Press, 1971), chap. 5.

7. Ralph Tymms, *Doubles in Literary Psychology* (Cambridge: Bowes & Bowes, 1949), chap. 2, 3.

8. For this term and "double by duplication," see ibid., pp. 16–17.

9. Sigmund Freud, "Psychoanalysis and War Neuroses," in *Miscellaneous Papers, 1888–1938*, vol. 5 of *Collected Papers*, ed. James Strachey (London: The Hogarth Press and The Institute of Psycho-analysis, 1950), p. 85.

10. Diary, 1914–1917, John Dos Passos Papers (acc. no. 5950-AC), Manuscripts Department, University of Virginia Library. Used by permission of Mrs. John Dos Passos.

11. Rank, *The Double*, p. 76.

12. Tymms, *Doubles in Literary Psychology*, p. 41.

13. Rank, *The Double*, pp. 79–80.

14. This apparently simple dichotomy is actually the basis for Jimmy Herf's problems in *Manhattan Transfer*, where again "success" in the existing system is actually a negative value: "In the empty chamber of his brain a doublefaced word clinked like a coin: Success Failure, Success Failure." See John Dos Passos, *Manhattan Transfer* (New York: Harper & Brothers Publishers, 1925), p. 303.

15. Rohn S. Friedman, "A Whitman Primer: Solipsism and Identity," *American Quarterly* 27 (October 1975): 445.

16. F. O. Matthiessen, *American Renaissance: Art and Expression in the Age of Emerson and Whitman* (New York: Oxford University Press, 1941), p. 525.

17. The word "gesture" first appears in the second half of the novel—with the appearance of John Andrews. A rough (though representative) estimate is that the word appears in increasing frequency as the novel progresses, once every twenty-five pages between 201 and 300; once every seventeen pages between 301 and 400; and once every five pages between 401 and 433. In contrast, the word "gesture" appears only twice in *Manhattan Transfer*, on pp. 374 and 375.

18. *Rosinante*, p. 23.

19. Ibid., p. 185.

20. Ibid., pp. 185, 243.

21. Ibid., p. 139.

22. Ibid., p. 20.

23. R. P. Blackmur, *Language as Gesture: Essays in Poetry* (London: George Allen and Unwin, Ltd., 1954), p. 3. The title essay was written in 1942.

24. Ibid., p. 6.

25. Ibid.

26. James, *Psychology*, pp. 462–63.

27. Ibid., p. 7.

28. Ibid., pp. 464–66.

29. *Don Quixote*, of course, is the source of the title of *Rosinante to the Road Again*. In 1916, Dos Passos writes to a friend: "Have read 'Don Quixote' vol 1 & 2 in original and I intend to study it violently in the near future." See *Fourteenth Chronicle*, p. 39.

30. *Rosinante*, p. 229.

Chapter 8. *Manhattan Transfer*

1. John Dos Passos, *Orient Express* (New York: Harper & Brothers, 1927), pp. 36–37. This section of the book first appeared as "In a New Republic," *Freeman* 4 (5 October 1921): 81–83.
2. Blanche Gelfant, *The American City Novel* (Norman: University of Oklahoma Press, 1954), pp. 139, 148–49.
3. Wrenn, *John Dos Passos*, pp. 129–30.
4. Craig Carver, "The Newspaper and Other Sources of *Manhattan Transfer*," *Studies in American Fiction* 3 (1975): 169.
5. John Dos Passos, *Manhattan Transfer* (Boston: Houghton Mifflin Company, 1925). The page references cited parenthetically in this sentence and those which follow in this chapter refer to this edition.
6. Carver, "The Newspaper . . . ," p. 168.
7. Waldo Frank, *Our America* (New York: Boni and Liveright, 1919), p. 174.
8. Whitman, "Democratic Vistas," *Prose Works*, p. 245.
9. These seasonal references can be found on the following pages of *Manhattan Transfer*: 21, 45, 53, 72, 90, 96, 113, 129, 136, 137, 152, 153, 161, 170, 194, 197, 220, 237, 244, 246, 254, 255, 260, 276, 279, 291, 296, 298, 304, 308, 315, 321, 322, 329, 333, 344, 351, 352, 353, 379, 395, 401, 403.
10. Whitman, "Democratic Vistas," *Prose Works*, p. 210.
11. William Faulkner, *Three Famous Short Novels* (New York: Vintage Books, 1966), p. 288.
12. See *Fourteenth Chronicle*, pp. 21–23.
13. Maxwell Geismar, *Writers in Crisis* (New York: Hill and Wang, 1961), p. 101.
14. Ibid., p. 104.
15. E. D. Lowry, "*Manhattan Transfer*: Dos Passos' Wasteland," *The University Review* 30 (1963): 50.
16. Gelfant, *City Novel*, p. 151.
17. Wagner, *Dos Passos: Artist as American*, pp. 52, 56.
18. David L. Vanderwerken, "*Manhattan Transfer*: Dos Passos' Babel Story," *American Literature* 49 (1977): 253–67.
19. Whitman, "Democratic Vistas," *Prose Works*, p. 249.
20. Ibid., p. 230.
21. Ibid., pp. 229–30.
22. Ibid., p. 233.
23. William James, *The Varieties of Religious Experience* (London: Longmans, Green and Co., 1902), p. 87.
24. James, *Pragmatism*, p. 128.
25. Ibid., p. 144.
26. James, *Varieties*, pp. 30–31.
27. Ibid., p. 30.
28. Ibid., p. 35.
29. Ibid., p. 519.
30. Ibid., p. 501.
31. John Dos Passos, "Told by a Believer," *New Masses* 2 (March 1927): 30.
32. John Dos Passos, "Is the 'Realistic' Theatre Obsolete," *Vanity Fair* 24 (1925): 64.
33. Lois Hughson, "Narration in the Making of *Manhattan Transfer*," *Studies in the Novel* 8 (1976): 197.
34. John Dos Passos, interview, in *First Person*, ed. Frank Gado (Schenectady: Union College Press, 1973), p. 42.

35. James, *Varieties,* p. 267.
36. Ibid., p. 248.
37. Ibid., p. 317.
38. Ibid., p. 318.
39. Ibid., p. 248.
40. Ibid.
41. James, *Pragmatism,* p. 137.
42. James, *Varieties,* pp. 250–51.
43. Ibid., p. 254.
44. Ibid., p. 167.
45. Colley, *Dos Passos and the Fiction of Despair,* p. 59.
46. Carver, "The Newspaper . . . ," p. 171.
47. James, *Varieties,* pp. 498–99.
48. Ibid., p. 53.
49. Ibid., p. 499.
50. E. D. Lowry, "The Lively Art of *Manhattan Transfer,*" *PMLA* 84 (1969): 1634.
51. Ibid., p. 1637.
52. Hughson, "Narration," p. 186.
53. Sinclair Lewis, *John Dos Passos' Manhattan Transfer* (New York: Harper & Brothers, 1926), p. 5.
54. James, *Psychology,* p. 42.
55. Ibid., p. 370.
56. Susan Lyman, *The Story of New York* (New York: Crown Publishers, Inc., 1964), p. 215.
57. See Michael MacDonald Mooney, *Evelyn Nesbit and Stanford White* (New York: William Morrow and Company, 1976), pp. 31, 60. Note too that in speaking to Ellen about his early romance with Nellie McNeil, George Baldwin refers to Nellie as "a wild rose" (p. 220).

Chapter 9. The *U.S.A.* Trilogy

1. James, *Pragmatism,* p. 71.
2. Ibid., pp. 70–71.
3. Arnold Hoffman, "An Element of Structure in *U.S.A.,*" *The CEA Critic* 31 (October 1968): 12–13.
4. Barbara Foley, "From *U.S.A.* to *Ragtime:* Notes on the Forms of Historical Consciousness in Modern Fiction," *American Literature* 50 (March 1978): 90.
5. Barbara Foley, "The Treatment of Time in *The Big Money:* An Examination of Ideology and Literary Form," *Modern Fiction Studies* 26 (Autumn 1980): 456–58.
6. Dos Passos's shortcomings as historian concern this very fact: he had no difficulty recognizing the important events of the Jeffersonian era, say, but he had great difficulty in drawing realistic generalities about those experiences. See John P. Diggins, "Visions of Chaos and Visions of Order: Dos Passos as Historian," *American Literature* 46 (November 1974): 329–46.
7. Foley, "From *U.S.A.* to *Ragtime,*" p. 93.
8. John Dos Passos, *U.S.A.* (New York: The Modern Library, 1937), p. 81. Parenthetical page references cited in this chapter will refer to this edition. For convenience in notation, the three novels in the trilogy will be cited by the following Roman numerals: (I) *The Forty-Second Parallel,* (II) *1919,* and (III) *The Big Money.*
9. Dos Passos, *The Best Times,* p. 44.
10. Dos Passos apparently felt that his failure to skate with the Rovers was an important—

even symbolic—failure. Linda Wagner notes that in the novel's early draft Dos Passos had underlined this sentence every time it appeared: "I couldn't learn to skate and kept falling down." See Wagner, *Dos Passos: Artist as American*, p. 106.

11. John Dos Passos, interview, in *First Person*, p. 43. The importance of Dos Passos's answer is suggested by a footnote in an article by Townsend Ludington, although he doesn't pursue the matter. See "The Ordering of the Camera Eye in *U.S.A.*," *American Literature* 49 (November 1977): 446.

12. Townsend Ludington, *John Dos Passos* (New York: E. P. Dutton, 1980), p. 258.

13. There have been three notable studies on time in *U.S.A.* See Barbara Foley's astute observations in her two articles mentioned in this chapter. See also Claude-Edmonde Magny, "Time in Dos Passos," in *Dos Passos*, ed. Andrew Hook (Englewood Cliffs, N.J.: Prentice-Hall, Inc., 1974), pp. 128–44.

14. Malcolm Cowley, "Dos Passos: Poet against the World," in *After the Genteel Tradition*, ed. Malcolm Cowley (Carbondale: Southern Illinois University Press, 1964), p. 141.

15. Lois Hughson has examined this passage in detail and shows how it compares to Whitman's vision of America. See "In Search of the True America," pp. 179–92.

16. Charles W. Walcutt, *American Literary Naturalism* (Minneapolis: University of Minnesota Press, 1956), pp. 288–89.

17. John Dos Passos, "A Question of Elbow Room," in *Occasions and Protests* (Chicago: H. Regnery, 1964), p. 62.

18. John Dos Passos, *In All Countries* (New York: Harcourt Brace and Company, 1934), p. 175.

19. Ibid., p. 182.

20. Ibid., p. 186. As my analysis emphasizes, everyday politics seems less important to Dos Passos than does a redeeming mythic vision of life. Thus Sacco is significant to Dos Passos because he possesses this mythic vision whereas the authorities do not. Robert C. Rosen, on the other hand, sees politics as the motivating force behind Dos Passos's fiction. Rosen states that "politics is not inimical to art, and for Dos Passos it is in fact its very essence, what makes his art possible" (*John Dos Passos: Politics and the Writer* [Lincoln: University of Nebraska Press, 1981], p. x). It is not politics, I would argue, but a holistic vision of life that is made up of a poetic appreciation of nature and a solid pragmatic epistemology.

21. Theodore Dreiser, *The Financier* (New York: Boni & Liveright, 1927), pp. 3–4.

22. Quoted by Wrenn, *John Dos Passos*, p. 105.

23. Dos Passos, *In All Countries*, p. 188.

24. John Dos Passos, "Looking Back on '*U.S.A.*,'" *New York Times*, 25 October 1959, sec. 2, p. 5.

25. Daniel Hoffman, *Form and Fable in American Literature* (New York: Oxford University Press, 1961), p. 34.

26. Dos Passos, *Rosinante*, p. 93.

27. Interview with John Dos Passos, in *Talks with Authors*, ed. Charles F. Madden (Carbondale: Southern Illinois University Press, 1968), p. 10.

28. John Dos Passos, "The *New Masses* I'd Like," *New Masses* 1 (June 1926): 20.

29. John Dos Passos, "The Duty of the Writer," in *Writers in Freedom*, ed. Hermon Ould (1941; reprint, Port Washington, N.Y.: Kennikat Press, 1970), p. 26.

30. John Dos Passos, "A Note on Fitzgerald," in *The Crack-Up* by F. Scott Fitzgerald, ed. by Edmund Wilson (New York: New Directions Publishing Corp., New Directions Paperbook, 1956), pp. 399, 343.

31. Aldridge, *After the Lost Generation*, p. 72.

32. Quoted in Dos Passos's introduction to *One Man's Initiation: 1917*, p. 9.

33. Dos Passos, "What Makes a Novelist," p. 31.

34. Ibid.
35. James, *Radical Empiricism*, p. 19.
36. *Fourteenth Chronicle*, p. 68.
37. John Dos Passos, "Satire as a Way of Seeing," in *Occasions and Protests*, p. 20.
38. *Rosinante*, p. 100.
39. David Vanderwerken, "*U.S.A.:* Dos Passos and the 'Old Words,' " *Twentieth Century Literature* 23 (May 1977): 195–228.
40. Diggins, "Visions of Chaos," pp. 343, 344.
41. Near the time he was beginning the *U.S.A.* trilogy, Dos Passos remarked that "any novelist that is worth his salt is a sort of truffle dog digging up raw material which a scientist, an anthropologist or a historian can later use to permanent advantage." See his "Statements of Belief," *The Bookman* 68 (September 1928):26.
42. Dos Passos, interview in *Talks with Authors*, p. 7.
43. James, *Radical Empiricism*, pp. 31–32.
44. Ibid., p. 52.
45. Wagner, *Dos Passos: Artist as American*, p. 88.
46. Interview with John Dos Passos, "The Art of Fiction XLIV," *Paris Review*, p. 161.
47. Dos Passos, "What Makes a Novelist," p. 32.
48. Dos Passos once spoke of his role of recording the contemporary social scene in his novels for future generations: he would "focus" the scene that he sees onto "the screen of the future." See "The Duty of the Writer," p. 25.
49. *Fourteenth Chronicle*, p. 522.
50. John Dos Passos, "Mr. Dos Passos on *him*," *New York Times*, 22 April 1928, sec. 9, p. 2.
51. Dos Passos, "The Making of a Writer," *New Masses* 4 (March 1929):23.
52. Leed, *No Man's Land*, p. 135.
53. *Fourteenth Chronicle*, p. 266.
54. See the discussion of *lo castizo* and Spain in chapter 7.
55. Dos Passos, "What Makes a Novelist," 32.
56. *Leaves of Grass* (1965), p. 712.

Chapter 10. Conclusion

1. John Dos Passos, *Chosen Country* (Boston: Houghton Mifflin Company, 1951), p. 482. Subsequent parenthetical page references are to this edition.
2. John Dos Passos, *Century's Ebb* (Boston: Gambit, 1975), pp. 5–13, and *passim*.
3. John Dos Passos, *Midcentury* (Boston: Houghton Mifflin Company, 1961), p. 421.
4. *Century's Ebb*, pp. 113–25. In light of my comments in earlier chapters, it is instructive to note that in the course of discussing John Dewey and American pragmatism in general, Dos Passos mentions Walt Whitman's name no less than six times. Thus, he says that "John Dewey felt a kinship with Walt" (p. 121) and that "If Walt Whitman was democracy's poet, John Dewey was democracy's philosopher" (p. 117). Moreover, Dewey is one of the "avatars" of Whitman's democracy (p. 124).
5. Gelfant, "The Search for Identity."

Bibliography

Primary Sources

"Against American Literature." *New Republic* 8 (14 October 1916): 269–71.

"Art and Baseball." John Dos Passos Papers. Manuscripts Department, University of Virginia Library, Charlottesville, Va.

The Best Times: An Informal Memoir. New York: The New American Library, Inc., 1966.

Century's Ebb: The Thirteenth Chronicle. Boston: Gambit, Inc., 1975.

Chosen Country. Boston: Houghton Mifflin Company, 1951.

Diary, 1914–1917. Unpublished. John Dos Passos Papers. Manuscripts Department, University of Virginia Library, Charlottesville, Va.

Diary, Nov.–Dec., 1917. Unpublished. John Dos Passos Papers. Manuscripts Department, University of Virginia Library, Charlottesville, Va.

"The Duty of the Writer." In *Writers in Freedom,* edited by Herman Ould. 1941. Reprint. Port Washington, N.Y.: Kennikat Press, 1970.

The Fourteenth Chronicle: Letters and Diaries of John Dos Passos. Edited by Townsend Ludington. Boston: Gambit, Inc., 1973.

"The Great Tradition." University of Illinois Library Archives, Champaign-Urbana, Ill.

The Ground We Stand On: Some Examples from the History of a Political Creed. New York: Harcourt, Brace and Company, 1941.

In All Countries. New York: Harcourt, Brace and Company, 1934.

Interview. In *First Person: Conversations on Writers and Writing,* edited by Frank Gado, pp. 31–55. Schenectady: Union College Press, 1973.

Interview. *Paris Review* 46 (Spring 1969): 147–72.

Interview. In *Talks with Authors,* edited by Charles F. Madden, pp. 3–11. Carbondale: Southern Illinois University Press, 1968.

"Is the 'Realistic' Theatre Obsolete." *Vanity Fair* 24 (May 1925): 64, 114.

Letter to Arthur McComb, undated. American Academy and Institute of Arts and Letters, New York, N.Y.

Letter to Frederick Lowe, 27 August 1948. John Dos Passos Collection. Pennsylvania State University Library, University Park, Pa.

Letter to Griffen Barry, 28 April 1919. John Dos Passos Papers. Manuscripts Department, University of Virginia Library, Charlottesville, Va.

"Looking Back on 'U.S.A.'" *New York Times,* 25 October 1959, sec. 2, p. 5.

Manhattan Transfer. Boston: Houghton Mifflin Company, 1925.

Midcentury. Boston: Houghton Mifflin Co., 1961.

"Mr. Dos Passos on *him.*" *New York Times,* 22 April 1928, sec. 9, p. 2.

"The *New Masses* I'd Like." *New Masses* 1 (June 1926): 20.

"A Note on Fitzgerald." In *The Crack-Up,* by F. Scott Fitzgerald, edited by Edmund Wilson. New York: New Directions Publishing Corp., 1956.

Occasions and Protests. Chicago: H. Regnery, 1964.

One Man's Initiation: 1917. Introduction by John Dos Passos. Ithaca: Cornell University Press, 1969.

Orient Express. New York: Harper & Brothers, 1927.

"Revolution." John Dos Passos Papers. Manuscripts Department, University of Virginia Library, Charlottesville, Va.

"Romantic Education." *Harvard Monthly* 61 (October 1915): 1–4.

Rosinante to the Road Again. New York: George H. Doran Company, 1922.

"Seven Times Round the Walls of Jericho." John Dos Passos Papers, Manuscripts Department, University of Virginia Library, Charlottesville, Va.

"Statements of Belief." *The Bookman* 68 (September 1928): 26.

Streets of Night. New York: George H. Doran Company, 1923.

Three Plays: The Garbage Man; Airways, Inc.; Fortune Heights. New York: Harcourt, Brace and Company, 1934.

Three Soldiers. New York: George H. Doran Company, 1921.

"Told by a Believer." *New Masses* 2 (March 1927): 30.

Travel Diary, 1911. John Dos Passos Papers. Manuscripts Department, University of Virginia Library, Charlottesville, Va.

U.S.A. New York: The Modern Library, 1937.

"What Makes a Novelist." *National Review* 20 (January 1968): 29–32.

Secondary Sources

Aldridge, John. *After the Lost Generation: A Critical Study of the Writers of Two Wars.* New York: Farrar, Straus, and Company, The Noonday Press, 1958.

Allen, Gay Wilson. *The Solitary Singer: A Critical Biography of Walt Whitman.* New York: New York University Press, 1967.

Aspiz, Harold. *Walt Whitman and the Body Beautiful.* Urbana: University of Illinois Press, 1980.

Blackmur, R. P. *Language as Gesture: Essays in Poetry.* London: George Allen & Unwin, Ltd., 1954.

Brantley, John D. *The Fiction of Dos Passos.* The Hague: Mouton, 1968.

Burroughs, John. *Whitman: A Study.* Boston: Houghton, Mifflin and Company, 1896.

Carver, Craig. "The Newspaper and Other Sources of *Manhattan Transfer.*" *Studies in American Fiction* 3 (1975): 167–79.

Colley, Iain. *Dos Passos and the Fiction of Despair.* Totowa, N.J.: Rowman and Littlefield, 1978.

Cowley, Malcolm. *After the Genteel Tradition: American Writers 1910–1930.* Carbondale: Southern Illinois University Press, 1964.

———. *Exile's Return: A Literary Odyssey of the 1920s.* New York: The Viking Press, 1951.

Davis, Robert Gorham. *John Dos Passos.* University of Minnesota Pamphlets on American Writers, no. 20. Minneapolis: University of Minnesota Press, 1962.

Diggins, John P. "Visions of Chaos and Visions of Order: Dos Passos as Historian." *American Literature* 46 (November 1974): 329–46.

Dreiser, Theodore. *The Financier.* Revised edition. New York: Boni & Liveright, 1927.

Faulkner, William. *Three Famous Short Novels.* New York: Vintage Books, 1966.

Foley, Barbara. "From *U.S.A.* to *Ragtime:* Notes on the Forms of Historical Consciousness in Modern Fiction." *American Literature* 50 (March 1978): 85–105.

———. "The Treatment of Time in *The Big Money:* An Examination of Ideology and Literary Forms." *Modern Fiction Studies* 26 (Autumn 1980): 447–67.

Frank, Waldo. *Our America.* New York: Boni & Liveright, 1919.

Frazer, Sir James. *The Golden Bough: A Study in Magic and Religion.* Abridged edition. New York: The MacMillan Company, 1950.

Freud, Sigmund. "Psychoanalysis and War Neuroses." In *Miscellaneous Papers, 1888–1938.* Vol. 5 of *Collected Papers,* edited by James Strachey. London: The Hogarth Press and the Institute of Psychoanalysis, 1950.

Friedman, Rohn S. "A Whitman Primer: Solipsism and Identity." *American Quarterly* 27 (October 1975): 443–60.

Gayley, Charles Mills. *The Classic Myths in English Literature and in Art.* Lexington, Mass.: Xerox College Publishing, 1972.

Geismar, Maxwell. *Writers in Crisis: The American Novel, 1925–1940.* New York: Hill and Wang, 1961.

Gelfant, Blanche. *The American City Novel.* Norman: University of Oklahoma Press, 1954.

———. "The Search for Identity in the Novels of John Dos Passos." *PMLA* 76 (March 1961): 133–49.

Haig, Elizabeth. *The Floral Symbolism of the Great Masters.* London: Keegan Paul, Trench, Trubner & Co., 1913.

Hawthorne, Nathaniel. *The Blithedale Romance and Fanshawe.* Columbus: Ohio State University Press, 1964.

Hoffman, Arnold. "An Element of Structure in *U.S.A.*" *The CEA Critic* 31 (October 1968): 12–13.

Hoffman, Daniel. *Form and Fable in American Literature.* New York: Oxford University Press, 1961.

Hughson, Lois. "In Search of the True America: Dos Passos' Debt to Whitman in *U.S.A.*" *Modern Fiction Studies* 19 (Summer 1973): 179–92.

———. "Narration in the Making of *Manhattan Transfer.*" *Studies in the Novel* 8 (1976): 185–98.

James, William. *Essays in Radical Empiricism.* Cambridge: Harvard University Press, 1976.

———. *The Meaning of Truth: A Sequel to Pragmatism.* Ann Arbor: The University of Michigan Press, Ann Arbor Paperbacks, 1970.

———. *Pragmatism.* Cambridge: Harvard University Press, 1975.

———. *Psychology: Briefer Course.* New York: Henry Holt and Company, 1892.

———. *The Varieties of Religious Experience: A Study in Human Nature.* London: Longmans, Green, and Co., 1902.

Kepner, Diane. "From Spears to Leaves: Walt Whitman's Theory of Nature in 'Song of Myself.'" *American Literature* 51 (May 1979): 179–204.

Landsberg, Melvin. *Dos Passos' Path to U.S.A.: A Political Biography, 1912–1936.* Boulder: The Colorado Associated University Press, 1972.

Langer, Susanne K. *Feeling and Form: A Theory of Art.* New York: Charles Scribner's Sons, 1953.

Leed, Eric J. *No Man's Land: Combat & Identity in World War I.* Cambridge: Cambridge University Press, 1979.

Lewis, Sinclair. *John Dos Passos' "Manhattan Transfer."* New York: Harper & Brothers Publishers, 1926.

Lowry, E. D. "The Lively Art of *Manhattan Transfer.*" *PMLA* 84 (1969): 1628–38.

———. "*Manhattan Transfer:* Dos Passos' Wasteland." *The University Review* 30 (Autumn 1963): 47–52.

Ludington, Townsend. *John Dos Passos: A Twentieth Century Odyssey.* New York: E. P. Dutton, 1980.

———. "The Ordering of the Camera Eye in *U.S.A.*" *American Literature* 49 (November 1977): 443–46.

Lyman, Susan. *The Story of New York.* New York: Crown Publishers, Inc., 1964.

Magny, Claude-Edmonde. "Time in Dos Passos." In *Dos Passos,* edited by Andrew Hook, pp. 128–44. Englewood Cliffs, N.J.: Prentice-Hall, Inc., 1974.

Matthiessen, F. O. *American Renaissance: Art and Expression in the Age of Emerson and Whitman.* New York: Oxford University Press, 1941.

———. *The James Family.* New York: Alfred A. Knopf, 1947.

Miller, James E., Jr. *A Critical Guide to "Leaves of Grass."* Chicago: The University of Chicago Press, 1957.

Mizener, Arthur. Introduction. *District of Columbia.* New York: Houghton, Mifflin, Co., 1952.

Mooney, Michael M. *Evelyn Nesbit and Stanford White.* New York: William Morrow and Company, 1976.

Perry, Bliss. *Walt Whitman.* Boston: Houghton, Mifflin Company, 1906.

Perry, Ralph B. *Characteristically American.* New York: Knopf, 1949.

Rank, Otto. *The Double: A Psychoanalytic Study.* Translated and edited by Harry Tucker, Jr. Chapel Hill: The University of North Carolina Press, 1971.

Roads, Samuel, Jr. *The History and Traditions of Marblehead.* Marblehead, Mass.: N. Allen Lindsey & Co., 1897.

Rosen, Robert C. *John Dos Passos: Politics and the Writer.* Lincoln: University of Nebraska Press, 1981.

Symonds, John. *Walt Whitman: A Study.* London: John C. Nimmo, 1893.

Tymms, Ralph. *Doubles in Literary Psychology.* Cambridge: Bowes & Bowes, 1949.

Vanderwerken, David L. "*Manhattan Transfer:* Dos Passos' Babel Story." *American Literature* 49 (1977): 253–67.

———. "*U.S.A.:* Dos Passos and the 'Old Words.'" *Twentieth Century Literature* 23 (May 1977): 195–228.

Wagner, Linda W. *Dos Passos: Artist as American.* Austin: University of Texas Press, 1979.

Walcutt, Charles Child. *American Literary Naturalism, a Divided Stream.* Minneapolis: University of Minnesota Press, 1956.

———. *Man's Changing Mask: Modes and Methods of Characterization in Fiction*. Minneapolis: University of Minnesota Press, 1966.

Weeks, Robert P. "The Novel as Poem: Whitman's Legacy to Dos Passos." *Modern Fiction Studies* 26 (Autumn 1980): 431–46.

Whitman, Walt. *Complete Prose Works*. Philadelphia: David McKay Publisher, 1891.

———. *Leaves of Grass: Comprehensive Reader's Edition*. Edited by Harold W. Blodgett and Sculley Bradley. New York: W. W. Norton & Co., Inc., 1965.

Williams, William C. *In the American Grain*. New York: New Directions, 1933.

———. *Selected Essays of William Carlos Williams*. New York: Random House, 1954.

Wrenn, John H. *John Dos Passos*. Twayne's United States Authors Series, no. 9. New York: Twayne Publishers, Inc., 1961.

Index

Adonis, 45, 46
Aldridge, John W., 64, 73, 138
Apollo, 45, 47–48
Aspiz, Harold, 78

Baroja, Pío, 136
Behavioristic method, 52, 142
Blackmur, R. P., 92
Brantley, John, 67
Burroughs, John, 23

Carver, Craig, 98, 99, 116
Colley, Iain, 64, 116
Cooper, James Fenimore, 97
Cowley, Malcolm, 14, 128–29
cummings, e. e., 142

Davis, Robert G., 64
Descartes, René, 95
Dewey, John, 151, 154 n.19, 163 n.4
Diggins, John, 139, 161 n.6
Dionysus, 45, 46, 47
Don Quixote, 54, 96
Dos Passos, John R., Jr.: "Against American Literature," 15, 19; "Art and Baseball," 15, 18, 39; *The Best Times,* 15; *The Big Money* (See *U.S.A.* trilogy); *Century's Ebb,* 150, 151; *Chosen Country,* 150; *The Forty-Second Parallel* (See *U.S.A.* trilogy); *The Garbage Man,* 49; "The Great Tradition," 14; *The Ground We Stand On,* 27; *In All Countries,* 131; *Manhattan Transfer,* 28, 97–122, 123, 124, 125, 127, 142, 152; *Midcentury,* 151; *1919* (See *U.S.A.* trilogy); *One Man's Initiation: 1917,* 28, 53, 62–75, 76, 77, 88, 93, 98, 151; *Orient Express,* 97; "Revolution," 29–31, 45; "Romantic Education," 31; *Rosinante to the Road Again,* 90–92, 96; *Seven Times Round the Walls of Jericho,* 53–61; *Streets of Night,* 28, 32–52, 61, 62, 67, 74, 78, 87, 88, 94, 107, 123, 130, 150; *Three Soldiers,* 28, 54, 76–96, 119, 142, 150, 151; *U.S.A.* trilogy, 18, 25, 28, 52, 123–49, 150, 152
Dos Passos, John R., Sr., 27
Dostoyevsky, Feodor, 159 n.4
Dreiser, Theodore: *The Financier,* 133–34

Faulkner, William: "The Bear," 106
Fitzgerald, F. Scott, 44, 107, 137
Flaubert, Gustave, 89
Foley, Barbara, 124, 125
Frank, Waldo: *Our America,* 99
Frazer, Sir James: *The Golden Bough,* 45–47, 52
Friedman, Rohn, 90
Freud, Sigmund, 78–79, 85

Geismar, Maxwell, 107, 108
Gelfant, Blanche, 32, 98, 108, 152
Gesture, 90–95, 119, 139, 142
Grosz, George, 138

Hawthorne, Nathaniel, 48, 49; *Fanshawe,* 33
Hillyer, Robert, 53
Hoffman, Arnold, 124
Hoffman, Daniel, 135
Hughson, Lois, 110, 118, 154–55 n.30

James, Henry, 31, 45, 106, 120
James, William, 17, 22, 24–28, 32, 49, 51, 63, 67, 68, 69, 70, 71, 73, 74, 78, 108, 109, 110, 116, 119, 123, 138, 147, 151, 154 n.19, 155 n.30; *Essays in Radical Empiricism,* 27, 118, 140; *Pragmatism,* 113, 118, 123–24; *Principles of Psychology,* 26, 92, 94, 117,

Index

118; *Varieties of Religious Experience,* 26, 109, 111–15, 117–18. *See also* Pragmatism

Lawson, John, 110
Leed, Eric J.: *No Man's Land,* 63, 143
Lewis, Sinclair, 118
Longfellow, Henry Wadsworth, 48; "The Slave's Dream," 38
Lowell, James Russell, "The Shepherd of King Admetus," 48, 157 n.30
Lowry, E. D., 108, 118
Lyman, Susan, 120

Macbeth, 29
McComb, Arthur, 15, 27, 69, 74
Marvin, Rumsey, 26, 27, 54, 63
Matthiessen, F. O., 90
Melville, Herman, 97
Mitchell, Stewart, 16

Nature, 19, 23, 25; in *Century's Ebb,* 151; in *Chosen Country,* 151; in *Manhattan Transfer,* 98–103, 113, 122; in *One Man's Initiation: 1917,* 65–67; in *Seven Times Round the Walls of Jericho,* 56–58; in *Streets of Night,* 42–44; in *Three Soldiers,* 78, 87–89, 96; in the *U.S.A.* trilogy, 124, 127, 128, 129, 130–36, 141, 146–49. *See also* Whitman, Walt
Nesbit, Evelyn, 120

Peirce, Charles Sanders, 151
Perry, Bliss, 23
Perry, Ralph Barton, 16
Plato, 26, 71–72, 158 n.22
Poe, Edgar Allan, 48, 49, 80, 159 n.4; "Annabel Lee," 35–37
Pragmatism, 21–23, 24–28, 98, 151; in *Century's Ebb,* 151; in *Manhattan Transfer,* 105–6, 115–22; in *Midcentury,* 151; in *One Man's Initiation: 1917,* 63, 67–74; in "Revolution," 30–31; in "Romantic Education," 31–32; in *Seven Times Round the Walls of Jericho,* 58–60; in *Streets of Night,* 49–51; in *Three Soldiers,* 92–95; in the *U.S.A.* trilogy, 123–24, 125, 127, 138–46, 147, 148, 149. *See also* James, William

Rank, Otto: *The Double,* 78, 85, 86
Rosen, Robert C., 162 n.20
Royce, Josiah, 71

Sacco and Vanzetti, 130–31, 134, 162 n.20
Santayana, George, 22
Symonds, John Addington, 23

Thaw, Harry K., 120
Thoreau, Henry David, 97
Twain, Mark, 97; *The Adventures of Huckleberry Finn,* 14
Tymms, Ralph, 78, 85

Unamuno, Miguel de, 96

Vanderwerken, David, 108, 139
Vanzetti, Bartolomeo. *See* Sacco and Vanzetti

Wagner, Linda, 14, 33, 37, 40, 64, 108
Walcutt, Charles C., 18, 131
Weeks, Robert, 155 n.30
White, Stanford, 99, 120
Whitman, Walt, 14, 17, 18–23, 32, 39, 41, 42, 49, 63, 67, 73, 74, 76–78, 87–90, 99, 104, 108–9, 110, 128, 130, 149, 150, 151, 154 n.19, 155 n.30, 159 n.4, 163 n.4; "A Backward Glance," 13; *Democratic Vistas,* 99, 109; "Eidolons," 78; "1855 Preface," 19, 21, 67; "1876 Preface," 19; *Leaves of Grass,* 19, 23, 130; "Out of the Cradle Endlessly Rocking," 25, 40, 89–90, 92; "Pent Up Aching Rivers," 39; "The Sleepers," 77, 99; "Song of Myself," 18, 40, 41, 42, 67, 76; "Song of Occupations," 40; "Song of the Open Road," 41; "There Was a Child Went Forth," 20–22, 24; "When Lilacs Last in the Dooryard Bloom'd," 38–39, 87. *See also* Nature
Whittier, John Greenleaf, 37, 48; "Skipper Ireson's Ride," 36
Williams, Roger, 27
Williams, William Carlos, 16; "The American Background," 33–34
Wrenn, John, 74, 98
Wright, Frank Lloyd, 128, 141